D1317571

THE INTELLECTUAL VENTURE CAPITALIST

Photograph by John Mottern

LIBRARY
I.U.P.
Indiana, PA

HF
1134
.H4
I58
1999

THE Intellectual Venture Capitalist

John H. McArthur and the
Work of the Harvard Business School,
1980-1995

Edited by Thomas K. McCraw and
Jeffrey L. Cruikshank

HARVARD BUSINESS SCHOOL PRESS
Boston, Massachusetts

Copyright © 1999 President and Fellows of Harvard College

All rights reserved

Printed in the United States of America
02 01 00 99 98 5 4 3 2 1

Library of Congress Cataloging-in-Publication Data

The intellectual venture capitalist: John H. McArthur and the work of
   the Harvard Business School. 1980–1998 / edited by Thomas K. McCraw
   and Jeffrey L. Cruikshank.
      p. cm
   Includes index.
   ISBN 0-87584-900-8 (alk. paper)
   1. McArthur, John H. 2. Deans (Education)—United States.
3. Harvard University. Graduate School of Business Administration.
I. McCraw, Thomas K. II. Cruikshank, Jeffrey L.
HF1134.H4I58 1999
650′.092—dc21
[b]
                                                        98-42244
                                                           CIP

The paper used in this publication meets the requirements of the American
National Standard for Permanence of Paper for Printed Library Materials
Z39.49-1984.

A000000305136

A man of humanity is one who,
in seeking to establish himself, finds a foothold for others and who,
desiring attainment for himself, helps others to attain.

CONFUCIUS

Contents

Foreword

A T THE CLOSE OF THE twentieth century, the Harvard Business
School stands at an important inflection point in its history.
Changes in the nature of business have created a dynamic,
turbulent environment. There never has been a greater need for effective general managers with the capacity for leadership. As a result, the
mission of the School—to educate leaders who make a difference in
society—has never been more significant, nor the call for innovation in
general management education more crucial. While we remain true to
our fundamental strategy, we must be prepared to break new ground:
in information technology, globalization, entrepreneurship, leadership,
and a host of other areas.

As we face the challenges and opportunities ahead, research and
course development will lie at the center of our work. As it has always
been, building intellectual capital will remain our lifeblood. The future
we aspire to create, as we look across the portfolio of faculty and projects, demands that we focus on important problems, that we pursue
deep knowledge with power in practice, that we employ a broad range
of methods in our work (especially methods that take us into the field),
that we be ready to break new ground in projects of significance and

scope, that we be unconventional in our thinking and ready to cut across disciplines, and that we forge close links between course development and research, and between the classroom and the field.

This is not an easy path, but one we view with confidence. Ours is a legacy of challenges met, and we celebrate a powerful element of that legacy in this book. During his deanship, John McArthur laid the foundation of intellectual growth and development on which we continue to build today. This volume examines a few of the many ventures John supported and nurtured. And it is just a few. The work not discussed here is equally impressive, including:

- The Social Enterprise Initiative, which is creating new insight about the governance and strategic management of nonprofit organizations, and about business leadership in the social sector

- New concepts in Marketing, including brands and relationship marketing, and marketing and society (for example, understanding the role of marketing in combating socially destructive, addictive products)

- New research in Managerial Accounting, including activity-based costing and the balanced scorecard

- Pathbreaking work in Organizational Behavior, including leadership, power and influence, networks, careers, and managing diversity

- The impact of the Internet on markets, channels, and distribution, as well as the strategic impact of information technology in organizations

In these areas and in the initiatives discussed herein, the mission of the School shines through. As these stories of intellectual journeys make clear, it is a mission pursued by remarkable people working in a remarkable community. Moreover, it is a mission that requires investment. It is perhaps not surprising that John, the quintessential intellectual venture capitalist, should bring to his work a spirit of investment. I speak here not only of dollars for R&D (although he provided plenty of them), but also of his personal investment in time, energy, spirit, and heart, in both his colleagues and the Harvard Business School. John taught and lived a principle fundamental to the School:

If we invest in each other—even to the point of making what feel like sacrifices in the amount of our own work—with support, time, attention, training, and ideas, we will create an environment and a community that is so vital, so rich and fertile, that each of us will end up far better off than if we selfishly pursued our own interests.

The years ahead are bound to be exciting and challenging. We must carve out new domains of intellectual investment, taking our research and case work more deeply into the global arena and into information technology. We must pursue new methods of integrating field and experimental research, and extend our reach into research that more intimately connects knowledge and practice. We must bring new knowledge about the world of business into the classroom in powerful ways. Ultimately, we must pursue the mission of the School with energy and passion. I am confident that as we do, and as we look back years from now, we will see that John McArthur—the intellectual venture capitalist—launched vital initiatives that marked the beginning of a remarkable era in the storied history of the Harvard Business School.

KIM B. CLARK
September 1998

CHAPTER ONE

The Intellectual Venture Capitalist

JEFFREY L. CRUIKSHANK, LINDA S. DOYLE, AND
THOMAS K. MCCRAW

THIS BOOK HONORS *John H. McArthur, dean of the Harvard Business School from 1980 to 1995. The book grows out of a symposium conceived and sponsored by McArthur's successor, Kim B. Clark, and held during a period of three days during the fall of 1996. Almost the entire faculty of the Harvard Business School participated, in addition to a number of invited guests from business and academia. At the symposium, 18 of McArthur's colleagues sketched out their own intellectual journeys and recounted his contributions to their work. In the other eight chapters of this book these 18 colleagues describe that work in detail.*

It is no accident that all nine of this book's chapters are co-authored. McArthur himself constantly emphasized the need for teamwork. He was convinced that, if the whole of the School were to exceed the sum of its parts, then its members—faculty, staff, students, and alumni—would have to work together more closely than is usual in academic settings, where joint efforts sometimes prove difficult.

This introductory essay is itself a joint effort, by three people who worked with McArthur in different roles and contexts. We've given the essay and the book their unusual title because the phrase captures a key aspect of McArthur's leadership of the School: identifying promising generators of ideas and placing large institutional bets on them. Of course, there are big differences between what deans do and what venture capitalists do. But in McArthur's case, the analogy fits. He was, and is, an investor in other people's ideas, and the support he gave was often indispensable, as every chapter of this book demonstrates.

In this introductory essay, we try to analyze how McArthur had his special impact. We are explicit here in ways that he himself avoided whenever possible, because we think that many people, in both business and the academy, can benefit from a clearer understanding of how one person so greatly amplified the creativity of those around him.

In a short essay such as this one, we cannot provide much more than a glimpse of the work of McArthur himself, let alone that of the hundreds of faculty members and professional staff who contributed so mightily to the School during his deanship. So, rather than try to cover everything or to mention even briefly every person important in the School's experience from 1980 to 1995, we have focused exclusively on McArthur. We reluctantly decided to mention no other names of Harvard faculty and staff at all, except for some of McArthurs's predecessors, his successor as dean, and Harvard's presidents. (We do list in Appendix A the academic associate deans.) There is also this irony: a focus on the self-effacing McArthur to the exclusion of his co-workers is the very last thing that he would have wished. So we ask pardon from all concerned for the omissions that space constraints compelled us to make.

The Dean and His Legacy

McARTHUR WAS BORN in 1934 in Vancouver, British Columbia. He grew up in a rough-and-ready working-class environment in the suburb of Burnaby, at a time when Greater Vancouver had a population of about 200,000. (Today, after several decades of mushrooming growth, it is home to about two million.) During his high school and college years, McArthur worked part-time in a sawmill. The owners of the sawmill, recognizing the young man's uncommon promise, encouraged him to go to college. One of only a few members of his high school class to continue their educations, McArthur entered the University of British Columbia, where he specialized in forestry and graduated in 1957 with a bachelor's in commerce. Before graduation he married Natty Ewasiuk, and eventually they had two daughters, Jocelyn and Susan.

A star athlete in several sports throughout these years in Vancouver, McArthur ended up with a number of offers to play professional football in Canada before he decided to marry and focus on his academic opportunities. Once he settled down at college, he began to earn outstanding grades for the first time in his life. It became clear to him and his coaches that his academic brilliance should take priority over athletics.

At the age of 23, he came with Natty to Cambridge, Massachusetts, to pursue an MBA. He had been admitted to both the Sloan School of Management and the Harvard Business School, and he postponed the final choice until the last minute, even after the McArthurs' arrival in Cambridge. In a dramatic moment, he and Natty made up their minds as they stood on a bridge spanning the Charles River. They turned and walked south across the bridge and onto Soldiers Field, where he enrolled at Harvard. He graduated in 1959. Then, somewhat to his own surprise, as he had not contemplated becoming a professor, he decided to stay on at the School. In 1962 he completed his DBA and joined the faculty. Over the next 18 years, he moved up through the School's ranks—writing cases, teaching finance, and doing more and more administrative work.

When McArthur became dean in 1980, he was 46 years old, full of energy, and well liked by almost everyone who knew him. Because of his upbeat temperament and his obvious interest in other people, he had a knack for establishing quick rapport with nearly anybody, of any age or station in life. When Harvard's President Derek Bok named him the new dean, under the difficult circumstances described below, almost everyone at Soldiers Field rejoiced.

There had been several outstanding leaders of the Harvard Business School since its founding in 1908, and when McArthur took the helm in 1980, he had a solid base on which to build. But with one notable exception, no other dean had served as long as McArthur would end up doing. Wallace B. Donham had the longest tenure, serving from 1919 to 1942, and he put the Harvard Business School on the map, literally and intellectually. Donham oversaw the creation of its Soldiers Field campus, and he pushed his faculty into inventing a variation on the Harvard Law School's "case method." This new pedagogy, which became tightly linked to field-based research, charted a distinctive intellectual path for the Harvard Business School.

But in the realm of ideas, no one, not even Donham, exceeded McArthur's impact on the institution; and McArthur himself was unequivocal about his commitment to what we are calling intellectual venture capitalism. "Research and course development are the foundation on which this school is built," he told a graduating class of Harvard's Advanced Management Program in 1983. Although the School had long been internationally renowned for its superlative teaching, "Outstanding teaching programs can only remain responsive to changing times if they are driven by intellectual capital formation."[1]

Perhaps our argument will surprise those at Soldiers Field and elsewhere who know that McArthur wrote very little and never aspired to be a scholar. Understandably, some friends and colleagues still think of him not as a man of deep conceptual insight, but rather as an unpretentious, sometimes disheveled, aw-shucks, almost blue-collar "people person." Even in retrospect, some regard him primarily as a builder of the School's physical plant and its endowment. And certainly during his tenure there were ample clouds of construction dust, prodigious growth in the endowment, and a dramatic increase in the number of named professorships.[2]

But we think that these kinds of changes were effected in service to a larger goal that was driven primarily by *ideas*. McArthur's mind seethed with ideas. Most of them had little to do with traditional academic disciplines, and he himself was not a conventional academic. He was not an economic or social theorist. He constructed no abstract models. Rather, his ideas had to do with the arts of administration and management, and he implemented these ideas in the running of the Harvard Business School.

The eight topical chapters of this book provide abundant evidence of McArthur's guidance of the intellectual development of the faculty. They document his role in specific areas of the School's teaching and research programs, from finance and production to ethics and business history, and much beyond. They highlight the persistent theme of his intellectual venture capitalism. They incidentally provide a lot of evidence that deans and other individual leaders can have a profound impact.

Leadership is a much-studied subject, of course, and it has been shown that effective styles can vary over a wide range. They can stretch from the eloquence and self-deprecation of Abraham Lincoln, to the bombastic preening of Douglas MacArthur, to the confident and infectious merriment of Franklin D. Roosevelt. Of great leaders, we think that John McArthur as dean perhaps most resembled Dwight D. Eisenhower. Like Eisenhower, he seldom sought the limelight and was not an outstanding public speaker. Like Eisenhower, he had an extraordinary talent for persuading antagonistic interests to pull together for a common object. But to do it effectively required that McArthur, like Eisenhower, accomplish most of his work in private—one on one or in small groups—and that he pay extremely close attention to the personal needs of his faculty and staff. McArthur did this in such a way that he won the fervent loyalty of several hundred people at Soldiers Field.

How, exactly, does someone effect this distinctive kind of leadership? In 1982 the political scientist Fred Greenstein published a study of Dwight Eisenhower's style, arguing that both as general and president Eisenhower exercised "hidden-hand" leadership. Some of Greenstein's words apply with equal accuracy to John McArthur, especially if the word *administrative* is substituted in some places where Greenstein writes *political*:

> *No do-it-yourself book can teach a leader to manage to be vague and folksy in public yet precise and analytic in private, to exude an apolitical aura while constantly devising political strategies and accurately appraising political personalities and practices, to view his immediate associates and other political actors with analytic detachment while conveying easy openness in working with them, and to pour intense energy into his efforts while appearing in public to be reasonably relaxed.*[3]

During McArthur's tenure, the levers of management that were available to a dean were rarely discussed out loud, and the ways in which they might be applied to promote intellectual venture capitalism were seldom made explicit. But his hidden-hand style was an exceptionally good fit with what the School needed in 1980, when he became dean. To help the reader understand this fit, we must begin with a broad context and then work our way down to specifics. We will also have to communicate some sense of the paradoxical realities of the School in 1980.

One Reality: A Position of Dominance

McArthur began his deanship as head of the leading American institutional player in an international industry, business education, that was itself dominated by the United States. That industry had grown rapidly during the three decades prior to 1980.[4] In 1950 U.S. colleges and universities had granted about 75,000 business degrees, of which around 4,300 were MBA degrees. By 1980 the equivalent annual numbers were 220,000 in total, of which 60,000 were MBAs. When McArthur took office, more than 1,000 American colleges and universities were offering undergraduate degrees in business administration, and almost 500 offered MBAs. About 100 of these schools were proficient institutions, and about a dozen were acknowledged to be elite. This small group included Chicago, Columbia, Darden (Virginia), Haas (Berkeley), Harvard, Kellogg (Northwestern), Sloan (MIT), Stanford, Tuck (Dartmouth), Wharton (Penn), and one or two others.

In this landscape of elite business education, Harvard stood out along several dimensions. It was the largest graduate business school, measured by MBA enrollment, size of faculty, endowment, and operating budget. Its annual expenditure for course development and research (about $15 million in 1980) was by itself bigger than the entire operating budgets of most business schools. Harvard produced more cases for classroom use than did all other schools combined. Several million copies of these cases were sold every year, for use in educational and training programs around the world.

The Harvard Business School also had the most impressive physical resources. The core of its magnificent campus had been designed and constructed as a unified whole during the mid-1920s. Whereas some leading business schools were housed in one or two buildings in the midst of a larger university complex, HBS had more than two dozen buildings and its own separate campus alongside the Charles River. Baker Library was the largest and the best business research facility in the world.

In 1980 students were clamoring for admission to Harvard as to no other business school of its kind. Some 25,000 people per year requested MBA application forms, and about 6,600 actually applied. (By design these forms were, and still are, extremely long and laborious to complete.) Of the 6,600 applicants, about 1,000 were admitted. Of those admitted, about 80 percent actually enrolled, and this "yield" was higher than that enjoyed by any other graduate business school. (During the period 1980 to 1995, the years of McArthur's deanship, the number of requests for applications to the MBA program rose to 60,000, and the School's yield of admitted applicants enrolled increased to 87 percent.)

At graduation, Harvard's students commanded the highest starting salaries for new MBAs; ten, twenty, and thirty years out, graduates reported the highest personal net worth of MBAs from any school. Large numbers of HBS graduates started their own businesses. And by the late 1970s, the unusually focused and determined classes of the immediate postwar period (that is, the classes between about 1947 and 1955) had come into their own and had achieved a remarkable prominence in American business.[5]

Viewed with an eye to statistics such as these, the school that McArthur inherited from outgoing Dean Lawrence E. Fouraker was in excellent shape.[6] The superficial observer might have concluded that little more than a caretaker dean was now needed. If the School were not broken, there was no compelling need to fix it. But McArthur himself, and a few others at Harvard, had already reached a different conclusion.

A Second Reality: Puzzles and Challenges

McArthur's predecessor had implemented an innovative matrix management structure when he took office in 1970. For a variety of reasons, Fouraker at that time had turned to the younger generation on the faculty to fill his key administrative positions, and McArthur was one of these relatively junior people. During an impromptu visit to McArthur's house on a Thanksgiving Day during the early 1970s, Fouraker had asked McArthur to head up the MBA program under the new organizational setup, and McArthur had quickly accepted. Afterward he telephoned a colleague in organizational behavior to inquire about just what a matrix management system was.

Over time, McArthur's responsibilities steadily increased. By the late 1970s he was one of Fouraker's key lieutenants, serving as liaison with other parts of Harvard, the most important of which was the president's office. President Derek Bok was interested in improving coordination among the university's various schools and departments—including, for example, a move to a common calendar—and Fouraker deputized McArthur to represent the School in a series of discussions with Bok.

During the summer of 1979, after it became clear that Fouraker intended to step down as dean, these discussions suddenly took on heightened importance. At that time, Bok set off something of a firestorm at Soldiers Field with the publication of his annual "President's Report." In part because he had been trained as a lawyer, Bok liked to work out his ideas by writing long and closely reasoned "briefs." During his presidency he produced about 20 annual reports of this kind, often designed to spark debate and help him better understand the various schools and other entities for which he might soon have to choose a new leader. In light of Fouraker's impending retirement, the 1979 report focused on the Harvard Business School. Although mostly complimentary to the School, Bok's report also took HBS to task for being too ingrown and for failing to conduct sufficient research. To some readers it appeared that Bok might even be attacking the School's cherished case method of instruction.

Accordingly, some of the School's alumni and other supporters objected strenuously to what they saw as Bok's unjustified criticisms. During the summer of 1979, as the debates simmered on, McArthur continued his dialogue with Bok, trying to deepen the president's understanding of why the School did business in its particular way. As McArthur says in retrospect, "It wasn't that Derek didn't try his hardest, or even that the report was wrong." But the report was almost inescapably hurtful in "the way it handled Larry [Fouraker], who had taken on the really tough stuff—like our uncontrolled, low-quality, at-the-margin growth—and not gotten any recognition for his efforts."[7] Bok, for his part, was no doubt interested in broadening McArthur's frame of reference, and in persuading the young professor/administrator that the Business School should set its intellectual sights higher.

McArthur's Letter: A Blueprint

In August 1979, in response to a request from Bok, McArthur wrote a 14-page letter to the Harvard president summarizing their discussions over the preceding months.[8] A close student of history, McArthur framed his letter with several references to the efforts of Wallace Donham, the influential dean from the 1920s and 1930s. He seemed to be trying to stress for Bok the consistency of the School's mission over the years and the persistent nature of its challenges. The upshot of McArthur's letter, for a president who would soon be appointing a new dean, was that there would be no easy answers to the School's problems.

In his letter, McArthur addressed three types of issues: "the general conditions that we must meet to improve the overall framework and climate," the intellectual areas at the School most in need of help, and "the emerging fields that you and I have gone over so often."

In the first category, McArthur emphasized the need to rebuild the self-confidence of the tenured faculty. He knew that without the enthusiastic efforts of this sometimes inflexible group, progress would be difficult and perhaps impossible. The tenure system, which is essential to the maintenance of academic freedom in universities, nevertheless represents the greatest potential obstacle to change. McArthur did not go into this issue directly, but instead wrote that real progress at HBS depended on a shared conviction within the faculty that the School was on the right path. "The absence of a broad consensus in this very particular sense," wrote McArthur, "leads to many other matters that should be possible to handle easily becoming almost intractable."

Also in this vein, he decried what had come to be known as the "Harvard-Stanford game," whereby the School's critics asserted that it was falling behind in a competition with the Stanford Business School. McArthur argued that when an intellectual community fell victim to this kind of "siege mentality," it invariably "becomes defensive, loses sight of its own mission and traditions, is erratic, and eventually ceases to be effective."

He argued further that the existing method of appointing faculty members at Soldiers Field was narrow and inadequate. The failings, he wrote, were in part an outgrowth of recruitment efforts that were inconsistent from one area to the next. Among other bad outcomes, there were no standards to guarantee that the candidate proudly hired by one area at the School would be as good as the candidate rejected by another. The lack of consistent and understandable entry standards only exacerbated the problem of inconsistent quality from area to area.

Several pages of McArthur's letter were devoted to an analysis of the career paths open to senior and nontenured faculty members. Senior people who were unhappy at the School would simply linger on, he warned, unless attractive alternatives existed elsewhere. (More flexible benefits and retirement packages would be helpful here, McArthur suggested.) And a huge block of tenured people simply sitting in one place from age 35 or 40 to age 70 worked against the School's ability to take on new kinds of opportunities.[9]

Junior faculty members faced even tougher challenges. Many, McArthur noted, seeing the odds against becoming tenured, felt that they had to "hedge their bets" after they signed on at the School. They had to keep doing the kinds of things that would keep them attractive to other employers, because a new start elsewhere might become necessary. But by doing so, they sometimes decreased their chances of success at Harvard. "We must find a more satisfactory and realistic way of thinking about these people," McArthur concluded. "Failure to do so is unfair to them, and sows the seeds of great instability later on in the deliberations of the Appointments Committee."

McArthur devoted a lot of attention in his letter to those fields of inquiry at the School that were most in need of rebuilding, repair, or, in some cases, demolition. Among the troubled areas he listed General Management, Control, and Production and Operations Management (POM). Although General Management had distinguished itself in previous decades, the group had now become a victim of its own success and had grown too large and diffuse. As for the heterogeneous group called Control, McArthur predicted that it "may disappear as an area, with its subfields of Financial Accounting, Management Information Systems, and Computing going elsewhere." Other areas, including POM, Marketing, and Organizational Behavior, already were in various stages of rebuilding, but the jury was still out.

Finally, McArthur described what he called the "emerging fields" of interest and promise at the School, and he seemed to imply that he would like to become their advocate. (He didn't know exactly how to do this and only several years later found the answer in the concept of "interest groups," whose evolution is discussed below.) One emerging field was "Business and Its External Environment," a construct McArthur saw as an organizing theme that might cut across the boundaries of traditional areas. A second was "The International Environment," which McArthur felt should be viewed much more broadly than had so far been the case. "A real understanding of the significance and impact of the international context must suffuse most of what we are doing." A third category, "Managing People," was a field McArthur thought might someday comprise the existing areas of Organizational Behavior, Labor, and elements of Management Control and General Management. A fourth, "Governance and the Role of Major Private Enterprise," might focus on the "appropriate role and governance of 'big business' by the rest of society" and therefore play to the existing strengths of the School.

McArthur also advocated an increased emphasis on "Ethical and Moral Values" and on the need for understanding the ways in which such values could shape decision making in business. Attaching for Bok's perusal some old correspondence to and from Dean Donham on the subject of how ethics might be taught, McArthur stressed that he himself was convinced that it would be "more difficult for us to evolve an effective response in this direction than in any other you and I have discussed."

Finally, McArthur argued for a more effective approach to the teaching of entrepreneurship. Thousands of the School's alumni counted themselves as entrepreneurs, and each year hundreds of students at

Soldiers Field wanted training in the subject. In the broader society, entrepreneurship was increasingly being viewed as a wellspring of employment and economic growth. Perversely, though, within the academy the field was regarded as a dead end for young faculty members trying to build a career. "As a consequence," McArthur lamented, "we have no serious research and development initiative around this theme, and most of our MBA teaching is done by part-time visiting entrepreneurs. This is not satisfactory." He suggested that the School should commit significant resources to the field, and also find a way to "reconceptualize" it, perhaps by emphasizing "the entrepreneurial role . . . as opposed to the managerial role."

McArthur's letter to Bok, written a few months before he became dean, gives a remarkably prophetic outline of much that happened at the School over the next decade and a half. The subsequent chapters of this book—notably those on entrepreneurship, ethics, organizations and markets, technology and operations management, and competitive strategy—document in detail the maturation of some of the initiatives McArthur foreshadowed in his letter.

Based on this brief sketch of the state of the School in 1980, one might conclude that it was an institution with clear strengths and equally clear weaknesses. The Harvard-Stanford game notwithstanding, there were no immediate competitive threats to the School's preeminent position in management education. Its faculty was distinguished and productive. Its alumni were successful, generous, and quick to defend the School against perceived attack. Its "products" (not only the MBA program, but also executive education, case materials, and the dominant *Harvard Business Review*) were in great demand. The swings of the international and domestic economy that were bedeviling managers in the late 1970s and early 1980s presented intellectual challenges for the School's faculty, but no compelling cause for alarm. True, some large financial obligations were looming—almost the entire campus, built as a unit during the 1920s, was in need of renovation—but a reconstruction program begun by Dean Fouraker, who had been a very effective fundraiser, had started to address that problem. Still, as McArthur's 1979 letter to Bok makes clear, there were continuing weaknesses that threatened the long-term health of the School.

As for who the School's new leader might be; there were many predictions that Bok was poised to bring in a high-profile outsider as dean, and to give that person explicit instructions to shake the place up. Most people at the School, therefore, were immensely relieved in the fall of 1979, when Bok countered this expectation and picked McArthur. (Bok was astonished when McArthur, who always thought in the long term, insisted on taking three weeks to talk things over with his family, before finally deciding to accept the offer.) Certainly, a homegrown dean was more likely to understand how the place worked and less likely to introduce dramatic and unwelcome changes. But would the new dean have the vision, credibility, courage, and skills needed to exert effective leadership?

People

As he took over the reins in the corner office on the first floor of Morgan Hall, McArthur had two key nonfinancial resources at his disposal: *people*—faculty members, administrators, and others—and *place*—the campus itself. We'll look at aspects of both people and place, beginning with the faculty, which the new dean cast as the most critical resource of all.

McArthur quickly established himself as a master motivator of the faculty. His method was a complex mixture of personal attention, subtle rewards, and his own persistently upbeat attitude. Perhaps reflecting his athletic experiences in his formative years, he often behaved like a tough but benign coach. He was especially effective with the tenured faculty. He sensed, he *knew*, that if he could get his talented veterans to perform up to and even beyond their own abilities, then the younger players would follow and the game would be won. As he wrote in a memo to Derek Bok in the spring of 1985, "As long as we can maintain a truly remarkable faculty that is excited by the pursuit of our unique and very special mission in business education, the Harvard Business School will thrive." The faculty is the "whole ballgame," he said on many occasions, even to nonfaculty audiences who were no doubt expecting to hear that they themselves were an essential part of the game.[10]

Through his sometimes uncanny insights into the nature of people, McArthur managed to develop a genuine personal relationship with almost every member of his tenured faculty. And, as with a powerful coach, many of them became so strongly motivated that they would go through walls for him.

The careful cultivation of his senior colleagues was not McArthur's exclusive preoccupation, nor were those colleagues the only allies he cultivated. To a remarkable extent, McArthur commanded the loyalty of scores of staff members, from the gardeners to the most senior professionals. He had a knack for knowing who should be thanked, when, and how. The half-sheet of the dean's letterhead notepaper with McArthur's distinctive slanting scrawl on it became a fixture on staff bulletin boards around the campus. Flowers, bowls, certificates, books, cameras, and other recognitions from the Dean's Office were similarly prized. McArthur himself often turned up, unannounced, in hospital rooms and at family celebrations of faculty and staff members. The presence at their side of such a busy and prominent person, seemingly in no hurry to leave, was the most convincing proof that he knew about the situation and that their institution would stand by them. One employee who was seriously injured in a car accident had a visit from a concerned McArthur even before the victim's wife was able to reach the hospital. Some HBS-affiliated newborns were admired by the dean before they left the maternity ward.

Part of McArthur's motivation was a real interest in the people around him. "I like people, you know? Most people here, I like."[11] Because the School operated on a relatively small scale, it was possible to make personal contact with a substantial percentage of its people. Many other institutions—the Harvard Medical School, for example, with its multiple teaching hospitals and ten times the HBS faculty—are far too large to manage in this way. McArthur makes a political analogy:

> It's the difference between running for the Senate in 1996 and being Ted Kennedy's grandfather in Ward 17 in Boston. If you're dealing with Ward 17, that's a certain kind of manageable challenge. And I figured that this place was more like Ward 17.[12]

The Ward 17 philosophy, which for the faculty is documented in the other eight chapters of this book, dovetailed with another of McArthur's goals: getting the maximum contribution from every employee. He frequently said that quality is indivisible. "Our bet has been on quality," he told an alumni gathering in 1988. "Our bet has been that the markets we serve will come to understand and seek out the highest quality."[13] And quality, as McArthur saw it, began with mundane things. You couldn't have a first-rate MBA program if you had a second-rate library, a second-rate food service, or a second-rate maintenance staff. There were no second-class citizens, because there were no unimportant jobs. And the remarkable fact that every kind of person in the organization, from typists to athletic trainers to food-service personnel, sought McArthur out for career counseling suggests that these people believed that the dean understood them, valued them, and could give them good guidance.

A large part of McArthur's approach was predicated on his conviction that the faculty's time was the School's most precious asset. The "theory of the case," as he liked to put such things, went something like this: If faculty time is our most valuable asset, then we should never spend it on something that could be done by an administrator. The practical result was that, although a faculty member led every important activity at the School, he or she was usually "doubled" by an administrator who reported through a formal structure to the Associate Dean for Administration, who in turn reported to the Dean. The administrators did the budgets, deployed the support staff, and were held accountable for managing their areas.

Resources were managed from large common pools rather than within small fiefdoms. The Division of Research was directed by a faculty member (and, eventually, a team of four faculty members) who allocated available resources across all the various projects and requests. Administrators monitored expenditures, oversaw the training and supervision of research assistants, and carried out the multiple tasks associated with administering a research budget that came to exceed $40 million.

Place

The Harvard Business School campus is a singular *place*. It shares this characteristic with other distinctive environments that tend to elicit certain feelings—places as different from each other as Arlington National Cemetery, the Vieux Carré in New Orleans, and the waterfront in San Francisco. The Soldiers Field campus was built from scratch during the mid-1920s, on land reclaimed from the tidal basin of the Charles River. The School was designed as a unit by the famous firm of McKim, Mead and White, which had won a spirited architectural competition for the contract. Before that time, the School had been shunted about in Harvard Yard, wandering like an orphan from one temporary home to another. Even as late as the 1920s, business schools were a relatively new phenomenon, and it was not clear what they were supposed to look like. The new design by the McKim firm answered that question in noble style.

Nobody understood the role of the School's physical environment better than John McArthur, who felt its importance in his bones. The campus seemed to have an almost mystical significance to him, and his stewardship took on the quality of a spiritual duty. During his time as dean, first one part of the campus and then another was transformed into a beehive of construction activity. Old buildings were reconstructed, and major new facilities went up. As for the "grounds" component of buildings and grounds, McArthur encouraged far more than 100 flowers to bloom. For 15 years, he invested in new lawns, flower beds, parks, paths, walkways, banks of shrubbery, and circles of benches. In a controversial step, he banned vehicles from most of the campus and sealed his victory by removing the roads they had once traversed.

In particular, McArthur became notorious (there is no other word) for his love affair with trees. All over the campus, towering maples and pines materialized on plots of ground where, hours before, no sprig or sapling had been in evidence. Small groves of fruit trees sprang up overnight, many of them in miraculous full blossom.[14] What was his motivation here? For the amateur psychologists in residence, the answer seemed obvious: it was compensatory behavior. From his high school days, as noted, McArthur had worked in sawmills in his native British Columbia, cutting up innocent pines and firs. Now, decades later, he was providing sanctuary for as many trees as possible.

McArthur acknowledged that the basis of his arboreal fervor lay in the past, but insisted that he had a practical end in mind. During the late 1950s, on his first case-writing assignment as a doctoral student—

"the first time I went out with my hat on," as he later put it—he had traveled to the Johnson & Johnson headquarters campus in New Brunswick, New Jersey. There he was struck by the beauty of J&J's landscaped complex. When afforded an opportunity to meet the company's famous chairman, Robert Johnson, Jr., the first thing that popped out of McArthur's mouth was an effusive compliment on the beauty of the campus. Johnson was delighted. He explained to McArthur that a pleasant working environment was a prerequisite for happy employees and high-quality work. This lesson resonated with McArthur's own feelings about the Soldiers Field environment, and he never forgot it.[15]

Flowers and trees presented one kind of opportunity when he became dean in 1980, but there were more expensive projects to contemplate. Seventeen out of the School's 26 existing buildings needed either major or minor renovations. (Seven of them had not been renovated since 1926.) The first renovation projects were on residence halls, and were begun during the tenure of McArthur's predecessor Lawrence Fouraker. These efforts in turn underscored the need for a new approach to climate control within buildings, and in 1992 the School completed its new chilled-water plant, designed to meet its growing needs in heating and air conditioning. Next, a fiber-optic network was installed as a first step toward moving the School into the Information Age.

Throughout the 1980s and early 90s, McArthur took other steps to improve the quality of campus life for a broader segment of the Soldiers Field community—and, significantly, to make the School more competitive in executive education. McCollum and Baker, the major executive education buildings, were completely redone during the 1980s and early 90s. In 1989, the School's new fitness and community center, Shad Hall, was completed, and the Class of 1959 Chapel was finished in 1992. McArthur's advisers almost unanimously counseled against building this small but highly visible chapel, even though they agreed with his argument that spiritual values must remain paramount. He went ahead anyway.

The most ambitious construction project during McArthur's tenure was the complete rebuilding of Morgan Hall, the faculty office building. The new Morgan, expanded from 53,000 to 116,000 square feet, was made large enough to reassemble most of the faculty, which had become dispersed in eight separate buildings. Its designers were instructed to promote intellectual egalitarianism by making almost all faculty offices more or less equally desirable.

Approximately $200 million was spent on buildings and infrastructure between 1980 and 1995. McArthur oversaw the renovation of 500,000 square feet of existing space and the addition of 300,000 square feet of new space. The replacement value of the School's buildings increased from about $75 million to about $250 million. McArthur most often described these expenditures as investments in a *community*.

The pattern of McArthur's investments underscores, again, that his primary concern was managing and leveraging the faculty. If the faculty got the kinds of support it needed, including creature comforts, logistical help, and infrastructural back-up, then most other things were made much easier. If it did not, then many good outcomes might be precluded. Overall, he made the place serve the people, and for him the key people remained the faculty.

The Function of Publishing

Almost from the beginning, one of the School's most important sets of activities has centered around publication—of faculty research, of the *Harvard Business Review* (begun in 1922), and most distinctively, of cases. Perhaps more than any other school in the world, HBS produces its own teaching materials, a custom that has imposed a tremendous burden on the faculty and staff. They have to keep the materials relevant and up to date, and they must maintain a precarious balance between the needs of students on the one hand and the demands for scholarship by the broader academic community on the other.

When McArthur became dean, there was almost no coordination of the School's assorted publishing activities, which were scattered haphazardly across the campus. The *Harvard Business Review* was located upstairs from The Coop, the student bookstore and notions shop. Case production was done in the basement of Morgan Hall, the principal faculty office building. There the scene resembled a newspaper production room, with noisy printing machines constantly churning out endless copies of cases. Various other publishing activities were done in still other locations. The publication of books by the School had dwindled to almost nothing, because of Dean Fouraker's accurate perception that the whole process was taking on the character of a vanity press.

McArthur saw in this situation an opportunity for a special kind of intellectual venture capitalism. The other eight chapters of this book detail his customary approach, but in publishing he did something quite different. There he placed a large bet not on teams of faculty members but on a new and centralized institutional structure.

He saw several reasons for taking this kind of approach. Probably the most important, at least in the short run, was the opportunity to create a directed activity that could develop and market intellectual products outside a decision-making process run entirely by the faculty, whose time was severely constrained. Then, too, operational and editorial synergies could be gained and economies realized. Looking to the longer term, McArthur also could see that the competitive landscape for the Business School was changing. New technologies were making it possible for intellectual content to be packaged in ways different from traditional books and articles. This situation constituted not only an opportunity, but also a double-barreled threat. The course development and research activities of the School occur on an unparalleled scale, at least in the context of academia. But they are enormously expensive, and there was a danger, as McArthur once put it, that the School might "end up in the position of making most of the critical investments in this food chain and capturing none of the returns."[16]

For all of these reasons, he began during the mid-1980s to consolidate and rejuvenate the School's publishing activities. The Harvard Business School Press was inaugurated in 1986 and at once began to publish books of high quality. Other steps followed in regular succession, and the long process culminated on January 1, 1993, with the launching of the Harvard Business School Publishing Corporation. This new organization moved into a large building of its own located half a mile from the main campus, and rapidly began to expand and rationalize the School's publishing activities.

The Publishing Corporation's marching orders were simple on their face but proved hard to implement: Take advantage of your close relationship with the School, but don't drift into vanity publishing. Experiment with expensive new technologies and new forms of distribution, but continue to return a steady stream of income back to the School. Create an organization that has its own sense of identity, cherishes its independence, and embodies a spirit of risk taking, but don't wander so far from the mother ship that semaphores can't be easily read. Try to improve the editorial quality of the teaching cases, and market them more imaginatively. Amplify the independent voice that the *Harvard Business Review* has created over many decades, and strengthen the links that help give the *Review* early insights into emerging research.

At the time of this writing, it is too early to bring in a verdict on the publishing enterprise. Nevertheless, there are many positive indicators. About six million cases are now sold annually. In the last few years, the HBS Press has published numerous best-sellers, as well as important scholarly and professional works. Several HBS faculty members with longstanding publishing relationships elsewhere have switched their allegiance to the Press. By the late 1990s, the *Harvard Business Review* was enjoying its strongest reader loyalty in many years, as measured by rates of subscription renewal. Almost every one of HBS Publishing's interactive multimedia products so far released has won multiple awards.

This road was not without bumps, of course. It was a difficult task to integrate a wholly owned, not-for-profit subsidiary of the Harvard Business School, which itself does not exist as a legal entity, into the Harvard University system. Some of HBS Publishing's vicissitudes (particularly its adventures in hiring the right people to fill changing jobs, plus a rapid turnover of several *HBR* editors during the early 1990s) received widespread newspaper coverage. But throughout this period of growing pains, McArthur remained unflappable, keeping faith with his own experiment.

The Levers of Management

These, then, were the main components of McArthur's strategy for implementing his intellectual venture capitalism: managing the faculty and other human resources, managing the physical environment, and managing publications. Let us now dig one level deeper, and be more explicit about the tactics that McArthur employed, the levers he chose to pull.

We can point to a half-dozen or so of his preferred methods, and as a narrative convenience, we present them here as imperatives: *do this, don't do that.* McArthur himself was rarely inclined to be explicit or didactic in this way, and his reluctance in part reflects the unusual relationship between a dean and a faculty. All members of a faculty are equal, but the dean is more equal than others. Such a situation necessitates a deft use of both carrot and stick, and also a finely tuned sensitivity to the large but sometimes fragile egos that come into play when deans talk to professors.

Don't Give Direct Orders—Instead, Listen, Persuade, and Cajole

The salient aspect of McArthur's style was his persistent pattern of indirection. He usually had an opinion about whatever problem lay at hand, and he almost always had a strong feeling about where the solution should be found. But he preferred that a colleague discover that solution rather than have it dictated by the dean. And although McArthur had full confidence in the powers of his own intellect, he also was open to discovering that some bright colleague had an idea better than his own.

McArthur's habitual indirection, together with his continual quest for better information, were usually in evidence during his many meetings with colleagues. Often, one's meeting with the dean would overlap with the unrelated meeting that had preceded it and would blur into the meetings that were to follow. Lines of topical demarcation remained curiously fuzzy. An argument from meeting A would be carried forward into meeting B, and the conclusions reached in meeting B might be discussed again in meetings C and D. Often it took 40 or 50 minutes of a one-hour appointment before the announced topic of the meeting was even introduced. Meanwhile, confusion might prevail. One faculty member recalls a meeting A topic—the activities of someone named Warren—spilling over into his own meeting B. He spent most of the ensuing conversation trying to figure out which of three or four possible Warrens was being discussed. As it turned out, this was an entirely new Warren whom he had never heard of and who had no relevance at all to the agenda of his own meeting.[17]

Throughout these overlapping meetings, McArthur was always informal and unceremonious. Clad in his trademark short-sleeved blue shirt and loosened tie, he would lean back in his chair, arms overhead, one hand holding the opposite elbow or clasping the other hand behind his neck. From that posture he would lead a conversation that meandered unhurriedly through a kind of random stream of consciousness. Often McArthur would become engagingly indiscreet and blandly reveal one School secret after another. These indiscretions, which were too commonplace to have been inadvertent, seemed to serve several purposes. People correctly concluded that they were hearing inner-circle arguments, which made them feel that much more central to the organization. The dean clearly trusted them, if he allowed them to hear and participate in these kinds of deliberations. And they themselves reciprocated, as confidants. They provided McArthur with their best off-the-cuff reactions to the issue at hand, thereby giving the dean a quick read on how a broader audience might respond to an impending course of action.

Build Consensus on the Institutional Mission

In many ways, the Harvard Business School was *sui generis,* both before and after 1980. It marched to its own drummer. It was far more interdisciplinary, closer to practice, and more sensitive to the needs of general managers than most business schools. But this position on the frontier cut both ways. Young faculty were understandably anxious about betting their careers on getting tenure at HBS. Senior professors at other institutions were sometimes reluctant to accept offers of employment from Harvard, which they correctly saw as an idiosyncratic institution. The casewriting activity alone was enough to discourage a few, and some others feared that they could not teach well enough to be productive in a community that so emphasized high-quality instruction.

McArthur was convinced that a sense of community and shared purpose was crucial to a free exchange of ideas, which in turn was at the heart of his intellectual venture capitalism. "It is, of course, always important for an effective institution to be clear about its purpose," he wrote in 1982. "It is an *absolute necessity* that this be so in the case of a pioneering institution such as the Harvard Business School that seeks to be uniquely different."[18]

Accordingly, he took a number of steps to build consensus on the purposes of the institution. A typical step came during the mid-1980s with his commissioning of an elaborate history of the School. He defined success for this project as having two characteristics: first, that the book be accurate and complete, and second, that no one be made less productive by its appearance. Although this illustrated history was eventually distributed to several thousand people broadly defined as friends of the School, its target audience was the faculty, whom McArthur wanted to educate about the School's roots and its evolving mission. Many other vehicles of communication were used to this same end during McArthur's tenure, such as research booklets and the *Bulletin*, the School's alumni magazine.

Above all, McArthur refused to be stampeded by new fashions, trends, or crises of the month. After one of his first faculty meetings as dean, he returned to his office with a sense that a particular issue that had been under discussion was now approaching the crisis stage. He began planning a response that would nip the potential crisis in the bud. At that moment, a friend and colleague arrived at the office. The colleague had a feeling, he told McArthur, that now might be a good time for the new dean to review a particular passage from *The Functions of the Executive*, the 1938 management classic written by New Jersey Bell president Chester Barnard. The passage reads as follows:

> *The fine art of executive decision consists in not deciding questions that are not now pertinent, in not deciding prematurely, in not making decisions that cannot be made effective, and in not making decisions that others should make.*[19]

As a result of this colleague's intervention and McArthur's own subsequent experiences, *crisis* was a word that he rarely used. It was also a word that proved a particularly ineffective lever when others used it in conversations with him. In the mid-1980s, for example, it became clear that a book was about to be published that cast the School in a bad light. Faculty members and administrators proposed lawsuits and other preemptive strikes against the forthcoming book. McArthur gave them their hearing, and also took a series of steps to reassure offended individuals that they had his full support. At the same time, he quietly blocked all proposals for dramatic action by the School.

George P. Baker, who served as the School's dean for most of the 1960s, often said that at any given time the next decade was pretty well mapped out at the School. It was the *following* decade, 10 to 20 years into the future, that the dean had to be worrying about. McArthur agreed, and he himself almost always thought in the long term. "This [university] is the oldest corporation in the Western Hemisphere," he said on several occasions. The implication was that an institution like Harvard could weather the most serious of storms. Even today, he pulls *The Functions of the Executive* off his bookshelf and shows a visitor the key passage, marked with a blue highlighter.

Embrace a Strategy and Create a Short List

McArthur sometimes faulted the players in his own field, management education, for lacking a strategy and for playing follow the leader, or, worse, blindman's bluff. Even for the "marauding commercial privateers" who traded in the intellectual capital developed at Harvard, McArthur once said, the "me-too strategy" was certain to fail.[20] His broad conviction was based primarily on his work as a consultant and institution builder in a wide variety of settings, ranging from bankrupt railroads to thriving Boston-area hospitals.

> I go to these meetings, and I watch what's going on. And most of the time I find myself thinking, "Here are all these really smart people, and nobody's got a strategy." Not that they've got the wrong strategy; it's no strategy. They're not thinking in terms of, "This move could lead to this outcome or that, and if it's that, then you're really up a creek, so we'd better not start down that path." Well, that's how I always think.[21]

Almost from his first day in office, McArthur emphasized that he had a relatively brief agenda of things that would get most of his attention. "In my new role as dean," he wrote in his first annual report, "I have consciously centered my efforts in looking towards the future on only a few themes."[22] The corollary was that most other things would not get his attention, soon or easily. For the most part, he stuck to this self-imposed focus. The short list was in part designed to prevent McArthur and his small administrative staff from overextending themselves. But more important, it was intended to conserve the School's resources in the face of near-constant entreaties for a larger institutional agenda. "A small place like this," McArthur told the faculty in 1989, "can't go after everything in a major way that some one of us thinks is interesting, or that people outside our walls will finance."[23]

For the first half-dozen years of McArthur's deanship, he talked and wrote incessantly about the need for high-quality, ground-breaking research. Internal memos and notes for speeches from this period refer to the "research tilt."[24] But it took the HBS community some time to realize that research projects on entrepreneurship, ethics, and other large topics were more than mere flavors of the month. Those who inferred from the evidence of McArthur's own slender published output that he would not emphasize or even recognize rigorous scholarship could not have been more mistaken. Several years went by before the faculty fully believed that McArthur was serious about his emphasis on research. And by that time he had already begun to shove the pendulum in the other direction, toward a reemphasis on teaching and course development. "Reshift balance between research and course development," he noted to himself in the spring of 1990, while preparing remarks for a meeting of Harvard's Council of Deans.[25] The overall point was that choices had to be made and the list of high-priority goals kept short. "Our resources and capacity are limited," he told one of the School's governing boards in 1990. "We are pressed from all sides to do MORE. Well, we cannot!"[26]

Define the Partnership and Facilitate Productive Teamwork

As noted above, McArthur felt strongly that the faculty was the "whole ball game." In his first formal address as dean, he talked at length about making every effort to help the faculty do its work. At the same time, he asked his colleagues to avoid what he called a "dependency relationship" and to limit their demands on him. The "partnership" he envisioned would grow out of mutual respect and be built by contributions from all. An effective partnership would be straightforward, would avoid "nagging criticisms of others . . . in their absence," and would avoid "blow-ups."[27]

In a logical extension of the partnership theme, McArthur talked often about the need for people to work together, especially when it came to the kinds of issues that were growing beyond the capacity of one person to master and affect. "The demands of the research and development we must do on so many of the new fronts," he told one audience, "suggest that we must surpass our traditional ethic of going it alone."[28] Actually, the School had a powerful collective ethic in many of its activities. Far more than faculty at most other institutions of higher learning, HBS professors were accustomed to working together. Their cooperative efforts within teaching groups and in activities such as the Advanced Management Program and the Program for Management Development invariably struck senior recruits from other schools as highly unusual.

Why were people so much more willing to work together at Soldiers Field than elsewhere? What was the glue that held them together? The answer was complex, but McArthur knew that part of it came from a sense of their own good fortune at being at Harvard, a sense of being blessed with membership in a special kind of academic community. Accordingly, whenever and however he could, he worked to preserve and strengthen that sense—to instill a feeling of institutional excellence, almost as a Marine drill instructor instills in new recruits a sense of the eliteness of the Corps. McArthur constantly preached not only teamwork, but the excellence of the School, manifested in its people, its publications, and its distinctive physical environment.

Sometimes the teamwork might stretch across the breadth of Harvard and to other schools, when extremely complex issues such as energy and the environment came to the fore. As he said to another audience, "The notion that any single scholar can take on the world energy problem and have something very useful to say about it is, I think, outdated."[29] But

McArthur remained very cautious throughout his deanship about collaborations with other parts of Harvard, let alone other universities. At a September 1992 academic retreat sponsored for the University's deans by Harvard's new president, Neil Rudenstine, McArthur argued that teamwork among schools within the university shouldn't be attempted simply for its own sake, especially across disciplines or institutional boundaries that might prove hard to break down. McArthur recommended that advocates of such work ask a series of questions: *Why this effort? Why this effort in a collaborative way? How new is it? How unique is it?* And finally, *Who's paying?* Only when these questions could be answered in a satisfactory way should a proposed collaboration move forward. For the most part, the real teamwork went on within the confines of Soldiers Field, and there it sometimes reached extraordinary heights.

Enhance Creativity through More Flexible Organizational Structures

McArthur's consolidation of publishing at the School has already been described. He took similar steps to reorganize parts of the faculty, and for the same reason—to facilitate new thinking. But here he moved in the opposite direction, toward decentralization. Early in his tenure, he became convinced that the School's existing "area" (departmental) structure did not satisfactorily encourage the generation of ideas. Lacking any alternative, he continued to work within that structure.

In 1983, however, a breakthrough came. The School's Research Policy Committee, reporting on a multiyear study of the subject, argued that a new entity, the "interest group," was needed to supplement the area structure. This idea hit McArthur like a hammer. "It was the key to our problems," he later said. "It made everything else possible."[30] And it fit neatly with the imperatives he had outlined in his letter to President Bok some four years earlier.

McArthur proceeded over the next few years to encourage the formation of new interest groups. One of his first steps was to summon three young full professors whom he believed to be constrained within General Management, then an oversized area with about 45 faculty members. He invited each of the three to head one of the new interest groups. The alternative, he said, was to keep tilting at the ponderous windmill of General Management, honoring or overthrowing the young professors' mentors and others who had gone before, but never getting much done that would be of real importance. The three eventually agreed, and thus the first three interest groups were born.[31] From that point on, not only areas but also *ideas* were in a position to drive developments—especially as McArthur directed resources toward the interest groups. Between 1980 and 1984, these three new groups, along with the ethics interest group, experienced a net gain of nine faculty members.[32] By 1994, the number of interest groups had risen to eight, reflecting not only internal developments but also the recruitment of strong faculty leaders from the outside.[33] The work of several interest groups is described in subsequent chapters of this book.

Similarly, McArthur in 1986 created what informally became known as the "Gang of Four" to head the School's Division of Research. Rather than continuing the tradition of having one person serve as head of the School's entire research and development effort (which was in the process of growing from about $15 million in 1980 to $44 million in 1995), McArthur asked four professors to serve jointly as directors of research. Each would take responsibility for a quarter of the faculty, and make a serious effort to understand and support their intellectual work.

Bet on People

In pursuing his strategy of intellectual venture capitalism, McArthur chose his ventures very carefully, and the other chapters of this book provide rich examples. Sometimes McArthur put more than one person or group to work on the same problem simultaneously. In explaining his rationale for doing this, he liked to cite the early history of the Apollo space program. When President Kennedy announced in the early 1960s that the nation would put a man on the moon before the end of the decade, the engineers at NASA were flabbergasted. The odds against meeting Kennedy's challenge successfully, NASA believed, were overwhelming. The only possible way to do it was to launch multiple design projects along parallel tracks. For instance, there would have to be multiple engines under design in 1965 if the space agency was to have any chance that one of them would succeed by the time the clock ran out in 1969. The same was true of boosters, lunar landers, retro rockets, heat shields, and so on.

Creativity, McArthur believed, grew mainly out of talent, experience, and dedication. But it also depended on the vagaries of human existence. Even if all other factors came together in support of a particular creative endeavor, the person leading that effort could get sick. Or a family member could suddenly start demanding more attention. Or a marriage could collapse.

The School must bet on *people*, McArthur concluded. Most often, the problem was a lack of people to bet on. Engine projects were unlikely to succeed, he reasoned, unless they had a specified owner—someone who felt responsible for the project. "Saying that we'll all do something is the kiss of death here at HBS," he once told a group of alumni. "It almost always means that whatever it is will get lost in the shuffle." [34] Not just any owner would do. The bigger the proposed initiative, the more important it was to have a talented and relatively young person as its owner. "I only back new ventures with strong leadership from the next generation," he told another gathering. [35]

This "ownership imperative" extended to the careers of individuals, as well as to projects. At one meeting, McArthur refused to approve a scheme that had a former faculty member serving in an exclusively administrative role unless one of the professors in attendance at that meeting agreed to take personal responsibility. "Our track record in situations like this is terrible," he said. "One of you has to look out for this person." Not until someone volunteered for the assignment did the larger scheme move forward.

Think Big

A recurrent theme in conversations with both faculty and administrators about their experiences with McArthur is his continual admonitions to dream bigger dreams and hitch wagons to higher stars. A senior professor specializing in information technology recalls being asked sometime in the 1980s by McArthur to think about how the School could do more with computers. The professor began looking into different ways of wiring up the campus to make computer resources more accessible and flexible. "Then I got a call from John," he says. "He said, 'Maybe I wasn't clear. I want you to think really *imaginatively* about computers in our educational program. Think about how you can spend a *ton* of money and make a real impact.' It was only after that discussion that I began thinking that we could reach for having every MBA student and every faculty member owning their own computer—which is exactly what we did, nine months later." [36]

Another present-day senior professor was the head of the MBA program in 1989, the year when the Berlin Wall came down. This professor was convinced that the School should do something in formal recognition of this momentous event. He expressed his conviction to McArthur, who encouraged him to think about how to do it. A week later, at a meeting of associate deans, McArthur asked if anyone had any ideas about how the School should come to terms with the fall of the Berlin Wall. The head of the MBA program—evidently the only person in the room with advance warning of the question—presented his ideas, which included bringing together people from Eastern Europe with the MBA students.

"So I laid this stuff out," he recalls, "and John says, 'I think that's a great idea. Why don't we lease a 747, go around to each of those countries, and pick up the people and bring them back to Boston for a conference?'" In the end, the 747 was not leased, but a major event was held at Soldiers Field involving dozens of people from Eastern Europe. The point of McArthur's message—"think big, get it done, and get it done right"—was heard loud and clear. [37]

Say "No" Respectfully

McArthur was a firm believer in keeping one's options open as long as possible. He knew that an opportunity seized too soon might turn out to have excessive costs associated with it. But he almost never uttered an outright "no."

There are innumerable examples of McArthur's method here. One faculty member in the early stages of his career at the School was asked to help organize a group of HBS professors in a large-scale effort to teach business history to Harvard undergraduates. This prospective invitation from the Faculty of Arts and Sciences to participate in Harvard College's "core curriculum" was unusual, and the HBS historians believed that the opportunity should be seized. They were convinced that they could get across to thousands of Harvard undergraduates a number of vital messages about the exceptionally rich history of American business. The School's historians were unanimously enthusiastic: "This is something we really should do," they said to McArthur, whom they knew to be a voracious reader of history books himself.

But the dean, after listening to the proposal and nodding with apparent empathy, gave a nebulous response. He seemed oddly noncommittal, even though the School's historians made it clear that they were being pressed for an answer by their friends across the Charles River. On the second and third occasions when the project was brought up, McArthur remained similarly vague. He kept asking questions with little relevance to the issue at hand. He just didn't seem to be getting it.

But of course it was the historians themselves who weren't getting it. Ultimately, the proposal ran out of steam and died a quiet death, even though no one in the group recalls having heard McArthur say "no" to their proposal. In long retrospect, it became clear to the professors involved that the idea had been a bad one to begin with. During the intervening years they had been able to produce a large body of work that would have been impossible to complete had they been teaching legions of undergraduates in addition to their MBA students at Soldiers Field.

McArthur almost never said "no" to anybody. But in addition to drawing out time so that bad ideas would die of their own accord, he built a management system that said "no" quite effectively. At his retirement party given by the administrative staff, T-shirts were distributed to everyone. But there were two different designs. One shirt, to be worn only by McArthur, read "YES!" The other design, worn by everyone else, explained that "What John really means is, . . . "

By never saying "no" directly, McArthur was able to display his enthusiasm for one of the flowers that might actually bloom, and at the same time not break the bank. In time, too, this technique helped improve the quality of ideas that landed on McArthur's desk; and the best ideas, the ones most completely thought out, somehow made a more rapid passage to institutional support and reality.

More than the Sum of Our Parts?

A key lesson emerges from the deanship of John McArthur. An unusually cohesive *community* grew out of the cooperative interaction among members of the faculty, the coordination of effort between the faculty and the administrative staff, and the commitment of the students and alumni to each other and to the School. These characteristics have made Harvard a special place to work and study—an institution that, like a chemical compound, has become different from and more than the sum of its constituent elements.

From a historical perspective, it is unusual for an organization to add up to more than the sum of its parts. During the Napoleonic Wars, Bonaparte's French army and Nelson's British navy were organizations so well led and so finely attuned to their tasks that they far exceeded the sum of their parts. By contrast, and much more typically, the huge but disorganized Spanish Armada of the late sixteenth century and the inept Italian army of World War II were less than the sum of theirs.

The success of any human institution, from families to business firms to armies to symphonies, is contingent on the ability of its members to cooperate with and complement each other. When the members of an organization achieve this state, they can accomplish great things, few of which they could do by themselves. Conversely, superb individual talents are likely to be frustrated when their organizations are atomistic and uncoordinated. Recriminations and resentment set in. When the Boston Red Sox became a group of pampered and uncooperative individualists during the 1970s and 1980s, the team's fans recited a code phrase: "25 players, 25 cabs."

But exceeding the sum of its parts doesn't just mean that the army is conquering, the team winning, the company turning a profit, or the musical group pleasing its audiences. Any competent human organization can usually hit one or two benchmarks of success. But for an institution to be truly exceptional, its members have to help each other transcend their individual limitations. When they do so, they perform far better than they and their critics thought possible.

What about academic institutions? Do they typically exceed the sum of their parts? Viewed in one way, the answer is an obvious "yes." Almost by definition, a large assembly of more or less brilliant people in one place, comprising disciplines from anthropology to zoology, would seem to assure that exciting things will happen. And yet there is no such assurance. Many universities with outstanding faculties can't seem to deliver a high-quality education. Conveying knowledge, it turns out, is as much of an art as building knowledge. Even the most prestigious universities at times resemble feudal baronies whose warlords jealously guard their prerogatives. They hire only people who speak their rarefied language, write articles only for each other, treat institutional resources as components of a zero-sum calculation (your gain is my loss), and spend inordinate amounts of time on guard duty for their narrow disciplines. Often within the academy, the most common cry is not "Let's go for it!" but "Who goes there?"

Occasionally, into this kind of strange landscape of unrealized potential walks a character like John McArthur. How does such a person conceptualize his task? Where does he get the patience to cope with it? Today, after his retirement from the deanship, McArthur says, "Much of what I did had to do with releasing energy. The energy was already there; it was just looking for a way to get released."[38] So he placed bets, tried to create circumstances that would make new things possible, guarded against meltdowns, and pushed for good outcomes. McArthur's view of the interest group invention captures the essence of this energy releasing, in the context of cross-disciplinary opportunism: "Get things moving and take some shots as chance arises," he once wrote in some notes for a speech.[39] On the occasion of another speech, in his typically short and telegraphic messages to himself, McArthur summarized his approach: "Keep things moving. Try new things, take risks—KEY!—kill things, But, don't fall apart."[40]

People were everything in this kind of guided opportunism, the scarcest resource and the most valuable prize. It mattered less which disciplinary door they walked through, as McArthur once phrased it, than whether they had what it took. "In hiring and promoting people," McArthur wrote to President Bok in 1985, "we can afford to put much less weight than we do on narrow fit with an existing need at the School, and more on whether the person being considered for the faculty position is *truly* outstanding and special when measured against all comers."[41] Bok, over the entire span of McArthur's 15-year deanship, never vetoed a single one of McArthur's recommendations for hiring and promotion, thereby encouraging the dean to range far afield in his hunt for talent.[42]

This was in part because Bok believed that the School was the most *managed* part of Harvard. And in retrospect, McArthur himself gives Bok immense credit for making a focused effort to understand the School's distinctive culture: the necessity for it to manage its own promotions process, rather than relying on the relatively impersonal, "ad hoc" system followed by most of the rest of the university; the importance of preserving alumni loyalty; the relevance for the School of the ingenious Harvard system of "every tub on its own bottom," with all that implies about autonomy and financial self-reliance. Bok's unusual commitment helped Harvard in its own competition with other business schools. "Nobody else had a president like we did," says McArthur.[43]

It is appropriate, of course, that a school of business administration be the beneficiary of effective and thoroughgoing management. But McArthur aspired to a new standard for academic administration, and the heart of his strategy was intellectual venture capitalism. At the end of the October 1996 HBS symposium honoring him, McArthur offered an unusual analogy to explain his deanship:

> *I adopted a kind of Elizabethan strategy—Elizabeth the First, that is. She sent thousands of little ships down the Thames, and those sailors went all around the world. Some got boiled and eaten in the South Pacific. Others ran onto the rocks in New England. And in some cases, Elizabeth had to send the navy out to bring them back in chains. But somehow or other, they eventually got back home to the*

Thames—after three years, or thirteen years, or whatever. And that was my belief about this place. I thought we should try to encourage as many people as possible who had an idea to head down the Thames, and see what they would do with it.[44]

But people are fragile, and their ability to cooperate with each other is more fragile still. The choice of a title for the School's history printed during McArthur's tenure—*A Delicate Experiment*, a phrase borrowed from one of the School's founders—seemed curious to some readers. There is not much about the Harvard Business School that appears to be delicate, considering its faculty, professional staff, students, reputation, endowment, physical plant, and other assets. But McArthur believed that the School's great strengths could easily be dissipated. "We cannot assume safely that those who follow us are automatically going to bond, and make the kinds of organizational commitments that have made the Business School such an effective teaching and learning institution in the past," he cautioned toward the end of his tenure. *"There is nothing that is automatic about this at all."*[45]

What must be done when organizational commitments can't be taken for granted and when nothing is automatic? The answer lies in part in the strategies and tactics outlined in the previous pages and in the next eight chapters: managing available resources in ways that make the implicit contract fair for all concerned, defining the partnership creatively, betting on people, thinking big, saying "no" carefully, and so on. But it also lies in the hands of "teachers"—individuals who are willing to serve as embodiments and endorsers of the organization's most important attributes.

"I'm a case method teacher," McArthur told one of the School's governing boards toward the end of his tenure.[46] By serving as an organizational teacher—an exemplar—and by empowering others to serve in the same way, McArthur for a decade and a half made the Harvard Business School more—much more—than the sum of its parts.

John McArthur at age two, posing on his scooter.

Age six (right front), with his brother Kenneth, age four, and parents, Hector and Elizabeth McArthur.

On horseback at his grandfather's farm in Alberta.

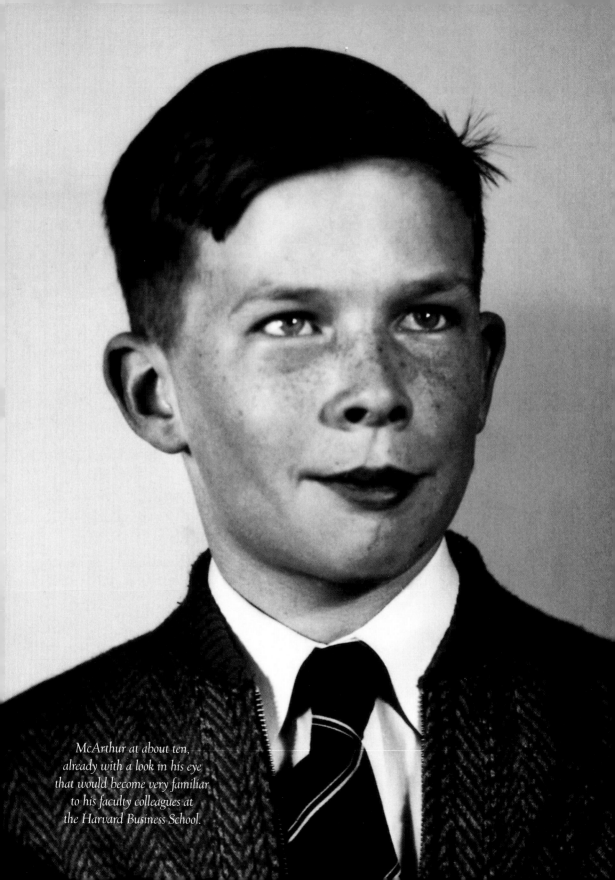

McArthur at about ten, already with a look in his eye that would become very familiar to his faculty colleagues at the Harvard Business School.

*John and Natty McArthur were college sweethearts, and John was a
star athlete in high school, college, and for a brief time in a semipro football league.
Here we see him in one of his football jackets. In a 1987 issue of* TV Guide,
*the writer Andy Meisler observed: "Sometimes even the unlikeliest of heroes are based on
real people. Eric, the leather-jacketed genius in [the ABC television sitcom]*
Head of the Class, *is based partially on a Vancouver high school acquaintance of cocreator
Rich Eustis. 'His name is John McArthur. He was the terror of the 12th grade.
He was a real tough, volatile type of guy. He played football. He was later rumored to be
the smartest kid ever to graduate from our high school. He's now the
Dean of the Harvard Business School.'"*

John and Natty out for a night on the town.

McArthur with friends at his graduation from the University of British Columbia in 1957. He majored in forestry.

McArthur just before
he began his doctoral
study in 1960.

Associate Dean for University Affairs, 1970s.

Speaking to a group of alumni in the fall of 1980, not long after he became dean.
(Photograph by Richard A. Chase)

*Fleshing out an idea
in a meeting during the
fall of 1980.*

McArthur laying out his ideas in a meeting in
his Morgan Hall office. Also pictured (left to right) are
Senior Associate Dean for Educational Programs
Thomas Piper, who carried an immense operational burden
during the McArthur years; and Dean Currie,
Associate Dean for Administration and Policy Planning
during the early part of the McArthur era.

Those who came to McArthur's office for meetings will recall this familiar posture.
(Photograph by Samuel S. Zanghi)

Presenting an MBA student with his diploma at graduation ceremonies.
(Photograph by Brooks Kraft)

CHEAP MONEY
THE DIFFERENCE
IT WILL MAKE
PAGE 30

SOFTWARE SPECIAL REPORT: THE GROWING GETS ROUGH PAGE 128

BusinessWeek

MARCH 24, 1986   A McGRAW-HILL PUBLICATION

Remaking An Institution

THE HARVARD B-SCHOOL

Plus a report card on the nation's top business schools
PAGE 54

DEAN JOHN H. McARTHUR
AND HARVARD STUDENTS

McGraw Hill

Business Week, 24 March 1986, when Harvard Business School and its dean were
featured in the cover article. (Reprinted from the March 24, 1986, issue of Business Week
by special permission. © 1986 by McGraw-Hill Companies.)

HBS is an institution with a strong sense of its history and traditions, where the coexistence of past and future is evident in the school's architecture. Here, the renovated Morgan Hall and the tower of Cotting House are reflected in the windows of Shad. (Photograph by Brooks Kraft)

The south side of Morgan Hall, facing Shad and the tennis courts. The renovation and new design of Morgan, and the reconsolidation of most faculty offices there, were milestones in the late years of McArthur's deanship. (Photograph by Richard A. Chase)

*A three-dimensional model of the design for Shad Hall, the HBS fitness
and community center completed in 1989. Shad won awards for its architectural design by Kallmann,
McKinnell & Wood, and it became a favorite haunt of MBA and executive education students.
(Photograph © Steve Rosenthal, Architect; Moshe Safdie Associates)*

The Dean's House, with its grounds in full summer bloom. McArthur oversaw a thorough renovation of this building and used it as a headquarters for visiting dignitaries and official faculty functions. (Photograph by Richard A. Chase)

At McArthur's direction, the school created an extremely attractive
Senior Faculty Center for emeritus professors. Here, Professors
C. Roland Christensen and Alfred D. Chandler, Jr. discuss their work.

The Class of 1959 Chapel, completed in 1992, pictured on the day of its dedication. McArthur wanted the Chapel to be a constant reminder of the importance of spiritual values. In the audience applauding the Dean, Natty McArthur stands toward the front wearing blue. (Photograph by Brooks Kraft)

The interior of the Chapel. The skylights in
the roof were designed to produce prismatic rainbows on
the Chapel walls, contributing to the celestial feeling of
the sanctuary. The only other ornament in the Chapel, aside from
the changing patterns of light that play on the walls, is
an arrangement of flowers, freshly cut every week. The acoustics
are ideal for the frequent concerts held for
the HBS community. (Photograph by Brooks Kraft)

The interior courtyard of the Chapel, enclosed by a glass pyramid. The flowers and trees planted around the edge of the courtyard and the walkways through its central fishpond infuse the space with a warm serenity bordering on the tropical. (Photograph by Brooks Kraft)

*When McArthur became Dean, he set about adding life to the campus through
a carefully crafted landscaping plan. Here, a tree and surrounding shrubs are planted outside
Baker Library in 1992. (Photo by Susan Young)*

Handsome old trees make a vaulted ceiling of leaves and branches over the walkway through the center of campus. (Photograph by Richard A. Chase)

One of the many archways around campus. The view through the arch looks almost idyllic with the sunlight and greenery; it was this kind of effect for which McArthur hoped when he began transforming the campus grounds. (Photograph © Kindra Clineff)

A woman walking by the bronze sculpture Presence *on an autumn day.*
As part of the campus landscaping plan, a patio was laid in the courtyard outside Hamilton Hall,
and McArthur chose this sculpture by the artist Mary Frank as the area's centerpiece.
The inspiration for the work, according to Frank, was a magazine photograph of a "primitive,
poignant" Himalayan doll she saw as a child. Frank used clay molds to cast the
300-pound sculpture in bronze.

McArthur genuinely cares about the people of HBS, and his feelings are reciprocated. Here he talks with staff members at the picnic given in his honor in July 1995. (Photograph by Richard A. Chase)

Staff members display the commemorative quilt they made for McArthur upon his retirement as dean in 1995. The quilt represents some of his contributions to the school through familiar HBS scenes and symbols. (Photograph by Brooks Kraft)

John and Natty McArthur at the Dean's Dinner in September 1995.
(Photograph by Richard A. Chase)

*Natty McArthur, with her husband in the background, accepts a gift
presented by Neil Rudenstine, Harvard's president, at the Dean's Dinner in September 1995.
(Photograph by Richard A. Chase)*

Deans Kim Clark and John McArthur,
enjoying a seminar at the three-day
Faculty Symposium sponsored by Clark
in McArthur's honor in October 1996.
(Photograph by John Mottern)

Technology and Operations Management

Life on an Academic Cliff Edge

ROBERT H. HAYES AND MARCO IANSITI

ONE SPRING AFTERNOON in 1984, Kim Clark, an associate professor in the School's Technology and Operations Management unit, went to Dean McArthur's office for a one-on-one conference. The subject of the meeting was Clark's intellectual agenda for the next several years.

Clark laid out his teaching and research plans, most of which had a common thread: his desire to find a home for the teaching of science management at the School. The young economist had perceived an increasing interest among his faculty colleagues in the management of basic research, technology, product design and development, and other important intersections of business and science. It seemed to Clark that developing a better understanding of science and technology management might also be an interesting way to attack the problems of productivity and competitiveness, which were then at the heart of the "Japan versus America" debate. He proposed a series of small-scale initiatives whereby he might discover productive ways to broaden the School's agenda.

But as he talked, Clark became aware that the dean—although not coming right out and saying so—was far from satisfied with the proposals. Finally, Clark asked McArthur why he looked disappointed.

"Kim," McArthur responded, "what you've come up with is acceptable, but I don't think it's the very best you can do. And in my experience, people around here never get anywhere unless they think big. So what I want you to do is go away, think some more about it, and come back with your big dreams."

IN RECENT YEARS, the Technology and Operations Management (TOM) unit has enjoyed a strong reputation, both inside and outside the Harvard Business School. But this has not always been the case, and chances are good that it will not always be the case in the future.[1]

In this essay, the authors undertake to explore how a rapidly changing discipline, carried forward by an ever-changing roster of diverse players, can be kept cohesive. We describe a field that has been held together by a number of integrating mechanisms, which we have discovered are themselves in need of constant reinforcement. We consider the paradox of inclusiveness—as we welcome members of new subdisciplines into our group, we run the risk of losing our focus—and we are aware that it was a cohesive agenda for research and teaching, in large part, that led to past successes.

We begin this essay with a quick summary of the TOM group's last 40 years. Maybe a recounting of four decades of Sisyphean labors will seem like overkill to some readers. Much of what has seemed to be of burning importance to those of us within the group may seem irrelevant to people outside the group. But we believe that there are useful lessons to be learned from our experience, applicable to a whole range of groups whose members must work together to solve tough intellectual problems that change rapidly over time.

John McArthur is the person who facilitated many of the most important changes in our unit during the 1980s and 1990s. He consistently provided his strong personal support and the School's financial backing. But to properly understand the nature and magnitude of the changes that occurred in the TOM unit during McArthur's deanship, it is useful to go back some 15 years before he became dean, to the mid-1960s. At that time the TOM unit (then called the Production area) was in the early stages of a battle for its very soul.

Surviving the 1960s

Through the 1950s and early 1960s, the Production area had focused on the nuts and bolts of running a factory, an approach that was captured effectively in our required first-year course. This course was essentially an amalgam of old-fashioned production management and industrial engineering. First-year students began their Production training by learning to read blueprints. Then they studied the operation of basic machine tools (such as the milling machine), and after that they plunged into analyses of the problems likely to be encountered in managing a metalworking business. Typical issues covered by the course included job definition and analysis, time-and-motion study, factory layout, work scheduling, shop floor control, inventory management, and personnel disputes.

Although practical and full of insights that often were applicable in other functional contexts—even in some general management contexts—the course gradually became less and less popular with our students. Fewer MBAs intended to work for metalworking companies, and not many were willing to invest in the extrapolations that were necessary to make Production relevant to other disciplines. At the same time, the course was becoming difficult to staff. In American companies and the academy alike, more and more observers were concluding that we had "solved the problem of production," as John Kenneth Galbraith phrased it.[2] As a result, production/operations management departments at business schools around the country were facing a crisis. Young people no longer were pursuing doctoral studies in either manufacturing management or industrial engineering. The future looked grim.

Meanwhile, the popular new field of operations research (OR) offered a radically different approach. OR and its philosophical siblings (such as systems analysis) addressed operating problems by abstracting them to core elements and creating mathematical or computer models to capture the interrelationships among those elements. The models were then analyzed using appropriate mathematical, statistical, or computer simulation techniques; and the resulting solutions were reinterpreted in light of the context from which the problems had been abstracted.

This approach often led to different types of solutions from those obtainable through the traditional production approach, the goal of which typically was to develop an incremental and "sensible" improvement over existing practice. Operations research, moreover, offered the promise of universality. By developing an effective solution for a single generalized problem, one ought to be able to solve a number of other, apparently unrelated problems in various industries, which might have different physical manifestations but which shared a common underlying logical/mathematical structure.

OR opened up the production field to people who were quite unlike those who long had dominated it. Direct hands-on experience working in factories was no longer required. An analytical mind and extensive training in mathematics, statistics, and computer techniques were what counted. As a result, it became possible for the field of operations management to become more "academic" (that is, discipline-based, rather than specific context–based) in nature. Young people were much excited by the promise of this new field, and they began pouring into doctoral programs that provided the relevant training. From there, they gravitated naturally into the operations management departments of business schools around the world.

Not surprisingly, a series of acrimonious disputes between the old guard and the Young Turks soon erupted. Several prominent schools, including Chicago, Columbia, Stanford, and Wharton, eventually resolved this problem by jettisoning the old guard. Those schools converted their operations management departments into operations research departments or did away with their operations management groups entirely.[3]

The Harvard Business School came close to making a similar decision in the late 1960s. Most of the new people who had been hired into the Production area during the 1960s came with an OR orientation. Meanwhile, as noted above, the area's required first-year course was becoming unpopular with MBA students. The area's hodgepodge of second-year elective courses generally attracted few students.[4] There was a total of nine such electives, ranging from the traditional (Management of Production Operations, and Operations Planning and Control) to the avant-garde (Systems Analysis: The City). Even Harvard's flagship executive program, the Advanced Management Program (AMP), which had deep roots in the production field, quietly dropped operations management from its required curriculum.

During the 1967–1968 academic year, the area renamed itself the Production and Operations Management, or POM, group. There is a saying at the School that a course that changes its name constantly is a course in trouble, and the same might be said about an area. It certainly proved true for POM. In 1969, after years of tension and discord, the POM area erupted into a full-fledged civil war over its future direction. One group, comprising those who embraced the traditional mission of the area, argued that it was expanding in far too many directions at once. As a result, it was losing its coherence and sense of community.[5] They contended that the area should henceforth refocus its attention on the kinds of managerial issues and approaches that it understood well, which were of demonstrated value to managers in the real world.

But another faction, those espousing the new approach based on OR and systems analysis, argued that "the kind of business world represented in most of our basic cases passed its peak in the 1950s." Therefore, the area must necessarily "become increasingly [concerned with] large and complex systems and changing technology and . . . move toward analytical, rather than just experiential, understandings of the managerial issues in our domain."[6] Members of this group went so far as to propose that the word *production* be dropped from the area's new name; henceforth, it should simply be called the "Operations Management" area.

The debate became so bitter that members of the first group eventually proposed a split into two distinct areas: "*Area Alpha* . . . a 'concept Area' whose primary focus will be upon those concepts, techniques and tools—quantitative and non-quantitative—that are not the primary responsibility of other Areas and are particularly applicable to any/all types of technologically based operating activities" and "*Area Beta* . . . a 'process Area' whose primary focus will be upon the management process in specific types of enterprises."[7] Each new area would offer its own required and elective courses. Others opposed a formal split, arguing instead that those who didn't like the way the area was heading should consider "withdrawal from [the] area, to reduce the friction . . . [and] affiliate with some other area . . . or withdrawal from the School, to find a new and more congenial environment."[8]

The School's faculty as a whole recognized that, although OR could bring some powerful tools to bear in solving certain types of problems, it was severely limited in the kind of problems it could deal with. At other schools, where the "Alphas" had won total victory, OR faculty tended to focus most of its attention on problems involving uncertain physical flows over time (such as demand forecasting, work scheduling, inventory control, the management of waiting lines, and physical distribution) or on the allocation of scarce resources among alternative short-term uses. These diverse problems had one thing in common: they were relatively easy to model. But problems involving longer-term strategic issues, and especially those associated with people—and with managing the interactions and conflicts among functional groups within a company, such as marketing and operations—were usually considered too difficult to model. So they were essentially ignored.

For those faculty leaders who had to deal on a day-to-day basis with the contentious field of POM, it was no doubt tempting simply to burn down this troubled house, perhaps through the wholesale expulsion of one of the two warring groups. Surely the HBS administration perceived an alarming deterioration in the external measures usually used to assess the success of an academic group and—closer to home—in the group's internal collegiality. To the School's great credit, however, it resisted the solution-by-elimination approach adopted at some of its competitor schools.

The Resurgence of the 1970s

Dean Lawrence Fouraker, John McArthur's predecessor, saw complementary strengths and weaknesses in the two POM factions and decided to try to maintain both perspectives within one larger group. In 1971 Fouraker appointed Professor C. Wickham Skinner as the new area chairman and simultaneously asked several of those who had been among the most active combatants in the civil war to shift their activities to other areas or programs. At the same time, four faculty members from other areas—all of whom were felt to possess a more or less dispassionate view of the Alpha versus Beta debate—were persuaded to join the area.[9] John McArthur, who was soon to be appointed faculty director of the MBA program, was involved in these decisions.

Over time, Fouraker's and McArthur's faith in the POM area's ability to resolve its problems was vindicated. The area experienced a remarkable renaissance. Under the successive leadership of two of the new transfers (Paul Marshall and Steve Wheelwright) in the early to mid-1970s, the first-year POM course was restructured, infused with new teaching materials, and staffed with new instructors. Students responded positively, and in their course ratings ranked the retooled POM course in the top half of the required curriculum. Two new second-year courses also were created, both of which proved highly successful: The Management of Service Operations and The Operating Manager. A required course on Operations Management was reintroduced into the Advanced Management Program.

Traditionally, students at the School have voted with their feet through their enrollment in electives, thereby signaling what is working in the curriculum and what is not. The School has paid close attention to these signals. Enrollment in POM's second-year courses rose from about 400 in 1969–1970 to about 900 in 1974–1975, and this was a very encouraging sign for the resurgent POM area.

But there was more to the story. These numbers did not include the students who took the popular elective course offered by the Labor Relations group, which became affiliated with POM during this period. Up until that time, Labor Relations had existed as a separate entity. The group consisted of three senior professors who were distinguished in their field. All three were approaching retirement, however, and Fouraker and McArthur became concerned about how the trio's legacy might be passed on. By affiliating with POM, the Labor Relations group improved its ability to recruit and develop new faculty (see below), and the area was able to introduce more labor relations issues into its first-year course.

The affiliation between POM and Labor Relations was not simply a marriage of convenience. At least from the days of the Luddites of early nineteenth-century England, workforce management and dispute resolution had been of intense interest to those involved in the production process. This interest was reflected in various POM courses over the years and sometimes resulted in overlap and awkward tensions between POM and Labor Relations. There was additional overlap with the Organizational Behavior (OB) area, one of whose principal interests was human resource management (HRM). The merger of POM and Labor Relations during the late 1970s helped resolve some of these tensions. It also fanned the interest in HRM among several area members—most notably Wick Skinner, who began offering an elective course on "Personnel and the Manager" in the late 1970s.

The success of that course, and its increasing attention to issues outside POM, attracted the attention of professors in other areas. During the early 1980s, the School's faculty decided to introduce a required course on HRM into the first-year curriculum, and Skinner co-taught the course with several members of the OB and General Management areas. The course and those teaching it soon affiliated with the OB area, and POM's formal affiliation with the Labor Relations group ended. The original problem, however, persists today: because operations involve people—generally lots of people—it is often difficult not to address HRM issues when dealing with operations/technology problems.[10]

Concurrently, area faculty were publishing a number of influential articles and books,[11] and reentered the "competition" in the marketplace of ideas. In 1976, for example, the area sponsored a two-and-a-half-day "POM/ME Workshop" on teaching operations management material using the case method, which attracted academics from all over the world. It also began to sponsor a new two-week summer executive program for manufacturing managers, which by the late 1970s was enrolling more than 100 attendees annually. Finally, and ultimately most importantly, the area was successful in recruiting several highly promising new faculty members—among them a young labor economist by the name of Kim Clark.

John McArthur deserves considerable credit for his behind-the-scenes efforts in support of the POM area's remarkable resurgence. His belief in the importance of the issues addressed by POM led him to get involved in persuading pivotal people to transfer into the area and to support the allocation of the resources required to implement its new initiatives. Unfortunately, McArthur's reward for this ongoing support was not to come until much later. A series of events conspired to cause the area to come unglued again in the early 1980s, soon after McArthur became dean. Far from being a successful area that the new dean could put on automatic pilot, POM quickly emerged as a pressing focus of concern for him.

The 1980s: Riding the Roller Coaster

To the outside world, the prestige of the HBS POM group had never been greater than it was in the early 1980s. During this period, many among the POM faculty seemed to be flying high. Their published work was receiving acclaim from almost all quarters.

Over the course of the preceding decade, many American industries had come under fierce attack from foreign competitors. First came steel and consumer electronics, then automobiles (that largest of U.S. industries and a potent symbol of the nation's industrial might), followed by machine tools, computer peripherals, office machines, and finally the pride of American technology: integrated circuits. All of these industries were losing market share to foreign imports. By the mid-1980s the U.S. merchandise trade deficit had soared to over $150 billion a year. In the eyes of American customers and consumers, imported products provided higher quality and greater reliability, variety, and value for the money. In short, the common weapon that foreign competitors were using to attack U.S. markets was primarily an ability to design, produce, and deliver defect-free products faster, more efficiently, and more responsively than domestic competitors seemed able to do. The problem of production clearly had not been "solved"; instead, it had grown to the point where it threatened many companies' survival.

Slowly, almost unnoticed, the unglamorous and taken-for-granted craft of operations management had emerged as the Achilles' heel of many American companies. When the competitive assault came, these companies were simply unprepared to respond. Their factories and equipment were aging, their workers dispirited, and their senior managers largely out of touch with operating issues. Never did managers have a greater need for guidance in improving and reshaping the operations side of their companies—and rarely had there been so few places to turn for such practical advice.

This was a historic moment, and the Harvard POM faculty rose to the challenge by writing a series of candid and penetrating articles and books aimed at managers.[12] The response was extremely gratifying. Between 1980 and 1986, POM area members were awarded the prestigious McKinsey Award, for the best article published in the *Harvard Business Review*, five times. In one year they captured both first and second place. The dates and titles of these articles suggest their content and the reason for their high impact:

1980　"Managing Our Way to Economic Decline," by Robert Hayes and William Abernathy

1981　"The New Industrial Competition," by William Abernathy, Kim Clark, and Alan Kantrow; (second place: "Why Japanese Factories Work," by Robert Hayes)

1982　"Managing as if Tomorrow Mattered," by Robert Hayes and David Garvin

1983　"Quality on the Line," by David Garvin

1986　"The Productivity Paradox," by Wickham Skinner

Within the space constraints of this essay, it would be impossible to summarize the depth and breadth of the area's intellectual accomplishments during this period. Professors William Abernathy and Kim Clark conducted a study of the worldwide auto industry (reported in the book *Industrial Renaissance,* 1983). Kim Clark and Robert Hayes supervised a study of the factors influencing monthly productivity and quality levels in 12 factories, belonging to three different companies, over periods of up to nine years (reported on in the book *Uneasy Alliance: Managing the Productivity-Technology Dilemma,* 1985). David Garvin conducted a study of the management policies influencing defect levels at essentially all the factories that manufactured room air conditioners in the United States and Japan (reported on in his book *Managing Quality,* 1988). Kim Clark and Takahiro Fujimoto studied the factors influencing the cost, speed, and effectiveness of product development at 19 automobile companies in Europe, Japan, and the United States (reported on in the book *Product Development Performance,* 1991). All four of these projects tackled big, complex, important problems. All consumed a substantial amount of funding from the School. All involved more than one researcher, substantial travel, and several years to complete. And all had significant impacts on management thinking.[13]

Early in this renaissance, Dean McArthur invited the POM area to sponsor one of the colloquia that were organized in the early 1980s to commemorate the School's 75th anniversary. Bill Abernathy, Kim Clark, and Bob Hayes agreed to organize this colloquium, which in March 1984 brought together more than 70 scholars and business practitioners from around the world. McArthur's support for the area was underscored throughout this ambitious venture. He ensured that funding was available for the nine major research projects that were conducted by HBS faculty and reported on in the colloquium. He made available ample administrative support to organize and host the event. And in the wake of the colloquium, he encouraged its organizers to invite Christopher Lorenz, management editor of *The Financial Times,* to spend a year at the School helping to review and edit the two dozen manuscripts, commentaries, and summaries that eventually comprised a book based on the event.[14]

Although the POM colloquium provided a wonderful opportunity for the faculty to showcase its breadth of interests, scholarly achievements, and concern with important issues, it was marred by one very sad note. Bill Abernathy, who had been one of the colloquium's architects and who had spent the previous ten years working on the linked issues of productivity and technology, lost his long battle with cancer three months before the colloquium took place. Because he was ahead of his time, international acclaim and recognition had come to Abernathy only shortly before his death. But his colleagues long continued to work the ground that he had first broken.

Abernathy's death was a blow to his friends and colleagues, who were accustomed to looking to him for stimulation and direction. More broadly, it underscored, vividly and painfully, the fact that the larger POM area itself was in a fragile state of health. The loss of this one colleague, who was relatively young and who was committed to the integration of multiple perspectives to deal with tough issues, was enough to jeopardize that health.

This was the paradox: by the mid-1980s, POM was projecting a vigorous image outside the School. There was no other academic group in the world succeeding so visibly at the task that POM had assigned itself. At the same time, however, serious problems had arisen for the area in its teaching program.

Again, real-world context played a role in this drama. The increasing ferocity of global competition, coupled with companies' growing recognition of the role that good operations management could play in corporate success, had forced operations managers to expand the scope of their activities. Instead of confining their attention to producing and delivering products and services, they were increasingly involved in developing products, managing global networks of plants and suppliers, coordinating and restructuring supply channels, and working with customers to meet their specialized needs.

In such a situation, the School faced the need to teach its students the new approaches to operations that had been developed by world-class companies in other countries, particularly Japan. This imperative, along with the expansion in scope of the operations manager's task, required that POM reconceptualize its first-year course from the ground up and infuse it with a new set of teaching materials.

This, in turn, raised a related challenge. The kinds of young people whom the School was hiring as new faculty members (and who would have to teach this new course) weren't prepared upon their arrival at the School to teach issues of such breadth, much less conduct research on them. The closing down of operations management departments at many of the traditional HBS "feeder" schools during the 1960s had reduced the number of potential faculty members who had a solid background in traditional operations management. The POM group's solution was to cast its recruiting net more widely and to seek out talented people from a variety of backgrounds: economists, political scientists, organizational sociologists, scientists, and engineers. This was a calculated bet. The POM area would assemble a group of outstanding people from disparate backgrounds, help them learn how to teach operations management, and get them to interact productively. If the gamble paid off, the core group might be able to develop an intellectual entity whose breadth of interests spanned the multitude of activities in which operations managers were expected to engage.

There were two keys to making such a strategy work. First, the area had to convince outstanding young scholars that associating with POM was a better career choice than joining a department at some other school that focused on the discipline for which their doctoral training had prepared them. This presented a chicken-egg problem: the young scholars who were most attractive to the area were often unwilling to take such a risk until they could see examples of others who had done so and succeeded—but it was difficult to produce such role models unless the area could attract people who had the highest potential for success in the HBS environment. As a result, the POM recruiters had to be very opportunistic in their hiring, seeking out the best people they could find and hoping a couple of them would succeed. The downside of this new strategy was that the possibility of failure was higher, and failure had sobering implications for the area's research productivity and the quality of its teaching.

The second key lay in providing effective mentoring. If young scholars from disparate backgrounds were to learn to teach in the HBS classroom, as well as to do high-quality research on important POM issues, the senior POM faculty would have to spend large amounts of time working with them. Unfortunately, at the same time that the demand for such mentoring was going up, the area's capacity for mentoring was decreasing. In 1979, a highly promising nontenured faculty member, Steve Wheelwright, was induced by Stanford to move to its Graduate School of Business. Then two of the area's younger and more effective tenured faculty members—Bill Abernathy and D. Daryl Wyckoff—died within a year of each other. Another of the area's pillars for many years, Wick Skinner, retired five years earlier than expected. Four other senior members followed their individual career paths into other areas and programs at the School. As a result, Robert Hayes and W. Earl Sasser were left as essentially the only tenured faculty members able to commit full time to the vast rebuilding task confronting the area. At one point (1982–1983), no tenured faculty member was available to head up the area's first-year course.

POM's staffing levels, as well as its visibility in the School's second-year program, were further reduced by events surrounding the Management of Service Operations course. Over the span of several years, this popular elective gradually had moved away from its origins, and beyond the operations side of service companies. As a result, in the latter part of the 1980s, the course's name was changed to Service Management. It became an increasingly attractive teaching assignment for people in other areas, and eventually its ties to POM loosened. Ultimately, those teaching the course formed their own independent Service Management area. Not only did POM lose the course, it also lost the course's originator, Earl Sasser, who had played such a critical role in holding the area together during the dark days of the early 1980s.

The point is not that individuals should not be encouraged to go where their ideas are taking them. (Sasser was so encouraged, even by his POM colleagues who hated to see him go.) Instead, the point is that *individuals* make up any scholarly community. The loss of even one of these individuals—by death, retirement, relocation, or change of intellectual focus—sorely tests the strength of a small community.

The predictable result of all these departures was a reduction in the average effectiveness of those teaching the area's courses. This led, in turn, to declining student ratings and second-year enrollments, as well as an unusually low rate of promotion among the area's nontenured faculty. Its morale undermined by a series of such setbacks, POM was again under siege. The area was beset by critics who asserted that it had become too unfocused and who questioned whether its increasingly complex subject matter could be taught to the new generation of MBA students.

Two positive forces countered this rising tide. First, in the face of mounting criticism, Dean McArthur stood firm. He conveyed his confidence in the area's leaders, provided resources for its teaching, research, and faculty development efforts, and kept encouraging the members of the area to keep their sights high. (The story that introduces this essay involved Kim Clark, but similar stories are told by almost everyone in the area at that time.) At one juncture, for example, McArthur agreed to fund a trip to Japan for the entire first-year POM teaching group, so that it could see for itself the advanced technologies and practices in Japanese factories.

The second positive thing that happened was that the area's efforts to recruit and mentor young faculty members gradually began to bear fruit. A series of remarkably talented and energetic people earned tenure and quickly took on leadership roles. Roy Shapiro, who had transferred over from the Managerial Economics area, took over the first-year course and gradually rebuilt its effectiveness. Kim Clark, a labor economist by training, rebuilt the area's doctoral program and—along with Jai Jaikumar, whose background was in Operations Research—spearheaded its research efforts. Dave Garvin, another Ph.D. economist, developed a highly successful second-year course in Operations Strategy. Steve Wheelwright, who returned to the School after almost a decade at Stanford, worked with Kim Clark to restructure and rejuvenate the Management of Technological Innovation elective into the popular New Product Development elective. Wheelwright then took over the first-year course. Building on the foundation laid by Roy Shapiro, he continued the transformation of that course, until it became recognized in the 1990s as one of the most effective required offerings at the School.

The 1990s: Success—and New Challenges

In 1990, the tenth year of John McArthur's deanship, Kim Clark took over as chair of POM. Even then it was clear that this was a watershed, in the sense that a new generation was now running the show, and that group was bristling with new ideas and initiatives.

In recognition of the growing importance of technology management—in companies and, by extension, in the area's course offerings—the first-year course was renamed Technology and Operations Management (TOM). The name was soon applied to the entire area, and technology now had the home at HBS that Kim Clark and others had been seeking to build.

Innovative recruitment continued, ensuring that the area would continue to evolve in new directions. For example, Kent Bowen, a chaired professor at MIT's school of engineering and one of the founders of that school's joint (with the Sloan School of Management) Leaders in Manufacturing master's degree program, was persuaded to join the TOM group. This move strengthened both the TOM knowledge base in the sciences and the area's ability to recruit scientifically trained people onto the faculty.

Neither Bowen's appointment nor Steve Wheelwright's earlier decision to return to Harvard would have been possible without Dean McArthur's active encouragement and support. McArthur had given the area a broad charter to hire faculty from a variety of science-and-technology-related disciplines. This had allowed it to bring in faculty members from many backgrounds, including mechanical engineering, solid-state physics, and materials science. Marco Iansiti, for example, had completed a Ph.D. in physics and a postdoctoral fellowship in solid-state physics research. David Upton, who held a Ph.D. in mechanical engineering, brought substantial firsthand experience in manufacturing and expertise in information technology. Their interests were complemented and reinforced by the promotions of Dorothy Leonard-Barton and Jai Jaikumar, both of whose work had focused on the introduction of new product and process technologies into organizations.

Before these young people could make a substantial contribution to the area and the School, they had to master a broad set of new skills, ranging from how to teach in the MBA classroom to how to conduct research in the social sciences. One of them (a co-author of this article) clearly remembers his first day of work. He had spent the previous five years working in semiconductor "clean rooms" and engineering new solid-state devices. Once unpacked and ensconced in his new office in the basement of Morgan Hall, he spent his first few hours in a condition of some anxiety and confusion, wondering what in the world he was actually supposed to be doing at this place.

That interlude of anxiety ended when Kim Clark, the head of the technology interest-group, walked into the newcomer's office. After chatting a bit about his own research, Clark said, in effect, "Look—I know this place must feel a bit strange to you, at this moment. Just remember that my door is always open, and that my time will always be available to you. When you have questions, just stop in and ask." Clark's behavior in subsequent weeks and months proved that the offer was genuine. Other senior faculty were equally accessible. They provided much-needed mentoring and advice to bewildered new arrivals.

The diversity of experiences and disciplinary expertise—ranging from organizational psychology to the history of science, from electrical engineering to materials science—presented real challenges to the senior POM faculty. Yet it was clear that these new junior faculty members were strengthening the area on a variety of fronts. For example, in the early 1990s, about half a dozen of the POM faculty were working on similar problems in innovation and product development, and they were focused increasingly on such high-tech industries as computer disk drives and pharmaceuticals. Their very diversity created unusual opportunities for cross-fertilization in research, and the beneficial results of their collaborations soon became apparent in a slew of co-authored papers and books. (One such work was *The Perpetual Enterprise Machine,* a book published in 1994 which represented a collaboration among five HBS faculty members; a half-dozen others from MIT, Purdue, and Stanford; and practitioners from five industrial companies.) The fruits of cross-pollination also became evident in the area's workshops and research seminars, whose topics ranged from the concept of "safety" in group interactions to the application of neural networks to business. The benefits of interdisciplinary collaboration were also apparent in course development. An impressive array of new cases, team projects, and exercises made their way into the area's first-year course. These exercises ranged from taking apart a videocassette recorder to discussing the sources of organizational capability.

The mentorship and sense of community provided by the area's new generation of senior faculty were central to its strength in the early 1990s. By its very nature, the interdisciplinary approach at the heart of the area's strategy entailed a commitment on the part of senior faculty to work with young colleagues. But in the early and mid-1990s, perhaps reflecting the area's success at collegial self-management, a number of those senior faculty were being drawn off into major administrative assignments at the School—first Bob Hayes, then Roy Shapiro, and then Steve Wheelwright. With Kim Clark's accession to the deanship in 1995, the area's senior ranks were again severely depleted. The ability of tenured faculty members to mentor young faculty was greatly constrained, and the area once again faced a period of rebuilding.

This was success with an asterisk. The area could point with pride to a record of strong accomplishment. At the same time, its members could acknowledge with a large dose of humility that the area's work was only beginning again.

1996: Looking to the Future

Let us emphasize that, despite all our talk of roller coasters and asterisks, the foundations of the TOM area established during John McArthur's deanship were sound and strong. Although the area was composed of people with diverse backgrounds, skill sets, and interests, it was cohesive in spirit and coherent in philosophy. Much of the 1970s and 1980s was dedicated to exploring the role that technology and operations management played in the success of a modern business. Ultimately, the area sought to demonstrate that, in today's increasingly competitive world, "good managers" cannot manage all aspects of their business simply by following a set of solid general management practices; they also had to have a firm grasp of the details and nuances of the core technologies that underpinned their businesses. Simple lessons, perhaps, but with profound implications for the School and for the world of business.

By 1996, these lessons had been largely accepted by academics and practitioners alike. As a result, the focus of the TOM unit's research and course development activities could now take a much more active stance toward shaping the firm: How, *exactly*, could an organization enhance or expand its capabilities to match the needs of its environment? This new mission, combined with the area's broad charter and heterogeneous faculty, presented the TOM faculty with a series of new challenges in its research, teaching, and faculty organization and development.

Research, as always, was a priority, and it presented major definitional challenges. The work of Abernathy, Clark, Hayes, Skinner, and Wheelwright, while grounded in specific industry contexts, produced lessons of general relevance to managers. These included, for example, the need to match strategy with operations, the need to streamline processes and align them more tightly with customer needs, and the need to cultivate internal capabilities. Strong parallels have been found between the conclusions of research into both innovation and operations. Will the same sorts of parallels recur in the next generation of innovation and operations? Will it provide a similarly compelling universal message?

Implications for Research

Some of the key research topics and questions for the late 1990s include the following:

Focus and core capabilities. Many of the advances in operations management that took place during the 1970s and 1980s were driven by the manufacturing strategy framework developed by Wick Skinner, who argued that *focus* was central to making a manufacturing strategy work. For example, Skinner used to challenge his students to imagine a plane that could travel at supersonic speeds, carry 500 passengers, and land in a small cow pasture. They quickly concluded that such a plane was impossible to build within the constraints of current technology. With Skinner's help, the students realized that every engineered system, whether a plane or a factory, had to be focused on accomplishing a restricted set of priorities that were not in conflict with one another. This idea led to an appreciation of the importance of identifying an organization's core capabilities. A business shouldn't try to do too many different things at the same time. Instead, it should focus its resources and management attention on the things it did particularly well compared with its competitors. Diversion of attention away from these core competencies, no matter how tempting or seemingly opportune, tends to dilute the organization's strengths. It produces undue stress and increases the chance of failure both within and outside the core business.

We can say that this is more or less "true" in industries where product life cycles are relatively long. But is it also true in fast-moving environments like software or pharmaceuticals? What if one's core capabilities threaten to become "core rigidities," in Dorothy Leonard's memorable term? For many decades, AT&T identified its telephone network as the center of its corporate existence. But alternative technologies like Internet-style networks or cellular telephony threatened to obsolete that core. AT&T was slow to enter the cellular business (which its own Bell Labs had invented in the first place) and eventually had to play catch-up through the costly acquisition of McCaw Communications.

Microsoft, at the other end of the spectrum, has entered a vast array of businesses in the past five years, ranging from computer peripherals to cable television, and from kids' toys to on-line services. Is this purposeful lack of focus appropriate for what is still only a medium-sized firm (of about 20,000 employees)? More generally, have changes in information technology increased the efficient scope of a single plant, a single R&D organization, or even a whole firm? Both the bumblebee and the Stealth bomber can fly, despite theoretical objections. How do we recognize the technological threshold at which Skinner's once-unlikely plane begins to be feasible?

MANAGING INCREMENTAL, GENERATIONAL, AND RADICAL IMPROVEMENTS. Generational improvement seems to have become increasingly central in a variety of competitive environments, often at the expense of incremental and radical improvements. In recent years, for example, Intel has adopted a practice called Copy Exactly when introducing a new generation of integrated circuit process technology. The new technology is developed in a single R&D fabrication facility ("fab") and painstakingly cloned in multiple production fabs. These facilities cannot alter the process in any way without authorization by a central task force (a cumbersome process). Any such improvement must be accepted by all fabs and implemented uniformly across the entire network. What does this mean for the concept of continuous improvement on the plant floor? Managers at Intel have knowingly sacrificed the potential for such incremental improvement in the name of greater control and faster technology transfer. How do we reconcile this philosophy with that of the Toyota production system? Are they simply driven by different technological environments, or are they also a function of differences in company culture and institutional context?

Similarly, we observe the decline of emphasis on radical improvement. In the last half of the twentieth century, industrial laboratories like Bell Labs, Xerox PARC, SRI, and IBM's T. J. Watson Research Center achieved an almost unbelievable string of technological breakthroughs, from the transistor to the UNIX operating system, from the graphics user interface to high-temperature superconductivity. In recent years, however, every one of these laboratories has been restructured, downsized, and focused on less radical discoveries. What will take their place? At least until very recently, Intel and other contemporary software and electronics firms have declined to make extensive investments in basic research. Will networks of small firms and universities truly be able to replace these once-formidable research institutions?

PROBLEM SOLVING, EXPERIMENTATION, LEARNING, AND FORGETTING. Academics and practitioners alike want to know much more about the mechanisms of innovation and learning. What are their roots, both in laboratories and on the manufacturing shop floor? How can we understand the nature of effective problem solving and experimentation? How do organizations (as opposed to individuals) learn? Why and how do they forget?

The relevant research so far has identified a variety of fascinating mechanisms and phenomena. Our work going forward should make use of the depth and diversity in our skill set to improve our fundamental understanding of how learning and innovation actually occur, and how they can be encouraged.

HOW IMPORTANT IS SIZE, AND UNDER WHAT CIRCUMSTANCES? The paradigm that dominated manufacturing management in the United States for at least a century prior to 1980 was based on a firm belief in the virtues of mass production. Managers extrapolated from this demonstrably valid belief and concluded that, in both R&D and operations, size created important advantages. During the past 25 years, however, that assumption has been questioned in a variety of contexts. Research into product development, for example, has consistently shown that smaller projects are typically also the fastest, even when performance measures are adjusted to account for differences in innovative content. This has been the conclusion of every study published in recent years, in fields ranging from biotechnology to automobiles, from semiconductors to software. On the operations side, research has challenged the need for building large, unwieldy manufacturing infrastructures, particularly in situations where information technology can be used to ensure integration across a complex operating network.

Additionally, while size advantages clearly exist in certain environments—for example, the paper industry—these economies of scale derive more from the effective application of massive amounts of equipment and capital than from the effective use of people. Is a bigger team a better team? The evidence appears to suggest that it is not the *size* of the team that counts, but the *nature* of individual skills and the range of experience on that team—particularly if the critical tasks are integrative in nature. This logic helps explain the remarkable success in recent years of small startup firms in a variety of contexts. If the advantages of size are indeed decreasing, some of the most basic assumptions about the bases of competitive advantage, and the appropriate way to structure and manage technology and operations, become open to challenge.

This suggests that we need to spend more time studying smaller firms. Although the TOM area traditionally has focused its research on large manufacturing firms,[15] course development efforts have begun to shift toward the concerns of smaller firms in industries such as health care and software that offer services as well as products. This shift sketches out a broad new research agenda. Do the concepts in technology and operations that we have developed for the General Motors of the world really apply to Yahoo!, Oxo, and General Scanning? What are the critical differences inherent in managing the operations of a small firm? The ability to create processes for R&D and operations that are both small *and* efficient is key to the viability of a small business—and, we suspect, critical to a useful understanding of the real threats to large firms.

THE DIVIDING LINE BETWEEN OPERATIONS AND TECHNOLOGY. Finally, getting to the very heart of the TOM area, what is the real difference between R&D and operations? How do we define the charter of an operations group in a way that differentiates it from that of the product/process development group? *Should* they be different organizations? Entire industries are implicitly arguing that they should not. In Internet services, for example, beta versions of new software products are routinely offered to customers through the regular operating network. The customers are expected to provide feedback, which is tracked by the same system that tracks problems experienced with released products. In many high-tech firms, the tasks associated with R&D—including the development of new processes and operations—are performed by the same organization, often by the same people. This increased integration of product/process development and operations is by no means limited to traditional high-tech environments. The quick-response network in the apparel industry which links the planning process to the distribution channel, for example, is essentially a product development and introduction process.

Similarly, the technologies with which TOM concerns itself increasingly represent various manifestations of *information* technology (IT)—whether they are embedded in the products and services provided by a company, in the processes that produce those products and services, or in the communication links among the various participants in the production/technology development process. But IT is not a technology that is defined and bounded by a scientific discipline, like those we have traditionally studied in papermaking or aircraft engines. IT is pervasive and often defined as much by the context in which it operates as by the configuration of the computers and information networks that comprise it. In that sense, it is not separate from operations; it is an indistinguishable aspect of operations.

THE BOUNDARIES OF OPERATIONS . . . AND ORGANIZATIONS. Where *are* the appropriate boundaries for our interests? Companies today are increasingly outsourcing critical parts and services, and establishing close, partnershiplike relationships in place of their traditional arm's-length relations with suppliers and even with competitors. Carried to the extreme, such loose assemblages become virtual organizations. How do we define the limits of operations in such groups? Some of our unit's faculty are now examining how the participants in various industry supply chains (such as food products) are organizing and governing their collective activities in ways intended to provide "quick/accurate response" to the demands of the customers at the end of the chain. Where, among such diverse yet integrated activities, do operations stop, and marketing and management control begin?

These are the kinds of questions that convince us that our integrative approach to research and teaching is increasingly important and relevant. Strong synergies *do* exist across the different disciplinary boundaries within TOM. Internet software development presents similarities to quick-response practices in the apparel industry. Concepts in logistics are applicable to the management of plant networks. Inertia in the realm of physics is not too different from inertia in organizations. Virtual factories are not that dissimilar to virtual product development teams. "Operations" today is spelled with a big O—a circle that encompasses a diverse set of disciplines and managerial problems. Of course, we can and should still focus our attention on specific topics within these broad pastures, but only after we have provided our students and our practitioner audience with a coherent framework showing how those topics fit into the whole.

Implications for Teaching

The earliest universities grew up around repositories of knowledge—that is, libraries. Scholars came to these repositories to examine the wisdom of the ancients and found that their attempts to understand and expand on this knowledge were strengthened by their dialogues and arguments with one another. Students gathered around the scholars (and the libraries) to learn from them. Eventually, as these groups of scholars stabilized and developed mores and standards, they evolved into what are now called faculties.

Over time, as knowledge became more dispersed and readily available, the focus of attention in academia shifted from the libraries to the scholars themselves, and a primary responsibility of the university was to attract the best faculty possible. This it did by providing them with the resources and physical facilities they needed to support their work: offices, laboratories, classrooms, stimulating colleagues, and, of course, libraries. Good faculties in turn attracted good students, which created the need for new kinds of resources: dormitories, student unions, and athletic facilities. So even as the physical proximity of the faculty to the sources of knowledge was becoming less important, its proximity to the students was becoming more important.

Today, for many business scholars, the information they need is in the field or on the Web. Their "colleagues" can be anywhere in the world. And if the promise of distance learning is realized, teachers someday may not even need to be where their students are. The university that once was compelled to huddle around a small collection of precious books is threatening to become a virtual organization, existing anywhere and *everywhere*.

Some scholars are wary of these changes, and understandably so. They want a clearer articulation of the proposed bargain—what they will be giving up, contrasted with what they will be gaining—before they will endorse it. But those of us in the TOM group are looking confidently into this technological future. Because of our understanding of technology and its implications for organization and management, we are almost uniquely positioned to exploit these kinds of changes. To us, they are *exciting*, and full of potential.

To benefit fully from these changes, however, we must first expand our notion of who our "students" are. Fellow academics at other institutions, business managers, and consultants should be able to participate in new kinds of exchanges, electronic and otherwise, which are comparable to those experienced by our traditional students. Similarly, we must expand our notion of who our "colleagues" are, to include consultants and practitioners and in some cases even our students, if we succeed in involving them in projects that generate data. And we must learn how to collaborate effectively with all these new students and colleagues.

Perhaps most importantly, we must learn the limits of these new technologies. No one knows exactly what will be gained and lost through distance learning, nor do we have even a rudimentary sense of which ideas are disseminated most effectively over the Net. How important is physical proximity and direct social interaction to the process of conveying the kind of broad-based knowledge that future managers will need? We don't yet know, and we are under ever-increasing pressure to find out.

What *do* we know about the future of TOM pedagogy? We know that we have to rethink the design of the courses and conceptual frameworks that we provide our students. In addition, we need to give our students

1. *A richer understanding of the problems faced today by managers in both large and small firms,* including firms in industries like health care that up to now have been largely outside our field of vision. Dave Upton's innovative combination of a written case with computerized video materials and simulation capabilities is an early, exciting example of the possibilities.[16]

2. *More direct interaction with managers and consultants,* whom we can involve in our courses via team projects, internships, and the Internet. (We specifically include consultants because their broader experience often makes them better informed about the latest management issues, because they are skilled at speaking to large groups, and because they *crave* exposure to our students!)

3. *More experiential projects.* These would include, for example, designing and experimenting with different work design or production scheduling systems, designing an actual product or service, internships, and so on.

4. *More, and more sophisticated, use of computer simulation.* Exercises like these are no longer optional, in an age in which our incoming students (for the most part weaned on sophisticated video games) have incredibly high expectations for computer-based products.

Similarly, we must retool our doctoral program to prepare its graduates to compete successfully in the world of the future, rather than that of the past. Most importantly, we need to help prepare them for the same transition in teaching that we face now.

The Challenge of Complexity

By 1996, the disciplinary content of TOM was incredibly broad. We were sponsoring research studies ranging from quick response in apparel to building scientific capabilities in East Asia. This diversity of disciplines continues to increase. In the past, we attempted to manage this diversity by informally dividing the unit into three major subunits: logistics, technology, and "core" operations management. Each subunit sponsored its own elective courses, while it collaborated in the design and teaching of our first-year course. Integrating the different sets of interests represented by these subunits was made easier by the fact that individual faculty members often bridged more than one, and "relocated" from one to another.

First-year TOM has long been the unit's principal integrating mechanism, providing the conceptual and social glue that holds it together. But as a result of larger curriculum revisions introduced at the School, that course has been both reduced in length and broken up into cohorts.[17] Increasingly, therefore, our faculty feels the need for additional processes that would serve to bring our expertise together. We can speculate on a few possibilities.

The first would involve extending the first-year teaching group mentality to the second year. This was intended to be a role of the Operations Strategy course, which traditionally enjoyed by far the highest enrollment among the TOM electives. However, in recent years, TOM second-year offerings have become a fairly balanced portfolio, with several courses having enrollments between 100 and 200 students. This means that a single course can no longer purport to be *the* integrating mechanism for the second year.

A second possibility would be to run a second-year teaching group that reaches across courses, sharing course development ideas and resources.

A third would be to encourage the design of courses that are not defined by traditional boundaries. For example, it might be interesting to offer a course on "operating speed and flexibility." This would reach across a variety of disciplines (logistics, product development, manufacturing) to address a critical, integrative topic. The course might be taught jointly by faculty from different backgrounds, encouraging the integration of research and course development materials.

A related possibility would be to create research efforts that cut across disciplines and industries. The same topic—"speed and flexibility," for example—could be used to integrate the research findings from environments as disparate as Internet software development and logistics in the apparel industry. This type of integrated effort seems particularly exciting in light of the fact that, over the past ten years, unit faculty members have accumulated a variety of field-based studies from many industrial environments, ranging from biotechnology to disk drives to paper making. This presents us with a rare opportunity to pull together these diverse results, integrate their messages in books or papers, and perhaps have the same kind of impact on academics and practitioners as did the research projects of the 1980s.

Additionally, as we attempt to integrate more effectively the research of our diverse base of faculty and students, we should use the TOM research seminar more actively. The seminar has long been a problem for the unit. The diversity of our interests has contributed to poor and unpredictable attendance, particularly for seminars that focused on narrow issues, which sometimes led to frustration and embarrassment on the part of the organizers. To make attendance more reliable and the exchanges more productive, perhaps more seminar efforts could be designed to lead directly to publications. As a "stretch" goal, for example, we could plan a series of volumes ("Research in Technology and Operations Management"?) to be published at a rate of, say, one every two years. The requirement for each of these might be to have at least two faculty members from different parts of the unit work jointly on each manuscript. The seminar would then become the vehicle for presenting the research and receiving feedback.

Such interdisciplinary efforts could, of course, easily encompass colleagues from other units, even other schools. One of the coauthors is currently working on a joint course with Professors Myra Hart and Ben Shapiro, which attempts to harness the combined expertise of TOM, Entrepreneurial Management, and Marketing. The effort, provisionally entitled Creating New Ventures, is currently only at the planning and conceptualization stage but has already given rise to a very productive interchange of knowledge and ideas.

Triumph or Tragedy?

By now, the reader has a sense of the cyclicality that has pervaded the history of Production/POM/TOM. Perhaps this cyclicality is the rule, rather than the exception in academia. But the history through which one lives personally takes on sharper relief, and is played out in brighter colors, than the stories told by colleagues here and elsewhere.

In a sense, we are back where we began this brief history—back in the mid-1960s, when the unit first attempted to assimilate a large number of new faculty members who brought with them different perspectives and a broader sense of the scope of "operations." Indeed, we have been dealing with that problem ever since. The central challenge for our TOM faculty, like that of many of the firms we study, is to cultivate and master an increasingly diverse set of skills and capabilities, while at the same time knitting them together through an organization and a set of coherent activities. Only through such integration can we leverage our collective impact on our students, the School, and the world of business around us. Preserving a sense of identity and community as our interests and perspectives on the world expand—and possibly bump into the well-patrolled boundaries of other groups—will not be an easy task. As noted at the outset of this essay, not all visions of our future are positive ones.

Perhaps we should avoid spinning a dismal scenario in this context. But those of us who have lived through previous unravelings feel compelled to retell this history. One scenario, informed by the memory of the divisions and acrimony that tore the area apart in the late 1960s, has TOM becoming increasingly fragmented by its diversity and complexity. The unit lingers on for a while as an umbrella organization, providing shelter for a scattering of loosely coupled subfields, and finally breaks up into smaller groups that focus their attention on traditional research disciplines or problem areas. (This landscape includes not just alpha and beta subunits, but gamma and delta as well!) Or just as unhappily, it loses its *raison d'etre* and is gradually absorbed into other groups (after all, "operations" take place everywhere!). In either case, TOM slowly becomes less than the sum of its parts and relinquishes its position of leadership in the academic and practitioner worlds. Its courses lose imagination and popularity, while its research projects—all working within rigidly defined (read "safe") functional boundaries—become incremental and sterile.

Is there a better script? Of course. The rosy scenario for the next five years envisions a unit that rallies around its diverse base, rebuilds its foundations, and redefines its research and course development agendas around integrative themes and processes. It is a unit that conceives and tackles important, challenging, multifaceted research issues and peda-gogical projects, which are both important in and of themselves and which create synergies across its various disciplines. It is a unit that truly mentors its students and junior faculty, providing both support and constructive criticism, while adding energy. And it is a unit that invests in bold, creative research with the same combination of rigor and relevance that made the 1980s so memorable.

Both futures are possible. Fortunately, today as in the past, the future is ours to shape.

CHAPTER THREE

The Global Financial System Project

ROBERT C. MERTON AND PETER TUFANO

I N MARCH 1992, *John McArthur sponsored a dinner at the dean's house on the HBS campus. His guests were William S. Edgerly, then chairman of the Boston-based State Street Bank and Trust, and several faculty members from the School's Finance area.*

They were meeting that night to discuss the possibility of setting up a research partnership between the School and Edgerly's bank, which was soon to celebrate its 200th anniversary. That evening's informal discussions led to a tentative plan to analyze the changes under way in the global financial and investment system, and to study the implications of these changes for the structure, management, and regulation of institutions in the future.

More discussions and planning followed, which eventually culminated in a "200th Anniversary Grant" to the School by State Street, to establish the HBS Research Partnership on the Global Financial and Investment System. This partnership was soon enlarged, with 14 other leading financial services firms joining State Street and the HBS faculty to collaborate on the increasingly ambitious project, renamed the Global Financial System project.

FOR A WIDE RANGE of players, the financial world has grown increasingly complex during the past few decades. Households, corporations, financial institutions, and regulators face both opportunities and challenges that grow out of the rapid pace of financial innovation, the blurring of distinctions between different providers of financial services, and the lowering of economic boundaries between countries.

The Global Financial System (GFS) project provides a framework for understanding this dynamic financial system. The GFS project adopts a *functional perspective*, anchored in the observation that financial systems in all times and places perform a basic set of functions. These functions include, for example, providing a payment system for the exchange of goods and services, providing a mechanism for the pooling of funds to undertake large-scale indivisible enterprise, and so on. (A complete list of the financial system's core functions as identified by the GFS project is included on pages 78–79.) The best ways of performing these functions tend to differ from country to country; and equally, they tend to evolve over time in response to changing technologies, costs, or social traditions. As a result, the financial institutions and regulations that we observe are both endogenous and dynamic.

Finally, by way of introduction, we note that the GFS project is a collaborative effort. It combines the efforts of several HBS faculty from the Finance area, as well as senior executives from some of the world's leading financial institutions.[1]

A Brief History of a Collaborative Effort

It was clear that a powerful unifying framework would be needed to address the fundamental issues raised at HBS in 1992. The initial project team considered several different approaches to organizing their work and soon concluded that the functional perspective was the best theme for structuring the research program.

One of the authors of this essay had provided some early thoughts on the functional perspective in a series of papers written between 1989 and 1992.[2] Communicated to a wide range of audiences through lectures and publications, these ideas—usually illustrated by means of simple, concrete examples—seemed to strike a resonant chord with regulators, financial executives, and academics. Among the most responsive were several of our colleagues at HBS, who soon attempted to use these ideas in their research and teaching.

A group of HBS faculty—consisting of Dwight Crane, Kenneth Froot, Scott Mason, Robert Merton, André Perold, Erik Sirri, Peter Tufano, and Zvi Bodie (of Boston University, who joined the HBS faculty in 1992 as a visiting professor)—served as the initial GFS project team. Their first goal was to develop the ideas and language of the functional perspective further and to test the concept by applying functional analysis to various aspects of the financial system. The group also agreed to write a joint monograph, which would set out the general notion of functional analysis and examine in depth the six core functions served by financial systems. The monograph was published by Harvard Business School Press in 1995 as *The Global Financial System: A Functional Perspective*.[3]

The members of the GFS project also committed themselves to producing original research and new educational materials that used the functional perspective to analyze issues that were important and relevant to users, producers, and regulators of the financial services sector. In this second phase of the project, we identified four substantive areas for further research:

- The role of financial markets and institutions in providing retirement income

- The changing structure of the property and casualty insurance industry, especially in terms of the bearing of catastrophic risk

- The allocation of capital and measurement of performance by financial services firms

- The role of financial engineering and risk management in the strategy and performance of nonfinancial firms

These projects (described in detail in Appendix B) would be carried out by many members of the HBS finance faculty, and the work would be disseminated through multiple channels, including conferences, lectures, and articles written for both academics and practitioners. The educational mission of the GFS program would be fulfilled through the development of a new MBA elective and new executive education programs, through the incorporation of functional analysis into existing finance courses at HBS, and through the compiling of a casebook for use by educators at other schools as well as HBS.

From the outset, the GFS team believed that the involvement of practitioners was essential to the project. They therefore sought to assemble an advisory board of CEOs and executive committee–level executives from several leading financial services firms. The commitment of senior executive attention, as well as pledges of major financial support to the project, helped to ensure that the project would address strategic issues of significance to managers. Among the first to join the GFS advisory board was Roberto Mendoza, vice chairman of J. P. Morgan and Company. Building on the enthusiastic early support of State Street Bank and J. P. Morgan, the GFS organizers eventually recruited 13 other leading international financial services firms: American International Group; Bancomer, S. A.; Dean Witter, Discover and Company (later to merge with another sponsor, Morgan Stanley); the Deutsche Bank; GE Capital; HSBC Holdings plc; The Industrial Bank of Japan, Ltd.; Mercury Asset Management Group plc; Mitsui Marine and Fire Insurance Co. Ltd.; Morgan Stanley Group Inc.; Prudential Insurance Company of America; Reuters Holdings; and S. G. Warburg Group plc (later to become SBC Warburg). At their frequent meetings with advisory board representatives from each of these firms, the GFS researchers actively solicited feedback on both the problem-finding and the problem-solving aspects of the research.

The remainder of this chapter focuses on the substantive *ideas* of the GFS project; namely, the functional perspective. However, we hope that this brief project history conveys the special character of the *process* that led to the creation of GFS. The project was conceived as a truly collaborative effort from the outset. Its initial monograph would be the work of a *team*, whose members actively tried to shape a common voice as they critiqued each other's work, with the ultimate objective of producing a coherent and unified book.

The team set an ambitious goal for itself: to change the way people think about the world financial system. Our progress so far has been neither continuous nor linear. The project has proceeded in fits and starts and has taken occasional detours, as is common with ambitious and collaborative intellectual endeavors. But throughout, we have continued to refine a unified concept—the functional perspective—which we believe serves as an effective framework for understanding and managing the financial system.

The Industry Context: Innovation Past and Future

To explain why we sought a new framework for interpreting and understanding the financial system, it is helpful to review the last quarter-century of changes in the world's financial system. It has been a period of extraordinary innovation. A prolonged burst of creativity has led to a host of new products, services, and institutions, and has made traditional institutional distinctions less and less relevant.[4]

Consider, for example: round-the-clock trading from Tokyo to London to New York, financial futures, swaps, exchange-traded options, mortgage-backed securities, "junk" bonds, shelf registration, electronic funds transfer and security trading, automated teller machines, NOW accounts, asset-based financing, and LBOs and MBOs. Changes in the structure of the financial system came about in part because of important advances in the theory of finance, in part because of a wide array of newly designed securities, and in part because of advances in computer and telecommunications technology that made possible the implementation of large-volume trading strategies in these diverse sets of securities.[5] Each of these ingredients has contributed to vastly reduced costs of financial transactions.

This level of innovation is likely to be sustained in the near future. It may even accelerate. There are two reasons for thinking so: continued technological improvements and further cost reductions. When we refer to reduced costs, we have in mind not only lower transaction costs, but also progress along the learning curve. After nine new products, markets, or institutions have been created, the tenth tends to come a lot more easily. For example, the rapid growth in over-the-counter derivatives (which are transacted away from a central market and therefore put greater pressure on the issuing institution's capability to price those derivatives correctly and manage their risk effectively) reflects a growing confidence in the modeling and evaluation skills on the part of the issuing institutions. That confidence comes from access to improved technology and also from the testing of these skills in real-world practice on a large scale for a considerable period of time. Moving down the learning curve is both efficient and rewarding.[6]

Our prediction of continued financial change also derives from what we call the "financial innovation spiral," in which two broad classes of institutions—organized markets and intermediaries—*compete* with each other in a static sense and *complement* each other in a dynamic sense.

It is widely understood, of course, that intermediaries and markets compete to provide financial products. Improved technology and attendant declines in transaction costs have only fueled that competition. A review of Finnerty's (1988, 1992) extensive histories of innovative financial products suggests a pattern whereby successful products that were first offered by intermediaries have ultimately moved to markets. Just a few examples:

- The development of liquid markets for money instruments such as commercial paper enabled money market mutual funds to compete with banks and thrifts for household savings.

- The creation of "junk bond" and medium-term note markets made it possible for mutual funds, pension funds, and individual investors to service those corporate issuers who had historically depended on banks as their source of debt financing.

- The creation of a national mortgage market allowed mutual funds and pension funds to become major funding alternatives to thrift institutions for residential mortgages. The creation of funding markets also made it possible for investment banks and mortgage brokers to compete with thrift institutions for the origination and servicing fees on loans and mortgages.

- Securitization of auto loans, credit card receivables, and leases on consumer and producer durables has intensified the competition between banks and finance companies as sources of funds for these purposes.[7]

This pattern suggests that successful new products will migrate from intermediaries to markets. In other words, once such products become familiar (and perhaps after some incentive problems are resolved), they will tend to trade in a market. Just as venture capital firms that provide financing for startup businesses expect to lose their successful customers to capital market sources of funding, so do the intermediaries that create new financial products.

Does this mean that intermediaries are doomed as an integral part of the financial system structure? We think not. An exclusive focus on the time path of individual products can be misleading. It can overstate the apparent secular decline in the importance of intermediation, and it can miss some of the subtle but vital complementarities between financial markets and intermediaries.

This is the essence of the innovation spiral: financial markets tend to be efficient institutional alternatives to intermediaries when the products in question have standardized terms or meanings, can serve a large number of customers, and are well enough understood for transactors to be comfortable in assessing their prices. Intermediaries, on the other hand, are better suited for low-volume, customized products. As such products as futures, options, swaps, and securitized loans become standardized and move from intermediaries to markets, the proliferation of new trading markets in those instruments permits the creation of new custom-designed financial products that improve market completeness. To hedge their exposures on those products, the producers (who are most often financial intermediaries) elect to trade in these new markets. Volume expands, and increased volume in turn reduces marginal transaction costs. This makes possible further implementation of more new products and trading strategies by intermediaries—which leads in turn to still more volume.

Ultimately, of course, the success of new markets and products encourages investment in the creation of still newer markets and products. And on it goes: spiraling toward the theoretically limiting case of zero marginal transaction costs and dynamically complete markets. The two key contributors to the financial innovation spiral—intermediaries and markets—compete with and complement each other.

Meanwhile, innovation drives the global financial system toward ever-greater economic efficiency. In particular, innovations in financial contracting technology expand opportunities for risk sharing, lessen transaction costs, and reduce information and agency costs.

Derivative securities provide a prime example. Some observers see the extraordinary growth in derivative securities over the past half-decade or so as little more than a fad. A more compelling explanation for this enormous increase is the vast reduction in transaction costs that results from their use.[8] The costs of implementing financial strategies using derivatives can be one-tenth to one-twentieth of the cost of using underlying cash-market securities. Further improvements in technology, along with growing breadth and experience in the application of derivatives, are likely to reduce transaction costs secularly as both producers and users of derivatives move down the learning curve. These efficiencies alone virtually ensure that derivatives will remain a permanent fixture in the mainstream global financial system.

But derivative securities also have provided effective instruments for controlling systematic risk exposures to interest rates, currencies, commodities, and equity markets. Financial engineering based on derivatives and special-purpose institutional structures has helped link individual national financial systems into a global system for capital and risk transfers. Derivatives are "adapters" that allow both corporations and sovereigns to tap global capital markets for financing. They provide a more nearly seamless transition across borders and facilitate flexibility across the widely different regulations, tax rules, and institutional practices that tend to characterize nations and economies.

Derivatives are only one example. A large number of other financial innovations have materially improved the performance of the world economy. Within the United States, for example, the development of a national mortgage market in the 1980s was accompanied by a wide array of mortgage-backed securities, which transformed residential housing finance from fragmented, locally based sources to a free-flowing international base of capital.[9] Another was the development of smoothly functioning markets for financial futures, swaps, and option contracts, a development that made it possible for business firms to hedge efficiently against the uncertainties of currency exchange rates, interest rates, and basic commodity prices.

Households, as well as institutions and economies, have benefited from innovation in the form of money market, fixed-income, international, real estate, and equity-indexed mutual funds, plus a variety of pension, life insurance, and annuity products. These are among the important innovations developed during the past 20 years, which have greatly increased the opportunities for households around the world to establish efficient risk-return tradeoffs. They have permitted much more effective tailoring to individual needs over the lifetime of individuals, including accumulation of assets during the work years and distribution of those assets in retirement.

Innovation, Oversight, and the Functional Perspective

Innovation can be threatening, of course, even when it promises to improve welfare. This may explain why managers, regulators, politicians, and the press have expressed so much concern over the risks inherent in the *new* activities of financial institutions, especially derivative-security products. This relative focus of concern seems particularly distorted in light of the substantial risks that are inherent in more traditional activities, such as real estate loans or LDC debt. Certainly, there has not yet been a major financial crisis associated with these new activities and instruments comparable to defaults by countries and by American savings and loan institutions in the 1970s and 1980s. In fact, based solely on the record, the rise of derivative products could have been depicted as greatly *reducing* risks in the system rather than increasing them.[10]

The implementation of derivative products has required major changes in the basic institutional hierarchy and in the infrastructure that supports it.[11] Not surprisingly, the knowledge that is required to manage in the new environment differs significantly from the traditional training and experience of many private-sector financial managers. The same holds true for the regulators who oversee the industry.

One "solution" to this problem, of course, would be simply to stifle innovation, but this would obviously have disastrous long-term implications. We advocate instead a two-track approach for accommodating the anxiety induced by financial innovation: first, a series of improvements to the financial infrastructure; and second, a new conceptual framework that will enable managers and regulators to interpret and understand the workings of the fast-moving financial system.

By "infrastructure," we mean the whole array of institutional interfaces between intermediaries and financial markets; regulatory practices; organization of trading, clearing, and other back-office facilities; and management information systems. Infrastructure improvements will permit innovation to proceed more efficiently and will also minimize the risk of disasters. Our point here is that innovations in financial products can be implemented unilaterally and rather quickly, whereas changes in financial infrastructure must be more coordinated and therefore take longer to implement.

Revisions of the accounting standards used in external risk monitoring, for example, often do not keep pace with derivative-product innovations. It is conceivable that, if carried to the extreme, the cumulative imbalance between new product development and continuing infrastructure could jeopardize the entire system. There is, therefore, a need for government policy to protect against such breakdown, even if the likelihood of such a systemic event is quite small.

But, as we have already suggested, it is far more important that managers and regulators involved in financial services possess a fundamental understanding of their field that can survive innovation at the margin—and even innovation at the core. What is needed is a conceptual framework broad and flexible enough to account both for differences in institutional structures across borders and for the dynamics of institutional change. We have proposed the functional perspective as this framework.

The Functional Perspective

People have engaged in financial transactions since at least the dawn of recorded history. Sumerian documents reveal the systematic use of credit for agricultural and other purposes in Mesopotamia around 3000 B.C., with barley and silver serving as the medium of exchange. The invention of money almost always prompted the invention of regulation. Hammurabi's code, promulgated in Babylon about 1800 B.C., includes many sections on the regulation of credit.[12]

Banking institutions arose in the city-state of Genoa in the twelfth century A.D. and flourished there (as well as in Florence and Venice) for several centuries. Those banks took demand deposits and made loans to merchants, rulers, and towns. Securities similar to those issued today originated in these same Italian city-states during the late Middle Ages. Long-term loans floated by the Republic of Venice, called the *prestiti*, were a popular form of investment in the thirteenth and fourteenth centuries, and their market price was a matter of public record. Even organized exchanges for trading financial futures contracts and other financial derivatives are not entirely new. Similar contracts were widely traded on the Amsterdam securities exchange in the 1600s.[13]

As this quick glimpse of historical context makes clear, some things have not changed.[14] Financial activities, such as borrowing, investing in securities, and other forms of financial contracting, are very old indeed. The institutional ways in which these activities are carried out, however, have changed considerably through the ages. As discussed in the introduction, the past few decades in particular have seen the pace of financial innovation and institutional change accelerate greatly.[15] The interesting question is, of course: What does the future hold?

Answering this question requires an analytical tool that deals explicitly with the dynamics of institutional change. The neoclassical economics perspective addresses the dynamics of prices and quantities, but it is largely an institution-free perspective. It has nothing to say directly about the institutions that perform particular functions or about how those institutions may change over time.[16]

At the other extreme is a purely institutional perspective, which assumes not only that institutions matter, but that they should serve as a conceptual anchor. From this perspective, the purpose of public policy is to help existing financial institutions survive and flourish. Adherents of this position talk in terms of *the* banks, or *the* insurance companies. Similarly, they define managerial objectives in terms of what can be done to make established financial institutions perform their particular services more efficiently and profitably.

Because this institutional perspective is fundamentally a static one, it cannot explain the dynamics of institutional change. From this perspective, moreover, financial innovations can appear to threaten the stability of the system, because they so often provide the means to circumvent institutionally based regulations at low cost.

Drawing on both the neoclassical and the institutional perspectives, the functional perspective adopted in the Global Financial System project focuses on the *economic functions* performed by financial institutions. It then seeks to discover the institutional structure best suited to performing those functions in a given time and place. It does not assume that existing institutions—whether private sector or governmental, operating or regulatory—will be preserved. Functions, rather than institutions, serve as the conceptual anchor. Because institutions "matter" but are not the anchors, institutional changes can be accommodated within this perspective.[17]

The GFS approach to the functional perspective distinguishes six core functions. As we see it, a financial system provides

- A payments system for the exchange of goods and services

- A mechanism for the pooling of funds to undertake large-scale indivisible enterprise

- A way to transfer economic resources through time and across geographic regions and industries

- A way to manage uncertainty and control risk

- Price information which helps coordinate decentralized decision making in various sectors of the economy

- A way to deal with the asymmetric-information and incentive problems when one party to a financial transaction has information that the other party does not

For a variety of reasons—including differences in size, complexity, and available technology, as well as differences in political, cultural, and historical backgrounds—the most efficient institutional structure for fulfilling the functions of the financial system generally *changes over time* and *differs across geopolitical subdivisions*. Moreover, even when the corporate identities of institutions are the same, the functions they perform often differ dramatically. For example, banks in the United States in 1998 are very different from what they were in 1928 or 1958, just as they are very different from the institutions called "banks" in Germany or the United Kingdom today. The financial markets in New York, London, and Tokyo today differ from what they were even as recently as 1980—before the widespread introduction of trading in fixed-income and stock-index futures, options, and swap contracts.

But the *basic functions* of a financial system are essentially the same in all economies—past and present, East and West. Because the functions of the financial system are far more stable than the identity or structure of the institutions performing them, a functional perspective provides a more reliable and enduring frame of reference than an institutional one, especially in an environment characterized by rapid change. And given the considerable institutional diversity across national borders, a functional perspective is more readily adaptable to a global setting for the financial system. Indeed, in light of the current rate of technological advance and the rapid integration of world financial markets, this approach may prove especially useful in anticipating the future direction of financial innovation, impending changes in financial markets and intermediaries, and likely regulatory bottlenecks.

Functional classification is surely not unique to the GFS team, and one can compare alternative classifications along a variety of dimensions.[18] But the final test of any functional approach (including ours) is the degree to which it can be applied to help users and regulators better understand the dynamic nature of the financial system. In that spirit, we were led to study how the functional perspective has been applied in the past and how it might be applied in the future.

Applications of the Functional Perspective

Our observations of companies and financial markets have found many instances where decisions enlightened by a functional approach have yielded private and social benefits to the core economy. Of these examples, perhaps the most intriguing have been in the energy sector.

The provision of energy and power is a prerequisite for development and constitutes a significant use of collective resources. For example, in the United States, as much as 5 percent of the gross domestic product goes toward the creation of fuels and power, 5 of *Fortune's* largest 25 firms are engaged in energy production, and 7 percent of all household disposable income is spent on energy.[19] Developments that enable societies to acquire power at lower costs or to manage unanticipated fluctuations in the price of power have enormous potential for improving social welfare.

The electric power industry is facing unprecedented deregulation—in the United States, Great Britain, Argentina, Australia, and elsewhere. The movement is aimed at giving consumers the benefits of decentralized competition without sacrificing the benefits of natural scale economies. In this dynamic context, a functional perspective has helped inform the decisions that firms have made, allowing them to profit from change rather than be threatened by it.

In the pages that follow, we will look at how two very different institutions in the energy field have used the functional perspective to their advantage.

Competing Functionally

A striking example of functionality shaping a company's strategy is that of Enron Capital and Trade Resources (ECT), a subsidiary of Enron

Corporation.[20] While ECT has gone by various names over the past decade, its primary mission is to serve the needs of users and consumers of natural gas. The vision for ECT came from its founder, Jeffrey Skilling, a Harvard MBA and a former McKinsey & Company partner.

As a consultant to both financial services firms and natural gas firms, Skilling saw a remarkable resemblance between the competitive states of these two industries. In both cases, deregulation had been accompanied by a substantial increase in volatility, which was proving disruptive to both buyers and sellers. Meanwhile, a number of institutional constraints were making it difficult for gas producers to acquire financing. Skilling sensed that there was a viable business in meeting these needs. In his first conception of the business that would become ECT, Skilling therefore drew on his analogy with financial service institutions, calling the new Enron entity "Gas Bank." The new firm he envisioned would act like a bank, except that its "currency" would be methane molecules, not dollars. Like a bank, it would intermediate between buyers and sellers. While the business was initially defined in institutional terms (a bank), its strategic orientation from the outset was to satisfy fundamental needs—in other words, it took a functional perspective.

As ECT has grown and prospered, it has begun to act like a universal bank in the natural gas business, performing the equivalent of commercial banking, investment banking, merchant banking, and investment management. Today, Skilling draws a triangle to represent the three major functions that ECT performs. At one corner is "Risk Management," whereby the firm allows buyers and sellers of gas to control price risk (one of the six GFS functions identified above). A second corner is what he calls the "Physical" business of moving gas molecules and settling contracts. This set of logistical activities combines elements of pooling, moving goods across time and space, and the payments system. The final leg of the triangle is the "Financing" business, whereby ECT provides capital to suppliers of gas.

Clearly, customers have needs that cut across these three activities. But thinking in these functional terms allows ECT to better define and organize itself around its competencies. As a result, ECT has been able to quickly move into a new business—electric power—where the key functions are quite similar to those in the gas industry.

Although not a direct customer service function, the collection of data and extraction of information from all of ECT's disparate activities lies at the heart of the company. A unit of ECT, Enron Risk Management Services, acts as the repository of the firm's knowledge of the rapidly changing gas markets, and all contracts to which the firm is a party must be approved by this group. This process of continual information collection and extraction allows ECT to carry out its other activities more effectively and permits the company to better price its services and manage its risks. According to recent press reports, this risk management activity has successfully limited the firm's exposures despite very large and sudden movements in the price of natural gas.[21]

Enron's business also reflects the relevance of the "innovation spiral" to businesses. Most of ECT's risk management service to customers involves writing over-the-counter contracts that are customized in some way. The development of the NYMEX natural gas contract in 1990 in one sense creates competition for ECT's risk management services. But in a more fundamental way, the public markets serve as an important ally to the firm. ECT can use the liquid, exchange-traded contracts to shed some of its short-term risks and benefit from the market's price-discovery process. And although the exchange is not the firm's only means of balancing its books, it contributes to ECT's ability to create customized contracts and thereby illustrates the innovation spiral.

The Tennessee Valley Authority (TVA), a major producer of electric power for the southeastern United States, provides a second example of a firm that has benefited from adopting a functional approach.[22] As noted above, deregulation of electric utilities is changing the industry in fundamental ways, introducing market-based pricing, competition among utilities, and higher price volatility than experienced in the era of regulation. While the social benefits of deregulation are large, individual firms in the industry now face more difficult decisions. Formerly, managers made major capital commitments, such as building new plants, with confidence that future output prices and quantities would be effectively determined by governmental fiat. In a market-based environment, by contrast, firms have to decide how to meet customers' demands for power over the coming decade—even as deregulation makes accurate predicting of demand considerably more difficult.

For TVA, these decisions are even more complicated. The company's capacity to construct new plants is limited by a budget cap imposed by the U.S. Congress and its own board. The uncertainty of the new marketplace, combined with these budget constraints, made TVA both less willing and less able to invest billions of dollars in new nuclear reactors or gas-fired turbines.

Stepping back, a group of engineers at TVA approached this problem *functionally*. They asked, in effect: What need are we trying to meet, and how can we meet it? The traditional answer to this problem was to build power plants. But now, the engineering group reconceived of power plants as real options, where by paying an option premium (the up-front investment), the firm would have the right—but not the obligation—to buy power at an exercise price equal to the variable cost of the production process, and then deliver this power to its customers.

From this functional definition of power plants, it was a short conceptual leap to considering the use of explicit call options on power, which would give TVA the right (but not the obligation) to purchase power from counterparties. The firm proceeded with this experiment, and it received bids that in total would give the firm the right to buy over 22,000 megawatts of power, the equivalent of 18 nuclear power plants. It accepted only a small fraction of these offers, but some analysts attribute the firm's subsequent decision to abandon plans for new nuclear power plants to its success with this "functionally equivalent" solution.[23]

Now let's return to where we started: the traditional financial services sector. In this sector, we see clear evidence of competition along functional lines not only at the firm level, but also at the industry level. For example, Dwight Crane and Zvi Bodie have analyzed the banking industry at a functional level (Crane and Bodie 1996). They decompose banking into its constituent functions, then describe the competition faced by banks from entities that offer functionally similar services, such as money market mutual funds and nonbank finance companies.

Because a major tenet of the functional approach is the notion that the ultimate provider of a given function will be the one with the most efficient institutional structure, Crane and Bodie also consider the reintegration of functions—how different sets of functions may be combined within new "banking" institutions. They point out that economies of both scale and scope, especially around information technology (but not physical facilities), will play an important role in the future reintegration of functions. New breeds of financial advisors and innovative technology-based products (such as Intuit's Quicken) may well serve as the agents of that reintegration.

The notion of functional competition also underlies our colleague Stuart Gilson's work (with Jerry Warner, University of Rochester) on the complementary uses of bank debt and publicly issued high-yield debt by corporations.[24] Whereas prior research has focused on these two tools as substitutes for one another, Gilson and Warner show that they are in fact complementary. A firm can dynamically switch from one financing vehicle to the other, depending on its current need for flexibility.

Substituting Functionally

What are the prospects for change in the institutional categories and classifications of risk? To answer this question, let's develop a single hypothetical example, drawn from a stereotypical situation in asset management. Imagine a bank that understands and manages credit risks, which has a special expertise in the evaluation of corporate debt. Let's assume that the bank's asset managers are able to outperform a standard corporate bond index by 200 basis points, or 2 percent, on a consistent basis, and that the bank does not have any investment managers engaged in the equity sector.

Now suppose a large pension plan inquires as to whether this bank wants to manage its equity portfolio. Ten years ago, the prudent response would have been to attempt to redefine the assignment, or to refer the client to another institution with expertise in equities. Today, however, a responsible institution with superior investment skills in any sector might be foolish to turn this business away. Indeed, it could credibly argue that it can consistently outperform a standard equity index.

How could our hypothetical bank become a superior equity manager when it has skills only in the fixed-income market? Consider the following scenario: the client gives the bank $100 million to invest. The money goes directly into the bank's bond portfolio, which the bank managers know how to manage effectively and on which it will earn a superior market-adjusted return. But because the client has made it clear that it is looking for superior *equity* management, the bank also enters into an equity "swap contract." This contract states that the bank will pay to a counterparty the total return on the standard corporate bond index each year as if that counterparty had $100 million invested in that index. In return, the counterparty will pay to the bank the total rate of return on the S&P 500 stock index, applied to the sum of $100 million. To avoid arbitrage, the price to either party for this exchange is set at zero (except for transactions fees), because each party is promising and being promised total returns on an equal market value of principal amount. Exchanging these returns is an even swap; therefore, neither party pays anything to the other for entering into this contract.

What is the effect of having entered into this contract? If the bank continues to beat the corporate bond market index, the $100 million invested in the bank's corporate bond fund earns, on average, the bond index plus 2 percent. The payout of the bond index as part of the swap agreement leaves the bank portfolio with just the 2 percent incremental return. However, the counterparty must pay to the bank in return whatever the S&P 500 earns (dividends plus appreciation). Adding these components, the bank's client will earn the S&P 500 plus 2 percent. Hence, without developing or acquiring any new analytic capabilities, investment managers who are superior performers in one arena (in this case, corporate bonds) can use a simple contract to transform themselves into superior performers in other asset categories (in this case, equities). And in fact, this type of asset management strategy is being practiced today.[25]

This simple example demonstrates an important potential for increased efficiency in the management of financial services. Finance professionals and their firms can continue to specialize in what they are good at—and not feel pressured by the need to offer a full range of products to expand into areas in which they have no comparative advantage. The swap/contracting vehicle just described is a very efficient tool both for achieving breadth and for retaining focus.

A second point made by this example is that some traditional institutional asset management categories are increasingly arbitrary. What does it mean to be a "fixed-income manager" if one can convert oneself into a superior equity manager by means of a simple swap contract? Where would our hypothetical bank locate the activity of the preceding example—within "fixed income" or within "equities"? Does it make sense to do either? The same problem pertains when one classifies assets according to geographical locations: "European equities" versus "fixed income in Japan." Through a series of swaps, superior performances on one of those markets can be transformed into superior performance in any other.

At first glance, this transfer of competitive advantage from one market to another (or "alpha transfer," as it is sometimes called) might seem relevant in only the most liquid of financial markets. But the concept already has manifested itself in product markets as well.[26] Enron Capital and Trade Resources, discussed above, has developed numerous competitive advantages in its "home" industry—the natural-gas business—including the ability to deliver methane anywhere in the continental United States within a few hours. The firm now seeks to establish itself as a significant force in the electric power market. It has done so by partially leveraging its competitive advantage in the natural gas market. Enron has negotiated contracts with generators of electric power nationwide, whereby they "swap" methane molecules for electrons (and a processing fee).

These swaps are conceptually similar to the equity swap described above, except that they transform physical products (gas into electricity) instead of returns. Through the swaps, ECT translates its logistical advantages in natural gas to the electric power business and makes itself able to deliver electrons around the country in a matter of hours. This ability (along with Enron's purchase of electric utilities and its planned marketing of its electricity to consumers nationwide) may prove to be important components for its success in the power businesses.

Regulating Functionally

As businesses find new ways to compete by delivering old functions in new institutions or products, the task of regulators will of course become more complicated. Determining appropriate relative comparisons of systemic risk exposure is the key challenge in the short run. Longer term, regulators will have to learn to think functionally and systematically, or run the risk of becoming irrelevant.

Furthermore, financial accounting needs fundamental revisions if we are to have effective external financial accounting and regulation. In particular, a specialized new branch called "risk accounting" (or perhaps "exposure accounting") needs to be created. Current accounting practices are focused on valuation, which is inherently a *static* measure of financial conditions. By contrast, with its focus on exposure, risk accounting is inherently a *dynamic* measure of financial condition. It indicates how individual balance sheet values are likely to change in response to changes in the underlying financial-economic environment. Pressed by reality, many of the financial institutions that deal extensively in these complex securities have already developed risk accounting systems as part of their managerial accounting. Those that we have studied appear to be effective and could well serve as prototypes for standardized risk accounting.[27]

As an illustration of static versus dynamic testing of financial health, consider a pension plan with a pension fund that holds assets to support the pension liabilities (the retirement benefits). In the traditional accounting perspective, one looks at the *current market values* of the assets and the liabilities at a given point in time and asks, "Are the assets adequate compared to liabilities?" Let's evaluate two hypothetical pension plans:

- Plan A has $105 in assets for every $100 in liabilities, both marked to market.

- Plan B has $101 in assets for every $100 in liabilities, both marked to market.

Based on current-valuation coverage, plan B appears less secure than plan A. But now suppose that you are given some additional information. The assets in plan A are held in common stocks. In plan B, they are held in fixed-income, sovereign-backed instruments with duration matched to the promised fixed payments on the pension liabilities.

Although plan A has a higher current ratio of assets to liabilities, it is more vulnerable to a stock market decline, especially one in which interest rates also fall. In that case, not only do plan assets decline but the value of plan liabilities rises, and what was formerly an excess coverage rapidly becomes a deficit coverage. In plan B, with matched funding to its liabilities, there is essentially no risk of this outcome. So although by traditional static measures plan A has "better" coverage than plan B, plan B is seen to be more secure when dynamic tests for changes in coverage are applied.[28] Risk accounting, focused on exposures, would make their differences apparent.

A second but related point: To avoid unintended consequences, policy implementation must be comprehensive, and must treat economically equivalent transactions similarly. For example, a proposed regulation to force marked-to-market collateral requirements on all OTC derivatives, but not on loans and other traditional investments, could actually cause a shift back toward structures like parallel loans (which were the functional predecessors to swaps). These parallel loans have total principal exposure, especially in cross-border trades, as well as aggregate gross-interest exposure in terms of default by either party. Swaps have *no* principal exposure (and only net interest exposure). As they say, the road to hell is paved with good intentions. By restricting derivatives and by *not* treating other functionally equivalent alternatives similarly, regulation intended to *reduce* those default exposures can actually *increase* that exposure.

The implementation of comprehensive regulation will be quite difficult. Consider the various ways of implementing a standard investment objective, taking a levered position in the S&P 500 stocks:

1. Buy each stock individually on margin in the cash stock market.

2. Invest in an S&P 500 index fund and borrow from a bank to finance it.

3. Go long a future contract on the S&P 500.

4. Go long an OTC forward contract on the S&P 500.

5. Enter into a swap contract to receive the total return on the S&P 500, and pay LIBOR or some other standard interest rate.

6. Go long exchanged traded call options and short puts on the S&P 500.

7. Go long OTC calls and short puts.

8. Purchase an equity-linked note that pays based on the S&P 500, and finance it by a repurchase agreement.

9. Purchase from a bank a certificate of deposit that has payment linked to the return on the S&P 500.

10. Buy on margin or purchase the capital appreciation component of a unit investment trust (examples are Super Shares or SPDRs) that holds the S&P 500.

11. Borrow to buy a variable-rate annuity contract that has its return linked to the S&P 500.

One could probably find many more ways to take the equivalent economic position of a levered position in the S&P 500. In the United States alone, the types of institutions involved in these functionally equivalent transactions include brokers, mutual funds, investment banks, commercial banks, insurance companies, and exchanges. The regulatory authorities involved include the SEC, CFTC, Federal Reserve, Comptroller of the Currency, and perhaps 50 state insurance commissions.

In the real world, attempts to regulate just two or three of these many ways of doing an equivalent thing are not going to be effective. In fact, they could be counterproductive. Regulators will find it increasingly difficult to organize their activities along traditional institutional lines in the future. In the longer run, regulation must follow functional lines, not institutional ones. Implementation will not be easy.

Financial Services in the Future: A Functional View

The goal of the GFS project is not only to document existing conditions, but also to use the functional perspective to address the major issues that are likely to face households, nonfinancial businesses, financial institutions, and governmental bodies as we move into the twenty-first century. Let's review our current projections in each of these areas.

The Household Sector

Households are the ultimate consumers of financial services. One major institutional change over the past two decades has been the disaggregation of financial services at the retail level. A second has been deregulation, combined with a reduction in government guarantees of financial performance. Those changes have imposed significantly more responsibility for risk bearing on the household. In other words, households are now called upon to make important financial decisions involving risk that they have not had to make in the past, and may be ill trained to make in the present or future. In this sense, the evolving structure of the financial system has a dysfunctional aspect. But it seems likely that the successful financial institutions in the impending future will be those that effectively address this problem, while still fully exploiting the functional benefits of new financial technology.

Households (and other "retail customers") will continue to move away from the types of direct, individual financial market activities—such as trading in individual stocks or bonds—where they have the greatest and growing comparative disadvantage. Better diversification, lower trading costs, and less informational disadvantage will continue to move their trading and investing activities toward aggregate bundles of securities, such as mutual funds, basket-type and index securities, and custom-designed products issued by intermediaries.

This secular shift, together with informational effects as described in Gammill and Perold (1989), will enhance liquidity in the basket/index securities, while individual stocks become relatively less liquid. With ever-greater institutional ownership of individual securities, there will be less need for the traditional regulatory protections and other subsidies of the costs of retail investors trading in stocks and bonds. The emphasis on disclosure and other regulations intended to protect those investors will tend to shift up the "security aggregation chain" to the interface between investors and investment companies, asset allocators, and insurance and pension products.

Overall, consumer financial products will become "user-friendly" and more tailored to individual profiles. Paradoxically, making the product simple is likely to create considerably more complexity for the producers of those products. Financial engineering creativity (and the technological base to implement that creativity, with reliability and at low cost) will be a key competitive element for financial-service providers.

The Nonfinancial Business Sector

The examples of Enron Capital and Trade Resources and of the Tennessee Valley Authority suggest that the managerial application of a functional approach can yield benefits for nonfinancial firms.[29] The development of low-cost financial tools that enable firms to hedge particular risks has profound implications for the investment, financing, and risk management strategies of these firms. Application of these tools is not limited to risk management; it can also support new business strategies. Furthermore, a functional approach may suggest different organizational designs for the financial activities of firms. In particular, it may help us to understand the relatively new phenomenon of outsourcing (the transfer of certain tasks to vendors outside the corporation).

The management of risk has traditionally focused on capital. Equity capital can be thought of as a cushion, available for absorbing the firm's risks. But the very characteristic of the equity cushion that makes it attractive to managers is the characteristic that creates a moral hazard for the shareholders who provide that equity cushion. The resulting agency and tax costs are the main reasons that equity financing can be expensive.[30]

The other fundamental means for controlling risk is through hedging. In contrast to equity capital, which is all-purpose, hedging is a form of risk control that is highly targeted. Hedging can be very efficient, but carries with it the requirement that users have a deep quantitative understanding of their business. They must understand much more about their structures than in the case of all-purpose equity capital. Developing this deeper understanding of their business often requires retraining managers in the ways they think about their business.

Many authors have written about how risk management can enhance shareholder welfare.[31] We focus on the role of risk management in helping firms to avoid carrying large, inefficient equity cushions. In particular, with effective risk management, firms may be able to remain private (by that we mean a firm with a relatively small number of owners) rather than becoming a publicly held firm with large numbers of public shareholders.[32]

The advantages of being privately held are obvious: reduced agency costs; lower costs of transferring information, including external reporting; protection of key information from competitors; and greater flexibility to optimize with respect to taxes and regulation. It is normally thought that privately held firms forfeit the opportunity to allow risk-averse owner-managers to diversify their risks, and also forgo the chance to raise additional funds so as to conduct their operations on a more efficient scale. Yet by hedging, the private firm may be able to enjoy both of these benefits. Furthermore, lenders are more willing to lend to hedged firms, allowing private firms to raise capital for funding larger projects.[33]

The benefits of financial market innovation to nonfinancial firms extend beyond hedging the risks of existing businesses. As the ECT and TVA examples show, firms can use financial markets to reconfigure their operations or to substitute for traditional activities. We also see opportunities where financial engineering can be used to support marketing programs, construct employee incentive programs, signal information to markets, and facilitate the process of industry transformation through mergers (see Tufano 1996b).

Developments in the financial system (in particular, financial engineering) may allow firms to take on strategic risks. By voluntarily bearing the risks of customers, employees, suppliers, or others, a firm may be able to reconfigure its activities or even its business strategy. For example, imagine that a real estate broker offers to sell your home, but instead of asking for the standard 6 percent commission, she offers you another alternative. Her firm will compensate you for any softening of the market from the time you sign the brokerage agreement to the time the home is sold, using a local real estate index as the basis for defining the protection. This feature (which would only be feasible as the financial system develops new customized contracts) would surely differentiate the firm from its rivals.

Finally, the functional perspective almost forces one to break a product, activity, or institution down into its basic components; that is, the functions it serves. It is not uncommon to discover, as a result of this disaggregation, that some of these functions are and should be separable. In finance, we see some activity toward decomposing the corporate finance function into its component parts and then outsourcing some or all of those parts to vendors.

This in turn may enable us to define what is distinctive about corporate finance—how it affects a firm's business strategy and whether it creates value. This may eventually give us greater insight into the seminal and startling work of Modigliani and Miller (1958), which held that, in terms of affecting shareholder value, much of corporate finance was irrelevant.

The Financial Sector

Whether the financial services industry will become more concentrated or more diffuse, as this scenario plays out, is unclear. The central functions of information and transactions processing seem to favor economies of scale, and therefore concentration. Similarly, the greater opportunities for netting and diversifying risk exposures by an intermediary with a diverse set of products suggest both fewer required hedging transactions and less risk capital per dollar of product liability, as size increases.[34] And finally, increased demand for custom products and private contracting services would seem to indicate that more of the financial services business will be conducted by principals instead of agents, which again favors size.

On the other hand, expansion in the types of organized trading markets, reductions in transactions costs, and continued improvements in information processing and telecommunications technologies will all make it easier for a greater variety of firms to serve the financial services functions. These same factors also improve the prospects for expanding asset-based financing, and such expanded opportunities for securitization will permit smaller, agent-type firms to compete with larger firms in traditionally principal-type activities.

Continuing the scenario, locational and regulatory advantages currently available to some financial institutions will be reduced. More firms will be capable of offering a broader range of financial products and of servicing a wider geographic area. Traditional institutional identifications with specific types of products will become increasingly blurred.

As in other innovating industries, competition to create new products and services, and to find new ways of producing established ones at lower costs, could make its R&D activity the lifeblood of the financial services firm. Along this hypothetical path, the need to distribute a higher volume and a more diverse set of products promises continued relative growth of the firm's sales activity.

Controlling actual and perceived default risk for its customer-held liabilities has always been a key requirement for the success of any financial intermediary. Customer expectations for higher service levels, as well as an ever-increasing complexity of products, will intensify the attention that firms give to this issue in the future. The finance function of financial services firms will be significantly expanded—to cover not only the increased working capital needs of the firm, but also the management of its counterparty credit risk exposure.

As technology advances continue to drive down trading and custodial costs, the posting and careful monitoring of collateral is likely to be more widely adopted as the primary means for ensuring counterparty performance, especially among financial institutions. Implementation of this practice will in turn require enhanced trading skills for the firm. The trading activity is also likely to expand, in order to meet the execution requirements for implementing more complex product technologies.

Governmental Bodies

As in the case of the private sector, the functional perspective provides a useful framework for analyzing the role of government in the financial system. The potential roles for regulation and other governmental activities in improving the economic performance of the financial system include promoting competition; ensuring market integrity, including macro credit risk protections; and managing public good–type externalities. The categories of potential costs for such activities are direct costs to participants, such as fees for using the markets or costs of filings; distortions of market prices and resource allocations; transfers of wealth among private party participants in the financial markets; and transfers of wealth from taxpayers to participants in the financial markets.

There are five ways that the government affects today's financial system: as a *market participant* following the same rules for action as other private-sector transactors, such as with open market operations; as an *industry competitor or benefactor of innovation*, by supporting development or directly creating new financial products or markets, such as index-linked bonds or all-savers accounts; as a *legislator and enforcer*, by setting and enforcing rules and restrictions on market participants, financial products, and markets, such as up-tick rules, margin requirements, circuit breakers, and patents on products; as a *negotiator*, by representing its domestic constituents in dealings with other sovereigns that involve financial markets; and as an *unwitting intervenor*, by changing general corporate regulations, taxes, and other laws or policies that frequently have significant unanticipated and unintended consequences for the financial services industry.

In the future, the impact of financial innovation on the way government undertakes its various financial market activities will be increasingly significant. As already discussed, a prime venue will be the way government regulates financial institutions. A second venue will be the valuation and management of government financial guarantees. A third will be government's role in promoting socially beneficial financial innovation. And a fourth will be the use of the new financial technology by government to make more effective implementation of macro stabilization policies.

Conclusions

The Global Financial System project was initiated to help give managers and regulators an approach for dealing with innovation and complexity in the financial system. It matches institutions with functions and functions with institutions. In each case, it asks whether the matches are effective and whether they can be improved.

The functional perspective encourages us to ask: Given the function that needs to be served, what is the best institutional structure to use? It also helps us frame the same question in a significantly different way: Given the institutional structure in place, what is the best set of functions to offer?

The first question assumes that we are working with a blank slate. The second question acknowledges that most firms approach most problems with significant organizational assets in place, and they seek the most effective way to deploy those assets. In either case, the issues raised by a functional analysis are intended to be strategic.

From its inception, the GFS project has sought to change the way academics, managers, and regulators understand the financial system, and thus to help them make better decisions. The project has been characterized by a close collaboration among the academics involved. It also has been characterized by a sustained interaction with some of the most successful senior executives in the financial services sector, which ensured that our work would remain relevant to all and focused on issues of prime significance over the long term.

These focuses have helped to make the GFS project a highly productive one. In Appendix B, we present a summary, in essay form, of the five areas of recent and current research conducted by individuals or groups associated with the larger GFS effort. (References for the GFS group are included at the end of this volume as Appendix A.) Individually and collectively, these research activities represent a potential fulfilled—and in turn suggest even greater potential.

The seeds of the GFS project were carefully sown under John McArthur's watchful eye, and with his patient support. With continued watering, weeding, and occasional pruning, the project is likely to bear fruit for years to come.

CHAPTER FOUR

Competition and Strategy

The Creation of a Group and a Field

MICHAEL E. PORTER AND NICOLAJ SIGGELKOW

I N THE SPRING OF 1975, *John McArthur invited Michael Porter to a meeting in his office in Morgan Hall. McArthur was then an associate dean in the administration of Dean Lawrence E. Fouraker. He was responsible for a wide range of tasks, sometimes including staffing assignments. McArthur had called the meeting to work out a new assignment for his young colleague.*

Porter was then beginning his third year on the HBS faculty. His novel ideas about strategy in various industry settings were becoming known among the faculty, and were already being hotly debated. He had spent the previous two years teaching in the Business Policy course the School's required "capstone" course for second-year MBA students. This in-depth exposure to a succession of field cases had motivated him to rethink the economic theories of industry competition that he had explored in his doctoral work. Porter wanted to use his emerging ideas to improve on the intellectual architecture of the Policy course, but he wondered how he would ever learn enough about the "real world" to make such a contribution.

McArthur now made an unexpected proposal to Porter. Why not take a few years away from the MBA setting, he suggested, and test your ideas against the kinds of high-level, functionally oriented executives who attend the Program for Management Development?

Porter was taken aback. The MBA program seemed to him to be at the heart of the School. But McArthur persisted, arguing that seasoned executives would challenge Porter better than MBA students.

McArthur was right. In 1978, following his return to the MBA program, Porter for the first time offered his ground-breaking Industry and Competitive Analysis course, which was eventually to have a powerful impact on the MBA curriculum.

IN 1980, when John McArthur became dean of the Harvard Business School, the field of Competition and Strategy (C&S) was just emerging in the mind of McArthur's colleague, Michael Porter, and a few others. When McArthur passed the torch to Kim Clark in 1995, by contrast, C&S had evolved into a vibrant area, with 14 faculty members who taught a full range of first- and second-year MBA classes and a broad spectrum of executive programs.

The C&S group is a direct descendant of the School's general management tradition and heritage. It has emerged as an influential voice in the world of business and business strategy. Its research today spans a wide array of topics: industry and positioning analysis, the sustainability of competitive advantage, corporate (multibusiness) strategy, international trade and competition, locational influences on competition, and the interplay of technology and strategy. The C&S faculty has been able to create a new body of ideas, drawing on economics, game theory, and other disciplines to inform business practice in the area of strategy. Through rigorous theoretical and empirical research, the C&S group has contributed significantly to academic thinking in strategy, economics, and other fields. The group has also been successful in communicating its work to practitioners.

Our goal in this essay is to recreate and interpret the intellectual and institutional evolution of the C&S unit at the Harvard Business School.

Let us state at the outset that John McArthur played a critical role in the birth and growth of the unit. He created an organizational context that nurtured our group. He actively encouraged us to conduct fundamental research, in ways that required significant investments by the School. Even before the group achieved the status of an independent area, McArthur gave us extensive leeway in hiring and assignments, thereby enabling us to grow and establish an independent identity. And perhaps most important, he helped us survive and prosper amid the kinds of personal and collective struggles that always accompany innovation.

Because our essay is necessarily limited in length, and despite the fact that the C&S group from the very beginning has been greatly influenced by external intellectual developments, we have omitted contextual details and background that we otherwise would have chosen to include. Of necessity, we pay inadequate tribute to our predecessors. We concentrate mainly on the development of strategy at the business-unit level and offer less detail on the area of corporate strategy—which deals with issues such as diversification and corporate control—despite the fact that these issues have become an important part of the group's work.

The Field Prior to 1980

In order to appreciate the development of the C&S area during McArthur's deanship, the reader needs to understand the "state of the strategy art" in 1980, as well as some aspects of the intellectual landscape at the Harvard Business School prior to 1980.

The modern strategy field has its roots in two parallel streams of work. One of these efforts, which came to the forefront in the 1960s and focused on functional integration and company uniqueness, was led by Kenneth Andrews, C. Roland Christensen, and their colleagues at the Harvard Business School. The other was an effort on the part of a few prominent consulting firms to create an alternative approach to strategy. These two traditions—the School's more holistic approach and the stripped-down, more readily quantifiable concepts that arose within the consulting community—were the defining bodies of thought in the field throughout the 1960s and 1970s.

The antecedents of "strategy" actually date back to the founding of the School, and even earlier. Almost from the start, the School had attempted to think holistically about enterprises. Its leaders believed that there was a theory of business to be discovered, although where that theory might reside and what it might comprise remained mysterious. The School's faculty subscribed to the notion that business was a complex endeavor and that this complexity had to underlie all of the School's analyses and prescriptions. Theory, whatever it turned out to be, had to be immersed in context. These foundations served many subsequent intellectual pioneers extremely well—including those in the C&S group.

Business Policy: Origins and Traditions

In the School's curriculum, much of the evolution of the strategy field occurred in the Business Policy course. Business Policy (BP) was first offered at the School in 1912, after Chicago-based publisher Arch W. Shaw persuaded the dean, Edwin F. Gay, that an integrative second-year course was needed to organize and reinforce the lessons of the first-year program, and to instill in HBS students the perspective of the upper-level manager. Although the word *strategy* appears nowhere in course descriptions of the day, BP was explicitly conceived as the venue for considerations of executive decision making. This predated the formal introduction of the case method at HBS, and at first, discussions were led by visiting business leaders. In the early 1920s, as HBS embraced its particular version of the case method, adequate teaching materials became available for the first time, and BP—which evidently had proven its worth—was made a required second-year course.[1]

Thus began the most durable run of any course in the School's history, extending over more than half a century. BP gradually became known as the "capstone" course in a curriculum that year by year was gaining credibility and recognition. In part, BP's role was one of pedagogical innovation. In the 1930s, for example, BP professors acknowledged the reality that problems do not "come walking up to executives' desks asking to be solved," and that the process of diagnosis was critical to successful management. Over subsequent decades, this recognition permeated the rest of the curriculum.[2]

In the prewar years, Business Policy was also the port of entry into the HBS curriculum for a variety of new ideas. For example, almost from its inception, BP was the preferred home for considerations of business ethics. In 1927, Business History first entered the required curriculum as an extra, early morning BP course added by historian N. S. B. Gras. During the mid-1930s, BP became the first testing ground for some of the radical concepts in "human relations" that were then emerging from the celebrated Hawthorne experiments, conducted in part by HBS faculty.[3]

Postwar: BP and Strategy

During the first decade after World War II, BP's tradition of innovation faded somewhat but was reinvigorated in 1956 when a small group of faculty members, led by Edmund Learned, C. Roland Christensen, and Kenneth Andrews, undertook to revamp the course. Their experiments emphasized strategic issues, as well as a willingness to invest in new kinds of teaching materials. For the first time, Business Policy cases explicitly examined companies as economic entities within their industries, with separate "industry notes" examining the structure of the industries involved. Those larger frameworks were then reapplied to the companies' social structures, the psychological profiles of key executives, and other critical issues.[4]

In 1961 Learned, Christensen, and Andrews published their seminal text, *Problems of General Management: Business Policy—A Series Casebook.* This was a book that in its various editions would strongly influence the teaching of BP around the world in the coming decades.[5] In 1960 the BP faculty group enrolled its first doctoral students. Three years later, the McKinsey Foundation for Management Research sponsored a "Symposium in Business Policy" at the School, and it was at this conference that Ken Andrews's "SWOT" framework—for Strengths, Weaknesses,

Opportunities, and Threats—first gained substantial public notice. Andrews and other members of the School's strategy faculty argued that the task of top management was to understand a company's special strengths and weaknesses, which they came to summarize as its "distinctive competence," as well as the opportunities and threats that the company had to deal with in the marketplace.

Strategy was viewed as the unifying idea that pulled together a company's functional areas and linked them to its external environment. Formulating strategy meant juxtaposing a company's strengths and weaknesses with the opportunities and threats presented by its environment, and devising an action plan based on that understanding. This plan then would be implemented through an internally consistent effort that coordinated the firm's goals, policies, and functional plans. Strengths, weaknesses, opportunities, and threats: "SWOT" influenced the development of corporate strategies for years to come. It was more fully developed in its " internal" workings—that is, in the internal workings of companies—than in its analysis of environmental factors, but it was highly influential nonetheless.

In 1971, Kenneth Andrews summarized much of the learning of the previous 15 years in *The Concept of Corporate Strategy*, a book written explicitly for use by general managers. In his preface to the third edition of the book, Andrews commented as follows:

> *The idea of corporate strategy brings all the special functions of business to bear on the principal task of the chief executive. It is capable of including the most extensive combination of interrelated variables involved in the most important of all business decisions.*
>
> *This idea cannot be brought to final fruition in this book or any other. It is only in an industry, company, and specific situation that its power can be realized.*[6]

In retrospect, the publication of Andrews's book can be seen as the high-water mark for BP and for the first-generation "strategy group." One challenge was that the group's senior leaders were refocusing their attention: Ed Learned retired, Ken Andrews (in 1973) was named chairman of the editorial board of the *Harvard Business Review,* and Chris Christensen (beginning in 1968, and throughout the 1970s and 1980s) was increasingly called upon by HBS, Harvard University, and other educational institutions to help teachers learn to teach using the case method.

Consultants Take the Field

Meanwhile, the field of business strategy was also evolving outside the School. Companies had always made plans, of course. But the idea that a business had to have a coherent strategy, conceived in a specific context, was greatly reinforced by the experiences of World War II, during which the effective deployment of resources (military and industrial) was a matter of national survival. And in the early 1960s, many American businesses began to face a level of competition that forced business leaders to confront the issue of effective choice making: Where should we take our company, and how should we get there?[7]

Beginning in the mid-1960s, some of the prominent consulting firms developed a very different framework from that which was emerging at the School, and thereby entered into a de facto competition of ideas with the Harvard strategists. For example, in 1966, the Boston Consulting Group (BCG) began describing a universal market dynamic on which all strategy could be based: the experience curve.[8] This model held that competitive advantage was defined by a single variable: cost. Cost was inversely proportional to learning, which itself was proportional to accumulated experience. Experience, in turn, was in large part derived from market share. A firm's strategy, therefore, should be designed to satisfy the all-important imperative of increasing relative market share.

The experience curve concept was embraced enthusiastically by companies in many industries. But the model's most pronounced impact came in its next iteration—the growth-share matrix—which emerged from BCG in the early 1970s. This framework encouraged a diversified company to locate its various operating divisions on a matrix, of which the two axes were growth and market share. Divisions in the high-growth, high-share quadrant were "stars" to be cultivated, whereas divisions in the low-growth, low-market-share quadrant were candidates for divestiture. Companies with inadequate numbers of "stars" could milk their "cash cows" to feed "question marks" and transform at least some of them into stars. The growth-share matrix, in turn, gave way to portfolio analysis and other new tools for setting and implementing strategy at the level of the diversified firm.

What is most interesting about the transitional period of the early to mid-1970s is the sharp contrast between the approaches advocated by HBS and the consulting firms. The Andrews-Christensen-Learned framework argued that strategy was situation-specific. Every industry and company was different in fundamental ways. By contrast, the uni-dimensional models put forward by consulting firms offered precision, simplicity, and universal applicability—or at least the promise thereof. At a time when more and more companies were looking for *answers*, in the wake of the oil shocks of the 1970s and the intensification of com-petition from Japan and other nations, the analytical techniques of the strategy consultants met a clear need. But as researchers at Harvard and elsewhere were quick to point out, the track record of the consultants' solutions was questionable. In their 1980 article, "Managing Our Way to Economic Decline," for example, Robert H. Hayes and William J. Abernathy argued that the consultants' analytic tools were both over-simplified and shortsighted.[9]

Pioneering: A Group and Its Frameworks (1978–1986)

In retrospect, the decision to create a separate course that dealt exclu-sively with the *content* of strategy can be understood as the starting point for today's C&S group. In the first few years of the transitional period, as the curricular and conceptual rules were being rewritten in the late 1970s, faculty from other areas of the School were attracted by Michael Porter's new frameworks (described below). They, not Policy profes-sors, helped teach the new second-year Industry and Competitive Analysis elective in which those frameworks were being developed. Because Porter founded and has played a prominent role in nurturing the strategy interest group, it might be useful for the reader to under-stand the intellectual context that spawned not only Porter, but several other of his HBS colleagues in the strategy area. That context was Harvard University's Ph.D. program in Business Economics.

Initiated in 1916 as a joint effort of the department of economics and HBS, the program did not enroll students on a regular basis until the late 1960s, when HBS Professor John Lintner took the lead in shaping a new program design. The newly endowed George Gund Chair of Economics and Business Administration (a joint appointment first held by Lintner) helped "bridge the river" between the two departments. The program's next two chairmen—Michael Spence, who later became chairman of the Harvard Department of Economics, dean of Harvard's Faculty of Arts and Sciences, and dean of the Stanford Business School; and Richard Caves, a leading figure in the field of industrial organization economics and a former head of Harvard's economics department—continued to mold the Business Economics Ph.D. program into a remarkable breeding ground for researchers not only in strategy, but also in several other disciplines.

By providing access to two leading faculties, the program served candidates who wanted to combine formal training in modern economic analysis with training in the realities of business operation and management. Graduates of the program were well positioned to bring the rigor of economic analysis to the traditionally more qualitative study of business administration.[10] Porter, one of the first Business Economics Ph.D.'s to join the HBS faculty, was the first economist in the Policy group. Other HBS faculty with Business Economics Ph.D.'s have included Willis Emmons, Robert Kennedy, and Forest Reinhardt (in the Business, Government, and International Economy unit); David Collis, Michael Enright, Pankaj Ghemawat, Tarun Khanna, Anita McGahan, and Jan Rivkin (Competition and Strategy); William Sahlman (Entrepreneurial Management); George Chacko, Benjamin Esty, Paul Gompers, Carl Kester, and Peter Tufano (Finance); James Sebenius (Negotiations); and George Baker and Ashish Nanda (Organizations and Markets). To reiterate the obvious: this is a remarkable record of achievement on the part of one Ph.D. program among many in the larger university context.

In 1983–1984, Porter became course head for BP I and started to introduce the new frameworks into the required curriculum. Again in retrospect, this can be seen as a milestone, representing as it did the migration of new thinking about strategy into the core of the HBS curriculum. Over time, the still-informal "C&S interest group" started to attract its own dedicated faculty, with strong backgrounds in both economics and applied research. Meanwhile, the close connection between the emerging C&S group and the Business Economics Ph.D. program also played a crucial role in shaping a common culture in the new group. The shared values that emerged in the group included high research standards, a powerful respect for formal analysis, and a recognition of the necessity to conduct and present such analyses in ways that would be useful to practicing managers. All of these factors contributed to a common intellectual framework which became the centerpiece of the C&S group's evolution in these early years.

From Industrial Organization Economics to Strategy

During the 1980s, strategy became a full-fledged intellectual and management discipline. The infusion of techniques from the field of industrial organization (IO) economics into business strategy research played an important role in this development. Previous work in strategy either had ignored industries altogether, focusing on companies alone; had implicitly assumed that all industries were equal (as with the experience curve); or had incompletely analyzed industries by presuming that growth rate, size, or technological sophistication were synonymous with industry attractiveness. IO economics, by contrast, recognized the important role of industry structure in shaping the behavior of firms and their resulting profit performance.

That was the entry on the positive side of the ledger, and it was a significant one. But traditional IO economics also had some negatives. First, IO economics focused on only a few attributes of structure, especially those that were the most easily measurable, such as seller concentration and a few types of barriers to entry. Second, IO economics omitted consideration of intraindustry positioning, implicitly positing that all companies in a particular industry were roughly alike. And finally, IO economics tended to focus on public policy issues, rather than managerial concerns. Economists by and large saw their job as policing the activities of firms and protecting the interests of consumers. Managers, meanwhile, were concerned with the well-being of their organizations—with promoting growth, innovation, and the like. These diverging agendas made IO economics less compelling to researchers at HBS, and also of little use to business practitioners.

In his early work during the 1970s and 1980s, Michael Porter sought to integrate the rigor of economic analysis and the richness and multidimensionality embodied in the traditional HBS style of thinking and teaching. He sought to build on the foundation of IO economics to construct a dynamic map of the firm's external environment, while capturing the complexity of businesses in real-world situations—in other words, to draw upon the strengths of economics without falling into a deterministic, equilibrium-oriented economic model that abstracted competition to a few dimensions. As early as 1974, he had used the tools of IO economics to focus on profit maximization, rather than public policy issues.[11] In a 1979 *Harvard Business Review* article, "How Competitive Forces Shape Strategy," Porter pushed this effort further. He employed the tools of economic analysis in the context of strategy formulation, providing a powerful framework to inform the kinds of systematic analysis that had so often been called for by the preceding generation of strategy scholars.

For example, in their Business Policy casebook, Andrews and his colleagues had suggested that managers should "examine the economic environment of the company, to determine the essential characteristics of the industry, to note its developments and trends, and to estimate future opportunities and risks for firms of varying resources and competencies," and the "industry notes" included in the casebook implied the form that such an examination might take. However, despite their recognition that industry conditions played an important role in a firm's success, Andrews and his colleagues had not offered a systematic way of assessing the competitive environment.

The framework that Porter developed in the late 1970s (see Figure 4.1), which later achieved renown as the "five forces," focused on assessing the attractiveness of a given industry for an average incumbent competitor. In addition to drawing on economics research to identify the determinants of rivalry among industry competitors as well as the barriers to new entrants, Porter's framework also included the influence of buyers and suppliers (who had power to influence competitors) and the influence of substitute products and services. In each area, the framework laid out the industry structural characteristics that were governing.

The five-forces framework Porter developed was first a tool for analyzing profitability differences across industries. It addressed the question of what happened to the value created by a product or a service. Was this value bargained away by customers? By suppliers? Was it dissipated through rivalry? Was it appropriated by new entrants? Limited by the existence of substitutes? It was also a tool for understanding the most important elements driving competition in an industry, for analyzing industry evolution, and for examining important industry settings, such as fragmented industries, emerging industries, declining industries, and global industries. Porter's 1980 book *Competitive Strategy* was the vehicle for presenting this framework. In it, he also provided a framework for understanding and predicting the behavior of competitors, thereby pioneering the field of competitive analysis, which has since become a discipline in its own right.

FIGURE 4.1   *Drivers of Industry Competition*

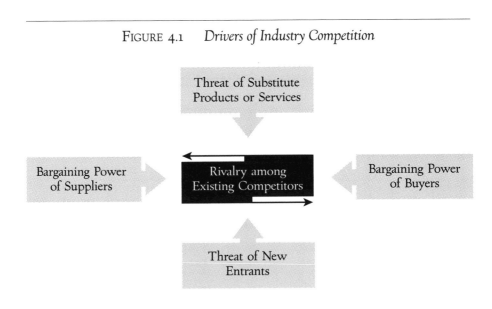

The five-forces framework also marked a new type of intellectual endeavor in the strategy field. At one end of the spectrum, economic models abstract competition down to a few variables, and for this reason are not particularly useful guides for business practitioners. They are highly sensitive to the assumptions underlying them; they depend on the "unrealistic" concept of equilibrium; they don't integrate easily with other analyses. At the other end of the spectrum, the tradition of HBS had been to eschew analytical reduction altogether, focusing instead on individual cases. Frameworks attempt to occupy a middle ground—respecting complexity while engaging in the "right" amount of reduction. Of particular note is the fact that frameworks do not assume equilibrium. In fact, the assumption is that there is a continually evolving environment in which a perpetual competitive interaction between rivals takes place. Frameworks share some characteristics with what were formerly called "expert systems"—guiding the user to the essential issues and choices in a particular competitive situation.

Mathematics and frameworks are not mutually exclusive. Indeed, they can be juxtaposed creatively to generate a constructive tension. Mathematics ensures logical consistency. Frameworks, for their part, can challenge the mathematics by highlighting omitted variables, the diversity of actual competitive situations, the range of actual strategy choices, and the extent to which key parameters are in flux.

Positioning: Intraindustry Profit Differences

The second major thrust of Porter's work in this period, which had just found its way into his 1980 book *Competitive Strategy*, was the positioning of the firm within an industry. Whereas the five-forces framework aimed to explain profitability differences *across* industries, positioning analysis attempted to explain differences in profitability among firms *within* a given industry. Up to that point, intraindustry differences in profitability had been little examined, except for some early efforts focusing on size and market share. A group of papers, including several written jointly by Richard Caves and Michael Porter, began to move this examination forward. One of the Caves/Porter papers, for example, introduced the notion of "mobility barriers," or the barriers to shifting competitive position within an industry.[12] Complementary work on the concept of strategic groups within industries was carried out by other students in the Business Economics and the Economics Ph.D. program, including Michael Hunt, Howard Newman, and Sharon Oster.

In 1980 Porter introduced the notion that all competitive advantages could be generalized to either lower cost or differentiation (see Figure 4.2). While management scholars had offered a number of taxonomies of strategies which concentrated on expansion options—such as internationalization and vertical integration—Porter reframed the debate around the concept of competitive advantage. The result was a framework called "generic strategies," which set up a number of positioning alternatives derived from the type of competitive advantage sought (again, either low cost or differentiation) and the scope of advantage pursued by a given firm—either serving a broad array of customers or offering a wide range of product types, or focused on a narrow customer or product segment.

Porter's theory emphasized that the essence of strategic positioning was *being different from rivals*. By this logic, a variety of positioning choices could be successful in an industry. A broad-line competitor, such as Toyota in automobiles, could be successful by offering good value at a low cost, while BMW could prosper simultaneously by offering customized high-performance cars at a premium price to a segment of customers that was very performance-sensitive (focused differentiation). This presented a sharp contrast to earlier approaches, such as the experience curve described above. As Porter saw it, these mostly unidimensional tools were not only misleading, they were also destructive, in that they encouraged all companies to compete on the same basis. In many cases, this triggered a downward spiral that hurt all participants.

The book *Competitive Strategy* offered an accessible way for managers to think about business as a system. It focused on the multidimensionality, interdependencies, fluidity, and dynamism that characterize much of business. By extending and integrating the concepts of IO economics with the general management traditions of the Harvard Business School, and by allowing the details to matter, *Competitive Strategy* captured a broad and influential audience. The success of the new approach created the momentum necessary to build a new interest group at HBS—attracting bright young people, and luring in interested scholars at a senior level.

FIGURE 4.2   *Choosing a Competitive Position*

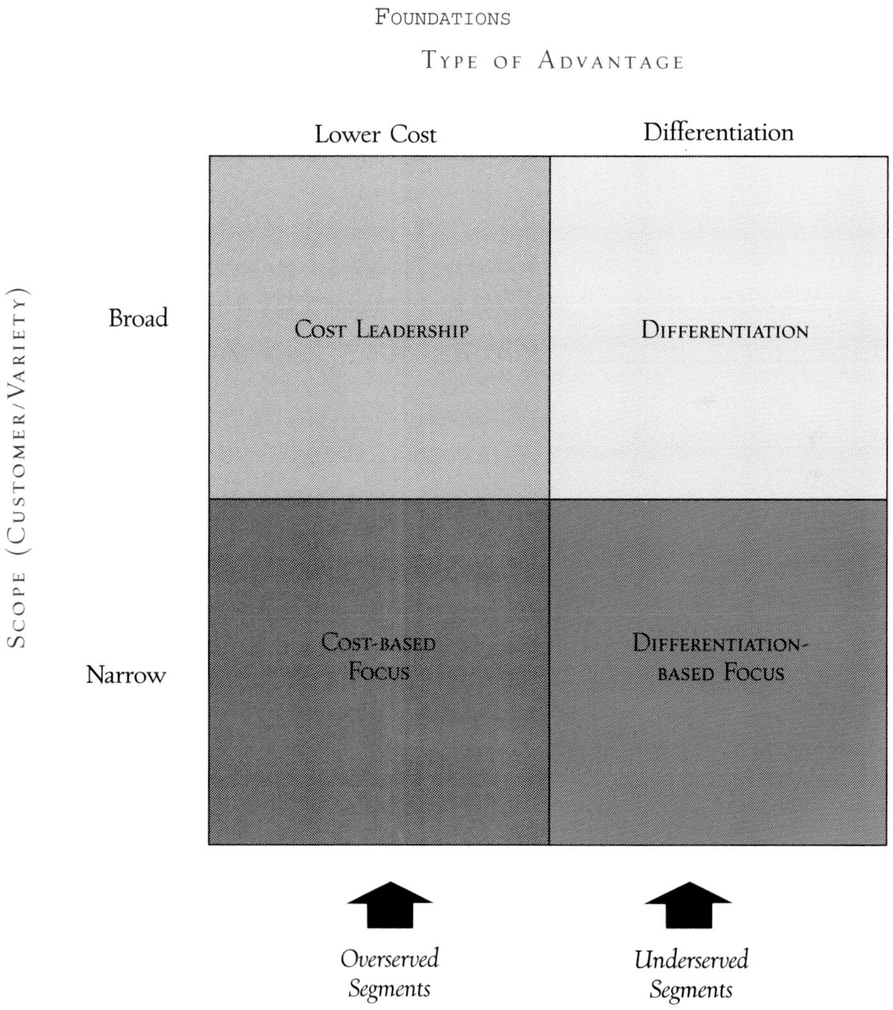

FOUNDATIONS

TYPE OF ADVANTAGE

	Lower Cost	Differentiation
Broad	COST LEADERSHIP	DIFFERENTIATION
Narrow	COST-BASED FOCUS	DIFFERENTIATION-BASED FOCUS

SCOPE (CUSTOMER/VARIETY)

Overserved Segments   *Underserved Segments*

Activities and the Value Chain

The first wave of Porter's work concerned itself mainly with external players, such as competitors, suppliers, and customers. In other words, Porter and his colleagues at first focused on competitive forces on the industry level, analyzing how those forces might be assessed and harnessed by a company within that industry. Over time, the early thinking about positioning led to a second strand of work focused on how to make positioning choices more operational.

This was in part an outgrowth of the realization, both at Harvard and in the business community, that industry-level analysis was only one piece of the puzzle. The IO economists had argued that certain industries were inherently more profitable than others. At the same time, empirical studies showed that a high-performing company in a lackluster (that is, low-profit) industry could produce better returns than an average company in a high-profit industry.

Another incentive for zeroing in on more operational issues was the emerging Japanese competition of the late 1970s and early 1980s, which had compelled companies to reexamine their ways of doing business. McKinsey & Company put forward a notion they called "the business system," in which the various functions (such as marketing and distribution) were arrayed as a system for doing business that could be modified. Other consulting firms during this period began focusing on various tools for more accurately understanding costs. (Portfolio analysis and other tools had tended to understate the costs that were shared by the various divisions operated by diversified corporations.) Functions that had been lumped together in experience-curve analyses were now broken into their constituent parts, allowing companies to identify "cost drivers" far more effectively. In his 1985 book *Competitive Advantage*, Porter drew upon these threads to present an overall framework for analyzing how a firm could actually attain the lowest-cost position and how could it create more value for buyers. Unlike *Competitive Strategy*, there were few antecedents in economics for this new line of inquiry.

Competitive Advantage developed the idea that competitive advantage was manifested in the discrete activities a company performed as it competed in a particular industry. Porter pointed to the array of tasks carried out by all corporations—such as order processing, process design, repair, sales force operations, and so on—which were narrower than the traditional business functions, such as marketing or production. He referred to these as "activities." Collectively, these activities comprised what Porter called the firm's *value chain*. A competitive advantage grew out of an internally consistent configuration of activities that was different from that of rivals. The process of assessing (and, where necessary, reconfiguring) activities made strategy operational.

Very important in the new Porter framework were the *linkages* among activities. Linkages transformed a collection of what might otherwise be independent activities into a value chain. Porter also explored how activities could be used to understand the advantages of focusing on a narrow segment, how activities could be shared in competing in distinct businesses, and how complementary products could affect competitive advantage. The value chain also provided a tool to develop the theory of global strategy—an issue of increasing concern to corporations in this period of time.

Embedding the New Frameworks at HBS

Most of these concepts were welcomed more or less enthusiastically into the strategy canon, and as we will see, some have since been extended in significant ways. But it is important to remember that, in the period when these ideas first began to be disseminated and debated—that is, in the late 1970s and early 1980s—they represented a departure from the Harvard Business School's traditional concept of strategy as an idiosyncratic plan about which no generalization was possible. Andrews and his colleagues had focused on the individual business level; now Porter was looking at companies in their industry context. In addition, as Porter saw it, a clear distinction was emerging between "business" or "competitive" strategy in a single industry and "corporate" strategy for a *diversified* firm.

In the spring of 1978, after returning to the MBA program from the PMD, Porter for the first time offered his Industry and Competitive Analysis (ICA) course. The course catalog promised that ICA would "present explicit conceptual tools for in-depth analysis of industries and competitors, drawing on new research in business strategy, industrial organization, market signaling, and game theory." In addition, "the course [would] begin with general analytical techniques that [could] be applied to any industry situation."

Phrases such as "general analytical techniques that [could] be applied to any industry situation" ruffled some feathers at Soldiers Field. But almost since the School's founding, the HBS faculty has placed great weight on student reactions to courses. And one gauge of student opinion is enrollments: HBS students "vote with their feet," thereby helping to determine the fate of new ideas. By this critical measure, ICA was a dramatic success. Soon, four sections were oversubscribed. By 1986, after the course had been offered for nine semesters and additional faculty members—including Richard Meyer, Hugo Uyterhoeven, John Wells, Elon Kohlberg, Mark Fuller, and Pankaj Ghemawat—had joined in teaching ICA, a total of almost 2,700 students had taken it.

Throughout most of the 1970s, Business Policy remained a full-year required course for second-year students. Most Policy professors held DBA degrees from HBS. And although many other graduate business schools were now offering BP-like courses, Harvard was one of the few business schools that "grew" and maintained a dedicated Policy group. (Most other schools relied either on experienced faculty from other functional areas or on seasoned businesspeople to provide the capstone experience to their MBA students.) This situation at Soldiers Field represented a double-edged sword. It guaranteed that the School would sustain a critical mass in the field, but it also presented the risk that the Policy group would become insulated and ingrown.[13]

During the 1979–1980 school year, the BP course was split into two component parts: Business Policy I, which became a first-year course; and Business Policy II, which became a required one-semester course taught in the fall of the second year. BP I would focus on strategy formulation, BP II on strategy implementation.

The motivation for splitting the course in two was both administrative and conceptual. Many faculty members found teaching the sole required course in the last semester of a four-semester program to be onerous duty. And from an intellectual vantage point, many faculty members felt that other areas, such as Marketing, had begun to address topics that had once been the sole domain of Policy. This situation argued for the presentation of an integrative course sooner in the curricular sequence—in other words, at the end of the first year.

In one sense, the split only codified a long-standing "housekeeping" division of the BP course. (Since its initial publication in 1961, the Business Policy casebook had been presented in two parts: Determining Corporate Strategy and Implementing Corporate Strategy.) But in another sense, the BP split can be seen as a critical event that is still shaping the development of the field today. Porter's ideas had begun to have an impact on the elective curriculum. The decision to decouple strategy formulation from strategy implementation created the opportunity to elevate strategy formulation into a field in its own right. The decision also entailed some costs, as we discuss at the end of this essay.

The Group Matures: Intellectual Diversification (1986–1995)

Historically, BP I and BP II had been part of the same faculty "area," or concentration of individuals with similar intellectual interests. This reflected Business Policy's origins as a single course with two component parts—a tradition which, as noted above, ended in the 1979–1980 school year when the course broke into two separate courses (policy formulation and policy implementation).

In 1983, with Malcolm Salter in charge of BP II and Michael Porter heading the BP I course, it appeared briefly as if the two parts, strategy formulation and implementation, might move closer together again. Both Salter and Porter had taught the "companion" course and understood it well. Their own backgrounds and interests were also complementary. As Salter put it, "Michael Porter had majored in markets and minored in firms, and I had majored in firms and minored in markets. It seemed like a great combination." [14] Unfortunately, Salter left the BP

II group in 1984 to take on an executive education assignment, and the two courses held to their separate agendas.

This situation changed in 1986–1987, although not in a way that had been anticipated by many of the participants. Reflecting the growth of an emerging field, a new area was formed: Business, Government, and Competition. The new area included 20 faculty members, all of whom had previously taught in the General Management area. The BP I group was part of this migration, moving to join the business historians and international business scholars in large part because all three groups shared a strong research and publication tradition. The ICA elective was henceforth part of this new area.[15] Business Policy I was renamed "Competition and Strategy" (C&S), and former PepsiCo president (and by then professor) Andrall Pearson was named course head. In 1988–1989, Porter again became course head of C&S and held this position until 1992–1993, when David Yoffie took over.

During its formative years, the C&S group had revolved around BP I and ICA. In that period, the group—still small and entirely informal—had a unified perspective, building on the frameworks outlined by Michael Porter. But the formation of the Business, Government, and Competition area signaled that the group had reached a stage of maturity with new opportunities and new obligations. Through its intense focus on a single set of issues, the C&S group had been able to make substantial progress in elaborating on and applying the new frameworks, such as the five-forces analysis and the value chain. The group had been notably successful in attracting scholars who shared the values that constituted the backbone of the C&S enterprise. Predictably, however, as soon as the group achieved the elusive and invaluable outcome of a certain coherence, it was time to initiate a new phase in the development of the C&S group. In that spirit, a very fruitful process of intellectual diversification got underway.

While the previous emphasis of the group had been on industry analysis and business unit strategy formulation, the group now expanded its scope to include issues such as the resources embodied by firms, game-theoretic analyses of competition and cooperation, the interface between technology and strategy choices, the role of geographic location in competition, and other themes. In the following sections, we sketch the rich variety of work that has taken place during the second phase of the C&S group's development.

Studying International Strategies

Almost from the beginning of his tenure, Dean McArthur had emphasized broadening the horizons of HBS to include new kinds of research and theory. In 1983 McArthur made a dramatic demonstration of this commitment. He used the 75th anniversary of the School as the backdrop for a year-long colloquium series, involving more than 450 academics and practitioners. Their collective assignment was to discuss and help define the research agenda for a wide variety of academic fields over the coming decade.

One of the faculty members to whom McArthur turned to make his vision a reality was Michael Porter. With encouragement from McArthur, Porter envisioned a research colloquium that would focus on the topic of international competition. The choice was not accidental, capturing as it did Porter's interests at that time, and also embodying the next logical frontier in the development of ideas about competition and strategy. Analysts of competitive strategy were then grappling with the fact that, to an increasing extent, both business units and corporations had to compete globally. "Global strategies" involved not only selling worldwide, but also producing and even conducting research in more than one location. Businesses could now locate these activities almost anywhere—or so it seemed.

Porter wrote a framework paper for his colloquium that laid out the architecture for a theory of global strategy. As the global firm deployed its once-centralized activities around the world, it had to decide how to *configure*, or spread, its activities worldwide to reinforce its competitive advantage most effectively. It also had to decide how these activities should be *coordinated*—or, conversely, how they should be allowed to operate autonomously—to reinforce competitive advantage. The dual issues of configuration and coordination were what distinguished global strategy from strategy generally. They gave rise to a host of global strategy alternatives whose appropriateness depended on industry structure and the firm's own competitive position.

Porter reunited colleagues from a variety of disciplines to explore global strategy issues from their respective perspectives. *Competition in Global Industries* (1986), the edited compilation of the research presented at the international competition colloquium, explored marketing, manufacturing, technology, alliances, finance, organization, government, and other areas. Many of the participating authors went on to write important books and papers that grew out of these compiled papers.

Sustainability of Competitive Advantage

Whereas it was Michael Porter who brought ideas from the world of IO economics into the business strategy field in the late 1970s and early 1980s, it was Pankaj Ghemawat who played this role in the second half of the 1980s. Ghemawat, as noted earlier, was a graduate of Harvard's Ph.D. program in Business Economics. He was determined to integrate recent advances in IO economics, which by then had adopted the framework of noncooperative game theory, into the business strategy context. This effort culminated in Ghemawat's book *Commitment*, published in 1991.

Ghemawat's inquiry started with the question of how a competitive advantage, once achieved, could be sustained. This had been a topic of general interest within the business world for decades. In an influential 1980 *Harvard Business Review* article, Ghemawat examined one of the key threats to sustainability—imitation—and explored ways of deterring it.[16]

Ghemawat's work next turned to a broader view of threats to sustainability and the irreversible commitments that were important to overcoming those threats. Important elements included an analysis of the short-run and long-run competitive positions implied by each particular strategic (irreversible) investment option, as well as an assessment of sustainability. Each option, Ghemawat argued, had to be evaluated with respect to its flexibility after implementation and its impact on the internal functioning of the firm—for example, its impact on the likelihood of both honest mistakes and deliberate distortions in the ranking of future strategic options.

Ghemawat developed his ideas while teaching the ICA course, in which he had been involved since 1983. He also developed the elective successor to ICA—Strategy, Commitment, and Choice (SCC)—which he taught for the first time in 1991. Porter's earlier ideas were now the basis of the required course, and the SCC elective became the venue for bringing Ghemawat's thinking on commitment and sustainability to bear on the advanced analysis of strategy.

In subsequent years, SCC was taught by Ghemawat, visiting professor Arnoldo C. Hax, and, most recently, Anita McGahan. Returning to teach the first-year C&S class in 1994–1995, Ghemawat became course head of C&S in 1995–1996. In his newest book (*Games Businesses Play*, 1997), Ghemawat has continued his work shaping noncooperative game theory into a useful tool for analyzing business interactions.

Others in the larger C&S group have also attempted to translate noncooperative game theory into a set of more useful and widely applicable tools. Kenneth Corts's research, for example, has focused on competition in segmented markets and on the relationships between firms and their distributors. His industry studies have included the breakfast cereal industry, health care markets, the music industry, and the motion picture industry.

Cooperative Game Theory and Business Strategy

In 1991 Porter invited Adam Brandenburger—a game theorist then teaching Managerial Economics—to teach the first-year C&S course. Struck by the power of the frameworks the course offered for analyzing business issues, Brandenburger set out with his doctoral student Harborne Stuart (now an assistant professor in the C&S group) to establish some of the theoretical underpinnings.

Not surprisingly, given their intellectual orientation, Brandenburger and Stuart turned to game theory. They soon encountered two obstacles. One problem was that the game models in the literature tended to prespecify all the possible moves and countermoves available to players. The reality is that interactions in the marketplace are much more free-wheeling than that. Another problem was that the literature focused largely on competition among rivals. In reality, customers and suppliers are the first order of business; competitors come later.

Brandenburger and Stuart found a way to solve both problems at once. In "Value-based Business Strategy" (*Journal of Economics & Management Strategy*, 1996), they employed a game model that didn't talk about "moves" at all. Instead, it described how much value is created when different combinations of players come together and transact. Following Porter's lead, they conceived the cast of players as consisting of firms together with their customers and suppliers. Value creation was couched in terms of the difference between a customer's willingness to pay for the products or services of a firm, and a supplier's opportunity cost of providing resources to a firm. This put the intrinsically cooperative acts of selling to customers and buying from suppliers where they belonged: at center stage.

The forces of competition were not ignored. Brandenburger and Stuart went on to define the "added value" of a player as the difference between the overall value created when the player is in the game and the overall value created when (as a thought experiment) the player in question is plucked out of the game. They argued that a player can capture no more than its added value, provided that the forces of competition are unfettered.

In treating buyers and suppliers symmetrically, Brandenburger and Stuart meant to emphasize the importance of suppliers in particular. They wanted to engineer a shift away from the focus on buyers that typified many discussions of business strategy. This asymmetric treatment of buyers and suppliers was conceptually unsatisfactory. Brandenburger and Stuart also noted that it was out of sync with the attention being given in the business community to the issue of supplier relations.

The game model employed in"Value-based Business Strategy" drew on the nonzero-sum ("cooperative") theory that John von Neumann and Oskar Morgenstern had laid out in *Theory of Games and Economic Behavior* (1944). Cooperative game theory had fallen out of favor among economists, as attention had become centered on analysis of highly specified games. Still, Brandenburger and Stuart hoped that their work would help rekindle interest in this part of von Neumann's and Morgenstern's original version.

Brandenburger began testing these ideas in a second-year elective, Changing the Game, which built on a course originally created by HBS colleague Vijay Krishna. By 1994, he felt ready to put his work into a prescriptive package for managers, and teamed up with Yale's Barry Nalebuff to write a book on business strategy.

As Brandenburger and Nalebuff started their work, they realized that an important group of players in the "game of business" had been largely neglected. In addition to the firm's competitors, there were the firms from which customers buy complementary products and services, or to which suppliers sell complementary resources. The practical importance of this group of players was evident in the amount of attention being paid in business to the subject of strategic alliances and partnerships. Brandenburger and Nalebuff dubbed these players the firm's "complementors," and drew up a more complete map of the business landscape (the "Value Net") which depicted competitors and complementors, in addition to customers and suppliers.

The Value Net became the backbone of Brandenburger's and Nalebuff's book (*Co-opetition*, 1996). The book struck a particular chord among members of the high-tech business community. These practitioners quickly adopted the complementor concept to help them describe and shape the interdependencies (hardware/software, Internet/high-speed phone lines, and others) that were central to their businesses.

In addition to Brandenburger, others in the larger C&S group have focused on particular aspects of game theory and business strategy. Elon Kohlberg, for example, has been studying the foundations of game theory. His work addresses the equilibrium concept in game theory, which is problematic when measured against dynamic real markets. Specifically, Kohlberg has been attempting to describe a probabilistic process through which equilibrium could arise.

A Resource-Based View of the Firm and Corporate Strategy

Cynthia A. Montgomery, whom Porter had recruited from Northwestern to join the HBS faculty in 1989, has been studying corporate-level strategy for nearly two decades. Her econometric research (parts of which were conducted with Birger Wernerfelt of MIT and S. Hariharan of the University of Southern California), has been published in numerous academic journals and focuses on diversification, firm performance, and market position. The body of work demonstrates that the relationships among these variables are very complex. While diversification and firm performance are negatively correlated in the aggregate, that relationship is moderated not only by the attractiveness of the industries in which firms compete, but also by the quality and specificity of the resources a firm can leverage.

Harking back to Andrews, Montgomery's research underscores once again that corporate strategy must blend an internal and an external perspective. Just as the competitive landscapes facing firms differ in systematic ways, so, too, do the resources of firms. Understanding both, and how they (separately and in concert) impact a firm's ability to create value, is integral to forging successful corporate strategies.

These ideas were developed further in Montgomery's joint work with David J. Collis, another Business Economics Ph.D. graduate. Their inquiries led to the publication of *Corporate Strategy: Resources and the Scope of the Firm* in 1997. The book presents a unique framework for analyzing and assessing corporate-level advantage. In addition to its practical significance, the book is notable for two integrating roles it plays in the field of strategy. First, it demonstrates the inextricable link between business and corporate level strategy, and shows that most corporate advantages ultimately are realized through enhanced performance at the business-unit level. Second, like Montgomery's earlier work, the book integrates resource-based theories, such as core competence, with market-based theories, such as industry analysis, to explain superior firm performance. The framework now forms the basis of Corporate Strategy, a second-year MBA offering, and Creating Corporate Advantage, an executive program for senior managers.

Collis has also explored issues related to corporate-level, multibusiness strategy. His field research generated teaching materials for the second-year MBA course, Corporate Strategy, which establishes a framework for analyzing and managing multibusiness corporations. Among Collis's research initiatives are a comparative international study of the sizes and roles of corporate offices; an analysis of the value of scope and coordination across businesses in the worldwide chemical and consumer electronics industries; a study of the evolution of the corporate domain of the regional Bell operating companies; and (with Stephen P. Bradley) an assessment of appropriate scope for firms in the emerging multimedia industry.

International Competitiveness

Michael Porter's initial work on global competition, conducted in conjunction with the international strategy colloquium of the mid-1980s, examined how firms could gain advantage by competing across locations in a global strategy. In his 1990 book *The Competitive Advantage of Nations*, Porter explored the importance of location in influencing a company's competitive advantage. In a theory that bridged strategy with the concerns of government in enhancing competitiveness, Porter's framework identified four aspects of a location's environment—the "diamond"—which tended to spawn productive and innovative global competitors: specialized factors, demanding local buyers, a critical mass of related and supporting industries, and intense local rivalry.

The new research brought microeconomic thinking to a subject in which macroeconomic analysis had dominated. It also added an interesting twist to work on strategy by demonstrating that the locus of some crucial corporate resources and advantages was not necessarily within the firm. Location, in particular, was established as another important variable in the analysis of competitive strategy. A firm's ability to choose and then to implement strategies, and also to innovate continually, was found not only within the firm, but also in its proximate local environment. Location not only affected the choice of strategies, but also played a large role in determining the firm's ability to configure activities and assemble capabilities or resources not available to rivals based elsewhere. Michael Enright, coordinator of the far-ranging Competitive Advantage of Nations project (and now at the University of Hong Kong), continued to develop this subject matter as a faculty member by developing and teaching a second-year course on this topic.

In addition to the implications of this research for economic policy in fostering, for instance, clusters of interrelated industries, the work demonstrated a significant underlying broadening of Porter's thinking. Whereas *Competitive Strategy* had focused primarily on the division of value created, *The Competitive Advantage of Nations* pointed to the important role of outside parties in creating value. Linkages among a critical mass of local institutions and firms, Porter asserted, could be captured by co-location in ways that were not available to more distant rivals. Suppliers, customers, and competitors were not only adversaries who competed for a portion of the total value created; they also participated in the ongoing creation of value.

Professor David Yoffie's research also has focused on competitive strategy and international competition, with a special emphasis on the role of government. From 1988 through 1992, he directed the Harvard Business School research project on global competition. Together with Debora L. Spar and John B. Goodman (from the Business, Government, and International Economy unit), he explored how foreign direct investment in the United States influenced American trade policy. Their study evaluated how huge inflows of foreign investment from Europe, Japan, and elsewhere during the 1980s changed demands for protectionism in America in the 1990s. A second study focused on how foreign investment and alliances between foreign and domestic firms affected the political positions of U.S. competitors.

Tarun Khanna's research is explaining how national context affects strategy in developing economies. Depending on the state or locational circumstances—such as capital markets, information, and the supply of skilled managers—strategies that offer little advantage in advanced economies may create value. In particular, Khanna has been studying the corporate strategy of diversified business groups in several emerging economies in Latin America and in South and East Asia.

Technology and Competition

Richard S. Rosenbloom, a senior HBS faculty member who joined the C&S group after extensive experience studying the evolution of technologies, began a stream of work in the group on the strategic management of technology and in the relationships between technological change and competitive strategy. He has investigated the histories of radical technological innovations and their consequences for the competitive positions both of established firms and of rivals that enter markets by exploiting new technologies. Rosenbloom has also served as a vital sounding board for many of his colleagues in C&S, giving careful responses to preliminary drafts and other presentations. Elizabeth Teisberg, now a professor at the Darden School at the University of Virginia, built on Rosenbloom's initial course and created a second-year elective around these questions.

Another senior HBS researcher in this field, Stephen Bradley, has concentrated on the impact of technology on industry structure and competitive strategy. His most recent book, *Globalization, Technology, and Competition* (1993), deals with the technical and functional convergence of computers and telecommunications in the 1990s. The products of his research have included an article ("Winners and Losers—Industry Structure in the Converging World of Telecommunications, Computing, and Entertainment," 1997) and a book, *Sense and Respond: Capturing Value in the Network Era* (1998), an outgrowth of a conference held at HBS in 1995.

David Yoffie, cited above, has a second research focus in the merging fields of computers, telecommunications, and consumer electronics. Yoffie's close ties to the high-tech field, and his intimate awareness of how that industry is structured and operates, have provided his C&S colleagues with an invaluable window on a vital industrial landscape. Yoffie led a research effort involving a dozen Harvard Business School faculty members who were exploring a variety of aspects of this process of convergence, including the competitive dynamics within and between standards, the role of alliances in multimedia technology, and the relationship between technology choices, scope of a firm, and financial decisions. This effort led to a published collection of articles on these related themes.[17]

Empirical Testing of Core Strategy Propositions

Anita M. McGahan's research involves the use of newly available, large-scale databases on company sales and profitability to investigate central issues in the determinants of company performance. The aim is to ground evolving theory in the facts about competitive outcomes in the economy as a whole. A series of papers with Michael Porter, employing data on all publicly held U.S. firms over the 15-year period from 1980 to 1994, examines the importance of industry, corporate parent, and positioning influences on firm profitability. This work is revealing important facts about how high or low performers emerge over time, the extent to which superior and inferior performance is sustained, and other questions. McGahan is also examining the determinants of financial market returns.

Strategic Tradeoffs and the Roots of Positioning

In his current work, Michael Porter is once again trying to challenge the predominant strategic focus of the business community. He has introduced the distinction between *operational effectiveness* (attaining and expanding best practice) and *strategic positioning* (competing in a different way from rivals to achieve different results). He is arguing that the current focus on operational effectiveness must be complemented by an emphasis on choosing well-defined strategic positions, and that doing so requires not the search for "best" practice but making tradeoffs. Porter asserts that, although it is true that operational effectiveness—as embodied by the "lean management," reengineering, and learning-organization movements of the last decade—is a necessary contributor to corporate survival, it is rarely sufficient to sustain superior performance. A strategic position must involve a different configuration of activities. Sustainability of a position, Porter argues, depends on tradeoffs with the way rivals are competing, which makes imitation undesirable. Both the extent of advantage and its sustainability rest heavily on the *fit* among a system of activities involved in implementing the position. The mutual reinforcement of a particularly configured activity system not only makes the firm highly effective in serving the target market, but also shields it from easy imitation by competitors. Individual activities, in other words, can be copied, but the *system* is far more difficult to imitate.

In a way, this work evokes the early expositions of Andrews, Christensen, and their colleagues. It attempts to make the notion of "fit"—which played a prominent role in the frameworks of Andrews and his colleagues in the 1960s—more precise and more easily operationalized. This intergenerational aspect of the strategy work is now being extended into the next generation of researchers. Just as Porter's work in the late 1970s was supported by various doctoral students, his current work is being extended by several Ph.D. students in Business Economics, among them Jan Rivkin (now a member of the C&S faculty) and Nicolaj Siggelkow. At the same time, the new work is building new bridges between strategy and implementation and is thereby continuing to close the gap that helped launch the group in the first place.

An Agenda for Future Research

Every human group includes multiple perspectives and therefore lends itself to multiple interpretations. Ours is no exception. Even among the current members of the C&S group, there are important differences of opinion about where we are today and where we should go next. That is how it should be.

One interpretation of the development of the C&S group is that it reflects a more general pattern in the evolution of organizations. The group started by rallying around a central framework—in this case, a set of ideas developed by Porter, based on his work with colleagues at HBS and elsewhere. Like most champions of a cause, this small but hardy band developed a set of core values, which reflected and were reinforced by the people it attracted. As a critical mass of mind power was assembled, this shared set of values provided a common intellectual underpinning and was leveraged across a whole array of research agendas and research methodologies. Not surprisingly, the unitary view gave way to a multitude of independent views. Again, this was how it should have been.

While the shared set of values guaranteed that various approaches would meet common standards, the branching out allowed each new set of ideas to be developed more fully. But as we suggested earlier, branching out also entailed some costs. One was inefficiency: similar concepts began to arise under different guises and with different terminology. A larger cost, sometimes the result of different emphases, was missed opportunities for collaboration.

The potential rewards for moving into a third phase—a phase of exploring the connections between the various research strands—appear to be large. Indeed, we assert that there is substantial room for exploring links not only between various strands of business strategy research, but also between strategy research and other areas outside the traditional domain of strategy.

For instance, the marrying of the models of organizational design and the frameworks of business strategy formulation could yield tremendous payoffs. Pertinent questions include: Which organizational structure could best implement a particular positioning choice? Or, from the other end of the telescope, which strategies are in the realm of implementable choices, given a particular organizational structure and culture?

At HBS, the marrying of these two sets of issues would most likely mean narrowing the gap that opened up in 1979, when Business Policy split into separate courses on formulation and implementation. Most still believe that the split was a fruitful one, as it facilitated the incorporation of more high-powered analytical techniques and the generation of a whole body of highly influential research. By the same token, many believe the divide should be considered a separation of convenience, which can and will diminish over time. Why? Because if we could harness the power of the analytical frameworks that have been developed both in the fields of organizational design and in business strategy, the result would be a huge conceptual step forward.

The School renewed its leadership position in the strategy field during a period when American businesses were awakening, belatedly, to the realities of global competition. The appearance of practical models for thinking through competitive strategy in the late 1970s and early 1980s was opportune, and those models were seized upon by practitioners eager to change the ways their companies did business.

This was important work. It goes without saying that much additional important work remains to be done. As the C&S group continues in its work, building for the future, we are mindful of the many things that John McArthur taught us during his time as dean. Perhaps the most important of these is the need to nurture the kind of entre-preneurial climate that gives outstanding people the room to innovate and grow. This is a tall order, but—as McArthur so ably demonstrated—not an impossible one.

CHAPTER FIVE

Entrepreneurial Management

In Pursuit of Opportunity

HOWARD H. STEVENSON AND TERESA M. AMABILE

I N THE FALL OF 1981, *Howard Stevenson was invited to lunch by an old friend, John McArthur. Stevenson, a former HBS faculty member, was then serving as vice president of finance and administration for Preco Corporation, an integrated pulp and paper man-ufacturer. McArthur had a proposition for Stevenson: return to the School's faculty and reinvent the field of entrepreneurship.*

Stevenson had mixed feelings about the plan. On the one hand, entrepreneurship was a subject about which he cared passionately. On the other hand, the faculty's commitment to the field was weak, at best. (One former colleague had condemned the field as an "intellectual onion": you peel away the layers only to find that there's nothing there, and it makes you cry.) Student and alumni interest in the topic had consistently exceeded the faculty's ability to deliver high-quality courses. Like real estate and related fields, entrepreneurship existed in a kind of intellectual purgatory. Because the field lacked a strong conceptual base, few academics focused seriously or systematically on it—which in turn ensured that it would continue to lack a strong conceptual base.

McArthur assured Stevenson that he would put the full authority of the dean's office behind the field. In December 1981, Stevenson returned to Soldiers Field to search for new ways to understand, research, and teach entrepreneurship.

THIS CHAPTER REVIEWS the development of the entrepreneurship field at the Harvard Business School over the past 60 years, with a particular focus on the 15 years comprising John McArthur's tenure as dean of the Harvard Business School.[1] Both a historical review and a focus on the McArthur years seem appropriate—the former because entrepreneurship is a venerable field, which has long tantalized and bedeviled those teachers and researchers who have ventured into it; and the latter because the field has evolved significantly in the 1980s and 1990s, with no small help from McArthur himself.

In the 1980s, there were an estimated 1.5 million business formations in the United States—in historical terms, an astounding burst of entrepreneurial activity. This trend has only intensified in the 1990s. In 1996 alone, something like 160,000 businesses were founded, which collectively were responsible for creating more than 800,000 new jobs.[2] And although many of these companies began as and have remained small enterprises, others have grown to a size at which they exert considerable economic influence. Table 5.1 presents a small sample of the kinds of entrepreneurial companies that have been responsible for significant job growth over the past two decades.

Much has been written in recent years about the "downsizing" of the largest U.S. corporations, and we will not restate that well-worn theme in this context. Suffice it to say that people from a wide variety of backgrounds have concluded that their best chances for job security and professional satisfaction are not to be found in the offices and factories of the established *Fortune* 500 companies.

For these and other reasons, entrepreneurship has been of increasing importance to the U.S. economy in recent years. It has also been important to many of the 60,000–plus alumni of the Harvard Business School. In recent surveys, for example, almost 40 percent of responding

HBS alumni claim self-employment status. Over half of our alumni identify themselves as entrepreneurs.[3]

These kinds of data show that the School and its alumni have long had a disproportionate impact on entrepreneurship. HBS graduates can take much of the credit for the creation of the spread-

TABLE 5.1   *Job Growth in a Sample of Entrepreneurial Companies*

COMPANY	FOUNDERS	Employees 1975	1985	1995
Amgen	George Rothman Gordon Binder	0	200	4,000
Circuit City Stores	Samuel Wurtzel Alan Wurtzel Richard Sharp	600	4,000	31,000
Compaq Computers	Joseph Canion Ben Rosen Eckhard Pfeiffer	0	2,000	14,000
Federal Express	Frederick Smith	0	34,000	107,000
MCI	William McGowan Bert Roberts	500	12,000	50,000
Nucor	F. Kenneth Iverson John Correnti	2,300	3,900	6,000
Oracle Corp.	Lawrence Ellison Jeffrey Henley Raymond Lane	0	600	17,000
Shaw Industries	Robert Shaw	1,600	4,000	25,000
Staples	Tom Stemberg	0	200	14,000
Thermoelectron	George Hatsopoulos John Hatsopoulos Arvin Smith	1,300	3,200	11,000

Source: From *Learn to Earn* by Peter Lynch and John Rothschild. Simon and Schuster, © 1996. Reprinted with permission.

sheet software business (Visi-Calc), the home personal financial market (Intuit), and the microbrew industry (Boston Beer). They have launched telecommunications giants such as MCI, Continental Cable, Capital Cities Broadcasting, Bloomberg, and Montreal-based Telemedia. In the financial world, they have founded or co-founded firms like Jemison, Batterymarch Financial, and Donaldson, Lufkin, & Jenrette. They have also established or played pivotal roles at hundreds of other companies with less recognizable names—like Preco Corporation, HCR Inc., Millipore, Raychem, Sunrise Corporation, Orbital Sciences, and INDIVERS—which have created tens of thousands of jobs and generated billions of dollars in revenues. HBS alumni entrepreneurs created impact each decade. The list is too large to read. Selecting among the many who would win any school's entrepreneur of the year award is a dangerous task, but some examples may give insight. Among the many notables, the '40s gave us Tom Murphy (Capital Cities Broadcasting), the '50s Arthur Rock (Intel, Apple, etc.), the '60s Amos Hostetter (Continental Cablevision), the '70s Tom Stemberg (Staples), and the '80s Shikhar Ghosh (Open Market). The '90s and beyond are the future in the making. Many thousands of other Harvard Business School alumni have changed their worlds.

HBS alumni have influenced the current shape of investment banking, money management, direct marketing, consumer products, consulting, and many other industries. This influence arose not only through startups, but also through entrepreneurial spinoffs, consolidations, and takeovers. In all of these different contexts, ideas about opportunity—where to find it, and how to exploit it—changed the nature of the game.

The indirect impacts of HBS alumni on entrepreneurship have also been important. For example, the School's graduates helped create and grow the venture capital industry. Through that mechanism alone, they have played a critical role in the emergence of semiconductors, personal computers, the biotechnology industry, and the communications revolution.

Given the complex web of relationships between the School and its graduates, and the unusual degree to which practitioners shape the School's agenda, we try in this chapter to tease out the common threads that make the larger HBS entrepreneurial enterprise distinctive. Arthur Rock, HBS '52 and a founding investor in Intel, Apple, Teledyne and many other firms, once commented that he tried to invest in "companies that change the way people live." Where did this impulse arise, and what are its implications? How should we teach and write about entrepreneurship?

Our guiding premise is that entrepreneurial success for individuals and organizations comes from

- A careful definition of available opportunities

- A motivation to pursue those opportunities to achieve some desired future state

- An understanding of the resource requirements for achievement of that desired future state

- A skill in negotiating for access to the required resources

To a considerable degree, these are learnable skills. The case method of teaching—within a conceptual framework developed from empirical research on entrepreneurial practice—is ideally suited to this task. Role models derived from cases demonstrate the broad range of the possible. Understanding the wide variety of successes and failures experienced by others encourages the development of skills. The driving motivation and vision for our group is that students will conclude that the HBS experience was instrumental in helping them both to dream bigger dreams and to accomplish things that they previously would not have thought possible.

Harvard and Entrepreneurial Studies: 1930–1980

The intellectual history of the entrepreneurial management field at HBS dates back to the 1940s and the Business History group's explorations of the entrepreneur. A distinguished group of scholars, including Joseph Schumpeter, Fritz Redlich, and Arthur Cole, gathered here to define both the "who" and the "what" of entrepreneurship.[4] Their scholarly focus was on the background of the entrepreneur and also on the accomplishments of the enterprises that notable entrepreneurs had created. Although Schumpeter's and Cole's "Research Center in Entrepreneurial History" achieved great renown, its work did not become fully integrated into the teaching or research traditions of the School. But these eminent scholars did leave a lasting legacy: one of the world's finest collections of business archives, providing business historians with a rich store of original documents that helped shape the understanding of business development.

The first pedagogical innovations in entrepreneurship at HBS began in 1946, when Professor Myles Mace detected a sea change that was being brought about by the GI's returning from World War II. Compared to students in earlier classes, these military veterans were older, more diverse, and less affluent. They were accustomed to leading and being led under stressful, sometimes terrifying, conditions. They had steeled themselves to grapple with an economy that might either boom or go bust. Pent-up demand for consumer goods and services seemed promising, but there was no guarantee that the nation wouldn't slip back into the depression of the prewar years.

Professor Mace realized that this new generation of students was unusually interested in creating and managing new enterprises. He therefore set out to develop a course that would teach the "how" of entrepreneurship. The resulting course, Management of New Enterprises, was immediately popular and was oversubscribed every time Mace offered it. The course focused on successful practice, and Mace played an essential role in bringing his ideas to life—inspiring and cajoling his students to think in new ways and generally broadening their sense of what might be possible.

Mace left the MBA course in 1950 to teach in the Advanced Management Program, an executive education program that had grown out of the School's wartime experiences. His ideas, and his attitude of relentless questioning of the status quo, again proved powerful in this new context. They were again tested and validated when Mace left the School in 1955 to work with two notable entrepreneurs—Roy Ash and Charles "Tex" Thorton—as they set out to create Litton Industries, one of the first entrepreneurial conglomerates.

In the wake of Mace's departure, the School tried a variety of approaches to staffing the entrepreneurship course. Visiting lecturers were brought in, many of them highly successful entrepreneurs who had created firms in the fledgling "high-technology" field and other cutting-edge sectors of the economy. (One lecturer, for example, was the founder of an experimental airframe manufacturer.) Other faculty came from within the School, drawing on their experiences as directors of or consultants to new firms then being formed by friends, neighbors, and former colleagues.

Soon, the entrepreneurial curriculum consisted of three courses: Management of New Enterprises, Small Manufacturing Enterprises, and Manufacturing. Some members of the HBS faculty saw the first two of these courses as little more than storytelling. Others saw them as comprising an interesting set of issues that were only marginally addressed and behind which stood almost no systematic research. Yet there was a high and continuous level of student interest in these two courses, which were taught by some memorable or soon-to-be-celebrated individuals.[5]

The third course, Manufacturing, was a story unto itself. It was offered by a man who became one of the fathers of the venture capital industry, Georges Doriot. By the 1950s, the French-born Doriot had been on the School's faculty for nearly a quarter-century, and was a unique quantity. Doriot lectured, rather than using the School's ubiquitous case method, and his lectures (delivered in a persistently strong French accent) covered all aspects of working life—from reading a newspaper, to the choice of a church and a spouse, to business etiquette (never be late; keep your shoes shined), to the actual running of a business. The course was very demanding—unlike most of the School's courses, it required the researching and writing of a publishable intellectual product—and it inspired great student loyalty. Many entrepreneurial graduates of the School attribute their success directly to the impact of "Le Grand General," and his course remains the stuff of teaching legend.

Doriot's status as a tenured professor freed him to experiment and to bring along a new generation of young teachers and scholars to carry on his tradition. For a variety of personal and professional reasons, however, Doriot did not succeed in mentoring young faculty and therefore failed to institutionalize his legacy. After he retired in 1966, his lecture notes were published by a group of admiring students.[6] But without a champion, the course died.

In 1965 Frank Tucker, a tenured professor, took responsibility for the School's small stable of entrepreneurship-oriented courses. Starting in 1967, he worked with Patrick Liles, who was then pursuing his doctoral degree at the School. Between them, Tucker and Liles developed new case material which they used to design and teach an extremely popular elective. Enrollments in the course (now called Management of Small Enterprises) blossomed to the 500 level in the early 1970s, and Liles's casebook became the standard for the field.[7] However, as a young professor subject to the increasing rigors of tenure review, Liles was advised to pursue teaching and research in topics more closely aligned with mainstream activities. As a result, the entrepreneurship course was taken over by a variety of tenured and visiting professors with only marginal commitment to the field. Despite the students' demonstrated interest in the topic of entrepreneurship, the School, as an institution, was not committed to it. Teaching entrepreneurship—and especially researching and developing courses in entrepreneurship—suffered accordingly.

During the 1970s, Howard Stevenson and others at the School collaborated to create two new courses focused on real estate. As with so many other courses in the larger entrepreneurship area, the two new real estate courses were grounded almost entirely in the work of practitioners. For the real estate courses, the practitioner was a Boston-based developer and investor named William Poorvu. Stevenson and Poorvu wrote over 60 new cases and began formulating the ideas that evolved into the conceptual framework now used in many of the entrepreneurial courses. Although the real estate courses also became very popular, the HBS administration conveyed the clear message that entrepreneurship (and, by extension, real estate) was not viewed as an important field of inquiry for the School's faculty. Liles and Stevenson—the entrepreneurship and real estate specialists, respectively—both left the School in the late 1970s. Liles became a successful venture capitalist, and Stevenson went on to the management of a rapidly growing manufacturing firm.

The McArthur-Era Initiatives in Entrepreneurship

When John McArthur was named dean in 1980, he took on the difficult challenge of investing in the field of entrepreneurship. At that point, the entrepreneurship courses either were in hiatus or were being taught by talented entrepreneurs. No entrepreneurship-related research or course development of consequence was then going on at the School.

Characteristically, McArthur launched efforts on several fronts at once. As noted above, he played the instrumental role in recruiting Howard Stevenson back to the Harvard Business School. Meanwhile, he took steps to institutionalize the field of entrepreneurship at the School. For example, one of the first endowed chairs raised during McArthur's tenure came from Arthur Rock and Fayez Sarofim, who specified—undoubtedly with McArthur's strong encouragement—that their gift was intended to support the study of entrepreneurship. Later, the MBA classes of '54, '55, '60, and '61 added entrepreneurship-oriented chairs.[8]

During the next two years, two other important events contributed to the development of entrepreneurship at the School. The first was a colloquium on entrepreneurship, held in 1983 as part of a larger celebration of the School's 75th anniversary. The colloquium attracted successful alumni entrepreneurs, faculty leaders in the field who had done their doctoral work at HBS (including Jeffry Timmons and LaRue Hosmer), and several nontenured faculty from HBS. The young faculty attendees in this last group included both Bill Sahlman and John Kao, who were later to play critical roles in the development of the courses and intellectual content in the field.

Among many other contributions, the colloquium renewed the School's emphasis on the *hows* of entrepreneurship. In addition, it identified several subfields as areas that demanded focused support for research and teaching. These included entrepreneurial finance, creativity, and the management of growing enterprises. Alumni attending the colloquium reaffirmed the importance of entrepreneurship courses in their own professional development. Many cited their exposure to entrepreneurship at the School as having helped define their own personal and professional possibilities.

A second major undertaking during this period was a data-gathering effort aimed at better understanding the School's alumni. Drawing on the general database, Paula Duffy—an MBA graduate working in the alumni office—helped Stevenson analyze the entrepreneurial component of Harvard alumni. The results of this work, made public in a preliminary form in 1984, surprised many people both inside and outside the School. It revealed a surprising level of entrepreneurial activity among the School's alumni, with something like half of all respondents labeling themselves "entrepreneurs." The second surprise lay in the survey's depiction of the *path* to entrepreneurship. The data showed that entrepreneurs often start down traditional career tracks, and many of the HBS entrepreneurs (by their own definition) had been successful managers prior to becoming entrepreneurs. The bulk of the self-employed became their own bosses between 10 and 20 years out of school. Thus hard data debunked the conventional wisdom that entrepreneurs are born and not made.

The results of this Harvard Alumni Study had a very interesting impact on the field. It directly refuted common beliefs that many entrepreneurs were less well educated than the general population, or tended to be loners, or had a history of failure before they achieved success. These notions had grown in large part out of earlier work by Collins and Moore.[9] The Harvard Alumni Study strongly suggested that those earlier results reflected a sampling bias: whereas Collins's and Moore's sample was drawn from a stratum of relatively less educated, independent machine-shop operators, the Harvard sample of 14,000 was drawn from across almost the entire spectrum of American industry.

The findings of the Harvard Alumni Study did much to begin changing entrenched beliefs about entrepreneurs as marginal characters. Entrepreneurs, it seemed, were more satisfied, wealthier, more energized by their jobs, and no more likely to have been fired or divorced than their counterparts with the same educational background who were employed by others. HBS Professor John Kotter's 20-year longitudinal study of the class of 1974 confirmed the Duffy and Stevenson findings.[10] Moreover, many of the findings have now been replicated by studies at

Wharton, the University of Virginia, Stanford, INSEAD, and MIT.[11] Overall, researchers have confirmed that entrepreneurship is a common career path for well-educated business practitioners.

That so many successful alumni were choosing the entrepreneurial path (and that in many cases they proved to be among the most loyal and generous supporters of the schools that had trained them) soon caught the attention of academic administrators around the world. During the 1980s, many schools began developing entrepreneurial centers, raising money for endowed chairs, and expanding on the annual research conference inaugurated by Babson College's business school in 1981. The number of schools offering formal entrepreneurship programs climbed from 6 in 1967 to 370 in 1993.[12]

Meanwhile, at HBS, with a senior faculty member once again dedicated to the development of entrepreneurial studies, a number of doctoral students undertook dissertations in the field. During this same period, assistant professors were hired into the area with primarily academic (rather than entrepreneurial) experience. In particular, course offerings were expanded to include functionally oriented entrepreneurial courses in the MBA curriculum, including those shown in Table 5.2.

By 1996, the courses offered by the Entrepreneurial Management unit enrolled a total of more than 1,100 students. The Entrepreneurial Management Unit faculty included five full professors, one adjunct professor, three associate professors, four assistant professors, and three senior lecturers. Six of the faculty members had joint appointments with other units, and many had informal affiliations with other units and programs at the School, including Finance, Organizational Behavior, Technology and Operations Management, Ethics, and Executive Education. These joint appointments and informal ties have helped integrate the ideas of entrepreneurship into the broader faculty. At the same time, they have enhanced the unit's ability to participate in the cross-disciplinary research that is required to understand the phenomenon of entrepreneurship.

In addition, faculty in the Entrepreneurial Management group began to play key roles in a number of executive education programs and external relations offerings. These included the following:

- Owner/President Management program

- President's Seminar

- Chief Executive Seminar

- American Electronics Association President's Seminar

- Symposium for Family Business

- Symposium for Venture Capital

- Symposium for Real Estate Professionals

- Venture Capital and Private Equity (in the Focused Financial Management series)

- Women Leading Business

- Entrepreneur's Toolkit

In this context, one executive education program—the Owner/President Management program (OPM)—deserves special note. With over 2,300 graduates, it has for more than two decades played an important role in the education of practicing entrepreneurs, even at times when the larger institution was reluctant to focus on issues of interest to entrepreneurs. Professor Dick Dooley began the predecessor program, Smaller Company Management Program, in the early 1970s, gearing its content to the professional management of smaller businesses. The OPM name was adopted in the early 1980s, when Professor Marty Marshall took over the program. Recognizing that a business ownership stake was important in ensuring high-level goals and attitudes among the program participants, Marshall decided to require both significant equity ownership *and* general management responsibilities on the part of OPM participants.

Staffed by faculty from across a broad range of the School's intellectual "units," OPM today is attended by the most diverse group of students in any HBS course. The participants—over half of whom are from outside the United States—range in age from 30 to over 65, and have education levels that range from a few years of high school to a Ph.D. degree. Their companies comprise all types of industries, and they vary in size from several million dollars in annual sales to over \$1 billion. Participating in three three-week sessions over a span of two years, and often returning for postgraduate programs, the OPM participants develop strong bonds with each other and with the School.

The success of the entrepreneurship course-development agenda can be assessed using a variety of criteria. We will cite only a few market-based examples. The Entrepreneurial Management unit has developed over 300 cases since 1982. Current members of the unit have published

TABLE 5.2   *Course Offerings in Entrepreneurial Management at Harvard Business School*

COURSE NAME	YEAR STARTED	MAXIMUM ENROLLMENT
Entrepreneurial Management	1983	400
Entrepreneurial Finance	1984	430
Entrepreneurship, Creativity, and Organization	1984	200
Venture Capital and Private Equity	1983	170
Building the Sustainable Venture	1993	90
Entrepreneurship in the Social Sector	1995	50
Entrepreneurial Marketing	1995	65
Real Property Asset Management	1971	300
Field Studies in Real Property	1991	60
Field Studies in Entrepreneurial Management	1984	65
Owner/President Management Program (Executive Education)	1975	120

five case collections that are used in more than 75 schools, with sales of over 10,000 copies per year. Cases and technical notes authored by members of the group sell approximately 175,000 units each year to outside users (through the Harvard Business School Publishing Corporation). If the voice of the market is to be believed, we are successfully meeting the needs of the entrepreneurship education community—which persuades us that, by extension, we are meeting the needs of entrepreneurs as well.

Intellectual Underpinnings

What are the roots of entrepreneurship as an academic field of interest? The term *entrepreneur*—literally, "undertaker"—has been around for over two centuries, having been introduced in the early eighteenth century by the Parisian banker Richard Cantillon.[13] Believing that the primary role of entrepreneurs was to bear risk, Cantillon focused his attention on the *economic* functions of entrepreneurship—a focus that was to hold sway until very recently. In various economic approaches to entrepreneurship, we can identify three defining schools of thought: those scholars focused on *risk*, those focused on *innovation*, and those focused on *new venture startup*.

Since Cantillon's time, many arguments have persisted about the risk-bearing aspect of entrepreneurship. Many studies of entrepreneurs (including autobiographies) tend to focus on foresight and the willingness to take risks as the essential prerequisites for entrepreneurship. But in recent years, increasing numbers of scholars (including Howard Stevenson) follow Schumpeter's lead[14] in arguing that most entrepreneurs bear risk only grudgingly. Instead, these scholars argue, entrepreneurs attempt to create deals that apportion risk among lenders, investors, suppliers, employees, customers, and so on. Recently this perspective has again been confirmed by Amar Bhidé's systematic study of the "bootstrap" entrepreneur.[15]

Schumpeter himself associated entrepreneurship with innovation. Schumpeter defined creativity as either a new idea or an old idea applied to a new setting. (More broadly and more famously, he described capitalism as a form of "creative destruction," often involving the dismantling of old modes of doing business.) Schumpeter's definition of entrepreneurship as innovation has enjoyed considerable popularity in the field.

Finally, some writers have implicitly "defined" entrepreneurship by restricting their study to the process of starting new ventures, apparently on the assumption that entrepreneurial activity is in large part confined to the phase of new business formation. We suggest that, although this approach greatly simplifies the life of the researcher, it is incomplete and distorting. We make an analogy between new business formation and child rearing: starting the task requires only a moment of enthusiasm, but successful completion generally requires decades of hard work.

As noted, each of the classical definitions of entrepreneurship—risk bearing, innovation, and starting new ventures—focuses on the economic functions performed by entrepreneurial activity. In the 1950s, following the work of Arthur Cole, attention shifted away from these economic functions in favor of more personal analyses of individual entrepreneurs. During this phase of development in the field, many researchers attempted to discover common character traits that might help distinguish "true" entrepreneurs from nonentrepreneurs. Jack Hornaday's work at Babson, as well as David McClelland's work on the entrepreneur's alleged "need for achievement," were seminal pieces in this genre.[16] Other traits that have been singled out and cited include a proclivity for risk seeking, an internal locus of control, and even one's place in the family birth order.[17] More recent studies have focused on overconfidence and other background characteristics.

Although this individually and psychologically oriented research has pointed to some interesting correlations, we argue that unfortunate consequences too easily result from such a focus. It implicitly suggests that, if one could only discern the psychological profile of an entrepreneur and then hold an individual up against that profile, one could predict whether that individual has the potential to become an entrepreneur, or is one already. Yet none of the proposed "profiles" applies to all entrepreneurs, and many entrepreneurs refuse to conform to any of these profiles.

Here we must confess to a bias. An emphasis on individual personality traits as the key to successful entrepreneurship leaves little room for either teaching or learning. We and our Harvard colleagues are in the business of educating young people to be better managers—entrepreneurial or otherwise. Based on our own experience and that of others, we believe that teachers with the right tools can make successful interventions and can increase the would-be entrepreneur's chances of success. To argue otherwise would be to argue against business schools in general, and against entrepreneurship courses in particular—an argument we will leave to others.

Entrepreneurship: A Behavior in Many Contexts

In summary, none of the past attempts to define entrepreneurship captures the range of activities that ought to be subsumed under that umbrella. Nor do they give much guidance to people wishing to become entrepreneurs. Richard Kilby, who in the 1960s studied the entrepreneurial phenomenon, likened scholars' attempts to define entrepreneurship to Winnie-the-Pooh's efforts to track down the elusive Heffalump. Wrote Kilby:

> [The entrepreneur] is a large and important animal which has been hunted by many individuals using various ingenious trapping devices. . . . All who claim to have caught sight of him report that he is enormous, but they disagree on his particularities. Not having explored his current habitat with sufficient care, some hunters have used as bait their own favorite dishes and have then tried to persuade people that what they caught was a Heffalump. However, very few are convinced, and the search goes on.[18]

About 15 years ago, Howard Stevenson resolved to catch the Heffalump by ignoring the beast itself and instead focusing on its behavior. More precisely, he set out to advance the field of entrepreneurial studies by defining a unified focus on which cumulative learning could be based. He proposed that the focus be the entrepreneurial act itself.

Rather than focusing on either functional or personal definitions, we have developed a behavioral model.[19] In this model, entrepreneurship is seen as a *way of managing*, rather than as a specific economic function or as an inborn characteristic of an individual. Our model suggests that entrepreneurial management does not stop once a company is formed. Rather, entrepreneurship is a never-ending process that comprises multiple phases: the identification of opportunity, the marshaling of required resources, the exploitation of opportunity, and harvesting.

In this behavioral model, entrepreneurship is defined as *the pursuit of opportunity beyond the resources currently controlled*. We have identified six dimensions of business practice along which entrepreneurial behavior can be distinguished from nonentrepreneurial (which we have chosen to call "administrative") behavior[20]:

- *Strategic orientation.* Entrepreneurial organizations are driven by the perception of opportunity, whereas administrative organizations are driven by the resources currently controlled.

- *Strategic experimentation.*[21] Entrepreneurial organizations are willing to experiment. They often make revolutionary, short-duration commitments to opportunity. Administrative organizations tend to make more evolutionary, longer-duration commitments.

- *Commitment of resources.* Entrepreneurial organizations make multistage resource commitments with minimal exposure at each stage, in contrast to administrative organizations, which tend to make single-stage commitments.

- *Control of resources.* Entrepreneurial organizations make (only) episodic use of required resources, whereas administrative organizations prefer to own or employ all required resources.

- *Management structure.* Entrepreneurial organizations employ management structures that are flat, with multiple informal networks, whereas administrative organizations employ formalized hierarchies.

- *Compensation systems.* Entrepreneurial organizations base compensation on long-term value creation and on team performance. Administrative organizations base compensation on individual responsibility levels (such as assets or resources under control) and on performance relative to short-term accounting targets (such as profits or return on assets). They rely heavily on frequent promotion as a means of reward.[22]

Our characterizations of administrative management practices are not intended to be pejorative. Entrepreneurial management is not necessarily "better" than administrative management. Nor are the distinctions between the two always sharp. Entrepreneurial companies (and the individuals who guide them) often exhibit administrative behaviors, and vice versa. So the appropriate question to pose is: Given the nature of the business challenge or opportunity at hand, and in light of the external economic context, which managerial mode makes more sense?

In our view, the current global economic environment almost requires that all companies behave more entrepreneurially. Specifically, increased international and domestic competition, natural resource supply shocks, economic deregulation, changes in the nature of the capital markets, technological change, and certain demographic and sociological changes demand an increased reliance on entrepreneurial management practices—no matter what the company or industry.[23]

Our research and teaching focus on entrepreneurial behavior in a variety of contexts. Almost everyone agrees that, during the early stages of a company's development, the new enterprise can tell us much about the process of identifying and exploiting opportunities.[24] We maintain, though, that there is as much to be learned about entrepreneurship during the same company's later phases. Entrepreneurship is also about companies' undergoing transitions well after they are formed—as they gain access to the required resources,[25] as they pursue new opportunities, or as they react to new information about the original opportunity. And finally, the Harvard definition of entrepreneurship extends to more mature companies that are coping actively with their particular competitive challenges and are searching for a new organizationwide approach.

The behavioral definition of entrepreneurship presumes that the entrepreneurial phenomenon should be studied from a variety of perspectives, and that the most important of these perspectives is the general manager's. The task of the entrepreneurial general manager is to create an organization focused on identifying new opportunities, marshaling required resources (inside and outside the organization), exploiting the opportunity, and harvesting the rewards. The general manager is responsible for assuring that this process never ends, lest the organization stagnate and fail.

Although we stress the general manager's perspective, we acknowledge that the entrepreneurial process can also be understood by the effective exploration of different functional perspectives. For example, developing an understanding of key functional tasks—how companies gain control over financial resources, how they structure incentives, how they foster ongoing innovation—can be critical to the improvement of management practice.

In some cases, successful entrepreneurship may depend on the application of a rigorous economic framework to understanding private equity investment organizations and the firms they fund; this thinking requires application of advanced option valuation techniques. Equally, the human resources practices of rapidly growing enterprises are different from those in stable or declining firms. The management of technological commitments in an entrepreneurial firm is different from the functional equivalent in a resource-driven firm. Thus research and analysis at the functional level can give valuable insight into the challenges facing entrepreneurial managers—and their responses to those challenges can be equally illuminating.

Human Capital in the Entrepreneurial Management Unit

Response to the model described above has been positive—at the Harvard Business School, in the broader academy, and in the business world. Meanwhile, as noted above, there has been an explosion of interest in entrepreneurship education throughout the world. As a result, one of our unit's critical challenges has been to conduct the necessary research and development, participate in the broader community of entrepreneurial scholarship, and still do the work of the School that sponsors us. The most demanding of these "domestic" tasks, of course, is finding ways to staff courses that enjoy ever-increasing enrollments.

The external demands on the members of the Entrepreneurial Management unit have grown enormously. Faculty members in the unit are frequently invited to serve as lecturers at the Price-Babson Symposium for Entrepreneurship Educators, the primary training mechanism for teachers of entrepreneurship throughout the world. (In a typical year, one-third of that program is presented by Harvard faculty.) In addition to the normal professional activities of journal reviewing, and presenting at conferences and research seminars, we have participated as advisors to the Kauffman Foundation, the National Association of Historically Black Colleges and Universities, the Center for Executive Leadership, the European Foundation for Entrepreneurship Research (EFER), and many others. "The Harvard way" provided the foundation for much of EFER's training of educators from the former Soviet Bloc.

To meet these many demands on our time, we have developed a three-pronged strategy for staffing. We have sought tenured and non-tenured candidates from other institutions, and we have recruited faculty from other units within HBS. We have participated in the doctoral programs at HBS, including the DBA program and the Ph.D. programs in Business Economics and Organizational Behavior. Finally, we have sought business leaders who can perform well in the classroom and who also exhibit a solid interest in creating intellectual capital.

The record of accomplishment in all three areas has been very satisfying. Since 1982, By Barnes, Norm Berg, Bill Sahlman, and John Kao have joined the Entrepreneurial Management unit from within HBS. (Sahlman assumed significant leadership in the unit with his creation of the Entrepreneurial Finance course.) Teresa Amabile, Jeffry Timmons, and Greg Dees all joined from other academic institutions. We have had extensive involvement with entrepreneurship research and teaching conferences, the Academy of Management, the Strategic Management Society, and the Society for Socioeconomics. Forging relationships in all of these external contexts helps stimulate insight into important problems in the field; it also helps us to uncover future intellectual leaders.

Over the past 13 years, members of the unit have served on over 20 doctoral dissertation committees. Our former doctoral students are leaders at HBS, INSEAD, the London Business School, IMD, the University of Virginia, Duke, and elsewhere. As a result of our involvement in the doctoral programs, we have hired into our unit faculty such HBS graduates as Mike Roberts, Amar Bhidé, Josh Lerner, Paul Gompers, Myra Hart, and Walter Kuemmerle. In each case, one or more members of the unit served on the dissertation committee. Other members of the present HBS faculty on whose committees members of the units served include George Baker, Clay Christensen, and Ashish Nanda.

We have been very fortunate in our search for outstanding practitioners. For example, both William Poorvu[26] and Irv Grousbeck[27] have published widely used texts and casebooks in their fields. The current practitioner faculty members—all of whom possess doctorates and also have extensive business experience—include John Davis, Joseph Lassiter, Paul Marshall, and Ed Zschau.

As a result of these many outreach and recruitment efforts, we currently have a faculty with 12 earned doctorates teaching 10 MBA courses and a series of executive programs. The unit maintains an active course development and research agenda (see below). Overall, we believe that our faculty is unique in the field of entrepreneurship, both in the depth and breadth of our academic and entrepreneurial experience, and in the strength of our educational backgrounds.

Research and Teaching: Goals and Guidelines

The behavioral approach to entrepreneurship guides most of the current research and teaching of the HBS Entrepreneurial Management unit. As with most academic endeavors, our goal is to gain insights into the phenomenon being studied by searching for generalizable patterns of success and failure—in our case, in the individuals and organizations exhibiting entrepreneurial behavior. A number of interrelated questions distinguish the research programs of our faculty:

- What is an opportunity?

- How do companies organize themselves to identify opportunities?

- How do companies develop and maintain innovative systems to identify and pursue opportunities?

- What resources are required to exploit the opportunity?

- How can the company gain control over those resources?

- How can companies establish structures, systems, and cultures that will support ongoing innovation?

- How should opportunities be exploited?

- When and how should opportunities be harvested?

Our research into these questions attempts to uncover complex, path-dependent, interactive effects. Because its ultimate goal is the improvement of practice, our research serves as the natural foundation for our teaching, which is largely organized along functional lines. Regardless of the particular functional focus in the individual courses, however, we insist on four common learning objectives. They are:

- The conceptual framework (the entrepreneurial management model)

- Skills and tools (such as opportunity analysis, deal structuring, organization design, and innovation support)

- Specific knowledge (tax law, corporate governance rules, securities regulation, intellectual property rules)

- Attitudinal development (commitment to continuous improvement, belief in the importance of creativity and innovation, a sense of the possible, a belief in the possibility of many options for success, a sense of personal responsibility grounded in ethical behavior)

Our research has informed our teaching, of course. But equally, our teaching has shaped our research agenda, by making evident where we should seek more practical knowledge of how entrepreneurship happens. This experience has validated a somewhat counterintuitive approach to sequencing our activities. A decade ago, in recognition of growing student demand, we established course development as our most urgent priority. We sought to develop three new courses as quickly as possible, which in turn required the researching and writing of more than 100 cases. These cases were chosen to illustrate diverse enterprises, including variety along the following dimensions: industry setting, growth potential (both high-potential ventures and lifestyle ventures), geography (both domestic and international sites), demographics (age, gender, ethnicity, and educational background), personality type, deal structure (partnerships, corporations, sole proprietorships, joint ventures), and success/failure (both initial and long term).

Consistently, we sought to expose students to the widest possible range of alternative opportunities and to show many entrepreneurial tools at work. We wanted to help students scan opportunities widely enough that all would be able to identify a good fit for their own skills and personal motivations. Of necessity, and by design, our cases exposed our students to seemingly contradictory messages—for example, always be in control versus have a partner; go public versus keep the business private; reach for the stars versus watch out for disaster; money is easy to raise versus money is difficult to get; your HBS degree is a key ingredient to success versus forget your formal training and get on with developing "street smarts." Our goal was not to confuse students, but—by getting them comfortable with the complex interactions between environmental and personal factors—to help them avoid the kinds of simplistic messages and straightforward algorithms that might otherwise seduce them.

From the time of our earliest efforts, we identified one additional goal: to help our students understand the ethical responsibilities that they assume when they undertake entrepreneurial work. Entrepreneurs create entire cultures, often without guiding traditions or the insulation that can be provided by administrative staff. By almost any reckoning, entrepreneurs are on the firing line. They must face and resolve ethical dilemmas of all varieties, and they must set high and compelling standards for the enterprises they are building.

We also address the implicit time horizon of our target audiences. As noted previously, evidence from the field suggests that many of our graduates defer becoming involved in an entrepreneurial setting for up to 10 years after graduation. Often, this is the first juncture in their careers when they have sufficient experience, skill, attitudes, and contacts to identify an opportunity and gain control over the resources required to pursue it. In many cases, those resource requirements are significant. It is not surprising, therefore, that experience and deep knowledge are required in order to gain the confidence of the resource providers. We want our students to understand that entrepreneurship should not be attempted prematurely, which in many cases means not immediately after graduation from business school.

Looking again at the range of issues outlined earlier, the magnitude of our remaining research challenge is clear, and sobering. Several projects currently under way in the unit are designed to probe some key issues in greater depth. Myra Hart is expanding her dissertation work focusing on the resource acquisition process. Teresa Amabile is studying motivational influences on creativity, the ways motivation can be affected by specific events in the work environment, and the mechanisms by which individual or team creativity translate into organizational innovation. Diane Burton, Walter Kuemmerle, and Howard Stevenson are all looking at various aspects of cultures, structures, and systems. Amar Bhidé's work is focusing on the exploitation of opportunities and the ways entrepreneurs create options out of initial opportunities that might seem relatively unattractive in and of themselves. Josh Lerner and Paul Gompers are doing important empirical analysis of the relationship between private equity organizations and the institutions that provide them with capital. In addition, Lerner is studying competition and innovation in high-technology industries, with emphasis on intellectual property policy. Bill Sahlman continues to innovate in both course development and theoretical work on the logical consequences of deal structures. Bill Poorvu is focusing on the changes that have beset the real estate industry as a result of the rapid restructuring of financial markets and of the globalization of many industries.

The Future: Toward a Unifying
Conceptual Framework

Since the fundamental intellectual work in the field of entrepreneurial management was first undertaken at Harvard in the 1940s, progress in the field has been marked by a wide variety of research paradigms across a broad spectrum of academic disciplines: economics, finance, organizational behavior, psychology, sociology, and general management, among others. To state, explore, and challenge these paradigms, researchers have employed an equally varied array of tools: focused teaching cases and exploratory case studies of entrepreneurial undertakings; archival studies of the personal, behavioral, and situational predictors of entrepreneurial success; survey and interview studies of specific entrepreneurial behaviors; and both qualitative and quantitative studies of the attitudes, motivations, experiences, and circumstances that appear to foster successful entrepreneurial efforts.

It might seem reasonable to conclude from this lengthy list that the field of entrepreneurial management is fragmented, disorganized, and weak. But we believe that the opposite is true—that this diversity enriches rather than undercuts the study of entrepreneurship. Multiple research perspectives are essential because, as noted earlier, the study of entrepreneurship is at its heart the study of management and requires attention to all aspects of management.

Entrepreneurial management is differentiated from broader approaches to general management because it focuses on particular types of behaviors that are desirable under certain sets of conditions. The business environment must be one in which new opportunities actually exist—such as when there is rapid change in technology, consumer economics, social values, or political rules—and where significant gains can be achieved by

- Pursuing those opportunities

- Making (seemingly) sudden, short-duration commitments to those opportunities (as when there are short decision windows and a limited set of decision constituencies)

- Committing resources in stages, rather than all at once (under conditions of limited predictability in resource needs, or lack of long-term control)

- Making flexible use of borrowed resources (for example, when there is high risk of resource obsolescence)

- Managing through a flat, nonhierarchical structure (when human resources are not directly controlled but instead must be coordinated)

- Compensating on the basis of long-term value creation rather than individual responsibility levels or short-term financial targets (when there are individual expectations of equity)[28]

We believe that scholars must continue the current drive to extend the study of entrepreneurship beyond small businesses and new ventures to "corporate entrepreneurship," which should comprise *all* firms that find themselves in the circumstances described above. Many established firms are now striving to achieve corporate entrepreneurship. Given the process definition of entrepreneurship, these firms (or firm units behaving in this manner) are in fact entrepreneurial organizations.[29]

We aim to embrace multiple research paradigms, so that we will be able to recognize and accommodate entrepreneurship in its many forms—some of which, no doubt, have yet to emerge. At the same time, it seems important to develop a unifying conceptual framework for understanding entrepreneurship. This can be accomplished only by building theory on a solid empirical foundation and by extending beyond that foundation to build intellectual bridges into unexplored territory. The result will be a comprehensive understanding of entrepreneurship.

There are three conceptual cornerstones for our current work: (1) *resources*, broadly conceived, as a prime determinant of entrepreneurial decisions and ultimate entrepreneurial success; (2) *entrepreneurial skills*, creatively applicable across a range of entrepreneurial activities; and (3) *human motivation*—specifically, intrinsic motivation and the power of predictability in motivating behavior. Let's look at each in turn.

Resources can be defined as all of the raw materials available to the entrepreneur: reputation, experience, people, and information, as well as funding and other material resources. Creative entrepreneurial skills can be considered as the set of operations that will, ideally, be applied to these resources in order to effect a successful outcome. Motivation is the driving force that brings creativity and all other entrepreneurial skills to bear on the resources.

For each of these components, our theoretical work is informed by (and in turn stimulates) our empirical research. Resources occupy a central position in our conceptualization of entrepreneurship and, indeed, in our process definition of entrepreneurship. Because entrepreneurial behavior is marked by a pursuit of opportunity regardless of the resources currently controlled, it requires finding, gaining control of, and effectively utilizing resources as necessary. This conceptualization of the central role of resources arises from several important empirical findings in our recent research:

- The design and consummation of deals for funding new ventures are crucial determinants of success. The way this process unfolds can have lasting consequences for the growth and health of an enterprise—and, indeed, for the economy as a whole.[30]

- The resources that are available to startup entrepreneurs at the conception of their enterprises can have a powerful impact on their chances of making it beyond the startup phase and experiencing high growth—particularly because those resources include not only funding, but also the experience, reputations, and networks of the founders.[31]

- The diversity of information sources available to new undertakings, including cross-functional and cross-cultural flows of data, positively predicts the success of business innovations.[32]

- The ways in which entrepreneurs manage their human resources and structure their organizations indelibly shape the ways in which those organizations will develop.[33]

In other words, resources must be considered from a number of viewpoints: those personal resources that business founders bring with them in the form of their own expertise, experience, contacts, and tangible goods; those material, human, and informational resources that entrepreneurs will find and for which they will negotiate; and those human resources that they will manage as they build their firms.[34]

In our view, the prime entrepreneurial skill is the identification of opportunity—the ability to continuously scan the world outside oneself, assess the environment accurately, and identify gaps between people's needs and what actually exists. This identification of gaps—this seeing something new that no one has seen before—is a hallmark of creative thinking.[35]

Creativity is the generation of novel and useful ideas. Innovation is the successful implementation of creative ideas by an organization. Unlike earlier scholars in the field who saw entrepreneurship as equivalent to innovation,[36] we argue that both creativity and innovation are necessary components of successful entrepreneurship. Entrepreneurs must be skilled both in generating new, workable ideas for their business (whether in the products or services, the marketing, the operations, or the funding of that business) *and* in executing those ideas effectively. In other words, it is unlikely that notable success can be achieved without some degree of novelty in some aspect of the entrepreneurial undertaking.

Therefore, rather than viewing creativity as a mysterious quality of the human personality, we view it as a skilled behavior that can be applied to the opportunities and resources available to the entrepreneur.[37] It is important to remember, however, that creativity entails novelty, and concurrent novelty in multiple aspects of an undertaking is often undesirable—too much of a good thing.[38]

A central organizing principle of human motivation is the desire for control. This desire is manifested in many ways, two of which have been the focus of our recent work: intrinsic motivation and the power of predictability. Intrinsic motivation is the drive to undertake something because it is interesting, intriguing, compelling, involving, challenging, or satisfying. Intrinsic motivation is fueled by—and in turn reinforces—feelings of competence and self-determination.[39] When people believe that by engaging in a particular activity they can increase their competence, pursue their interests, and control their own fate—whether that activity involves planning a research project or starting a business—they are less likely to need incentives or directives from others, and they are more likely to find creative solutions to problems.[40]

The human desire for control also illuminates a powerful related phenomenon: the desire for predictability in outcomes. In small social units, in organizations and in societies, people wish to understand the likely consequences of their own actions and the actions of others, in relation to some desired future state. Without this understanding, ongoing mutual progress is impossible.[41] We believe that theoretical models of entrepreneurship must take into account both intrinsic motivation and the power of prediction. Entrepreneurs are more likely to succeed if they can establish work environments that foster intrinsic motivation in their associates. Moreover, considerable entrepreneurial opportunity is open to those who can find ways to increase predictability for others, including their customers and their employees.[42]

Although there is growing empirical support for our current articulation of the role of resources, skills, and motivation in entrepreneurial processes, these are only pieces of a comprehensive map of the entrepreneurial landscape. Our efforts must be linked to theoretical and empirical work being done by other scholars, within and outside HBS, which collectively should address the entire range of questions about entrepreneurship: its *causes* (drawing primarily from psychology and sociology), its *processes* (drawing from basic studies in entrepreneurial management), and its *results* (drawing primarily from economics). These questions cannot be studied only in isolation, but must instead be connected by logical and pragmatic threads.

Although management scholars are an important audience for the ideas we are generating, we do not conceive of them as our primary audience. Ultimately, we want to have our primary impact on management practice—both by giving our students insight into and experience in grappling with the problems and opportunities they will face as entrepreneurs, and by communicating our findings effectively to entrepreneurs, aspiring entrepreneurs, and policy makers.

A Continual Questioning

Long ago, our predecessors at HBS realized the central importance of entrepreneurial activity in business practice, research, and education. They also perceived the possibility of first-rate scholarly work in the field. That tradition, greatly reinforced by John McArthur's founding of the Entrepreneurial Management unit, has placed the School in an excellent position to lead the field into what many expect to be the "entrepreneurs' century." We have strong interdisciplinary faculty within the unit, representing economics, finance, mathematics, psychology, sociology, organizational behavior, and general management, with many links to others outside the unit. Moreover, these faculty cumulatively represent several decades of actual entrepreneurial experience, founding, running, evaluating, investing in, and directing entrepreneurial ventures of various types.[43]

We believe that our evolving conceptual framework, illuminating the practice of entrepreneurship as a complex of attitudes and behaviors in response to opportunities in the environment, captures the essence of innovative management. But we also recognize our obligation to engage in a process of continual questioning. Are we serving the right people? How can we better integrate our efforts with those of other scholars and educators within and outside of the School? How can we better learn from and communicate to the entrepreneurial community? Are we adequately perceiving and acting on our own opportunities? How can we, as a group, improve our entrepreneurial efforts in scholarship and education?

Because HBS is the unique institution it is, we have unparalleled access to real entrepreneurs and real entrepreneurial activities. We believe that this unusual combination—cross-disciplinary scholarly rigor with practical experience and real-world access—will increase the probability that the individual and collaborative work of our unit will be not only intellectually pioneering, but also managerially important.

CHAPTER SIX

Organizations and Markets

MICHAEL C. JENSEN, GEORGE BAKER,
CARLISS BALDWIN, AND KAREN H. WRUCK

AT A BREAKFAST MEETING *early in 1985, John McArthur told a visiting professor, Michael C. Jensen, the story of how the Business, Government, and the International Economy (BGIE) and the Competition and Strategy initiatives had come together at the School in the previous decade.*

Jensen was then on leave from the University of Rochester's Simon School of Business, where he and colleague William Meckling had been working for more than a decade on a new model of organizations and markets. Jensen had been interested in testing his unorthodox ideas against the experiences of practitioners and had agreed to come to HBS on a temporary basis to get increased access to high-level decision makers in business. Now, at breakfast, McArthur was lobbying Jensen to join the HBS faculty permanently and run his own large-scale course development effort. But Jensen, although tempted by the chance to stay on in an environment that he found stimulating, felt a strong loyalty to his Rochester colleagues.

McArthur was prepared for this response. He had already sought out Harvard's President Derek Bok and told him that he had an unusual plan in mind. He wanted to offer Jensen a half-time tenured position, even though there was no group at the School that had yet agreed to take the controversial Rochester professor under its wing. Let's just get him here, McArthur encouraged Bok, and the housekeeping details will take care of themselves. Bok, trusting McArthur's instincts, agreed to the plan.

Jensen soon accepted the half-time offer and began reworking his ideas about organizations and markets for application in the HBS context. Several years later, as McArthur had hoped, Jensen joined the HBS faculty full time, and intensified his efforts to build a major new field of research and teaching at the School.

T HE ORGANIZATIONS AND MARKETS (O&M) unit at the Harvard Business School is devoted to the interdisciplinary development of a modern theory of organizations and markets which is useful to both social scientists and managers.

Organizations and markets are, of course, important topics in the social sciences and beyond. Researchers in economics, sociology, political science, psychology, anthropology, and biology have studied these phenomena from their different disciplinary vantage points, bringing their own intellectual traditions, methodologies, strengths, and limitations to bear. Economists, for example, traditionally have focused on how markets function. To make their theories tractable, they have reduced the behavior of organizations and individuals to a few overly simple axioms. In the last ten years, economists have been making progress in dealing with the complexities of organizations, but there is still much work to be done.

In contrast, researchers in the fields of psychology, sociology, organizational behavior, anthropology, and biology have focused on organizations of various kinds. They have developed complex theories and large bodies of evidence that shed light on individual and group behavior. However, with a few exceptions, the effects of competition and market-type selection processes on survival and adaptation by individuals and groups were not topics of primary interest to scholars in these fields.

It could be argued that treating organizations and markets as separate entities was justifiable as long as organizational boundaries were well defined and the preponderance of market transactions were simple and stylized. Today, however, technological and historical developments (including the development of high-speed information analysis and transfer technologies, as well as the emergence of modern high-capacity capital markets) are blurring key boundaries and making the relationship between organizations and markets much more complex and inescapable. Any rigorous and useful theory of organizations, we argue, must be embedded in an understanding of both human behavior *and* markets.

At the same time, more and more fields have demonstrated that they have something to contribute to one or the other of these two areas of study. As a result, over the last decade, scholars who have sought to play the vital integrating role between organizations and markets have had to embrace the divergent methodologies and vocabularies of a broad range of scholarly fields. Of necessity, their work has become increasingly interdisciplinary, drawing on economics, organizational behavior, finance, psychology, sociology, and linguistics, as well as neuroscience and evolutionary biology.

These are the exciting challenges that face the members of the O&M unit at the Harvard Business School. In developing our theory, we focus particularly on four interrelated areas: (1) the nature of human beings and their behavior; (2) compensation, career systems, and performance measurement; (3) task structure, organizational boundaries, and technology; and (4) governance, corporate finance, and organizational performance. Later in this chapter, we will present specifics in each of these four categories.

Because of the strong interdisciplinary nature of our research, and the close interrelationships among our research, course development, and teaching, our group's history has been intertwined with that of several other units at the School. The O&M faculty has at various times been associated with the Control, Organizational Behavior, and General Management units, as well as tangentially with Finance. In the fall of 1995, with the appointment of Kim Clark as dean, O&M became one of the operating units of HBS. The O&M unit currently consists of four senior faculty (Professors George Baker, Carliss Baldwin, Michael Jensen, and Malcolm Salter), two affiliated senior faculty (Chris Argyris, now emeritus, and Richard Hackman), and three junior faculty (Associate Professors Karen Wruck and Brian Hall, and Assistant Professor Ashish Nanda).

CCMO: A Course Defines a Field

The story of the development of the O&M unit is essentially the story of the development of a distinctive course—Coordination, Control, and the Management of Organizations (CCMO)—first at the University of Rochester and subsequently at Harvard. At both institutions, the research effort coincided with and was inseparable from the development of the course.

The first HBS version of CCMO was taught to 35 students in the winter of 1985. But before we take up the CCMO story at HBS, it is useful to look at the roots of this research/course effort, which began at Rochester in the early 1970s.

The Beginnings

In the early 1970s, the business school at the University of Rochester was dominated by economists. At the same time, it was a place where more or less frustrated students regularly questioned the usefulness of the price theory they were learning. This frustration also extended to the Rochester Executive Education Program, in which executives from the upstate New York area attended classes one day a week for two years to earn the MBA degree. In 1974, in response to this frustration, two Rochester professors—Michael C. Jensen and Dean William H. Meckling—launched a radical experiment. They set out to teach the executive students price theory in a way that would make the theoretical material relevant and immediately applicable to their jobs.

At its heart, the Rochester experiment attempted to teach price theory without once mentioning the kinds of public policy issues that had failed to connect with Rochester's highly practical students. Jensen and Meckling instead adopted a managerial perspective, using the organizational problems of a large multidivisional firm as the device for illustrating and teaching economic principles. In those early days, the principles taught tended to be pricing issues, such as transfer pricing, peak load pricing, and public goods theory applied to the production and pricing of computer software.

This experiment proved to be a success. The executives almost immediately began using the material in their everyday work lives. But, as is so often the case, solving one problem tended to create a new one. With less than a semester of exposure to the price theory material—now presented in a much more exciting and accessible way—the executives often did not know enough to put that material to full and proper use.

At the same time, Jensen, Meckling, and their students found that they were becoming more and more fascinated by the organizational problems they were discussing. The problems of a multidivisional firm, originally a pedagogical point of entry for studying price theory, were becoming the focus of the course. Meanwhile, the price theory that the Rochester faculty members were supposed to be teaching, and which their students were supposed to be learning, was increasingly being relegated to off-line discussion groups directed by Kenneth French, the teaching assistant for the course during its first two years (now the Beinecke Professor of Finance at Yale). By the end of the second year, Jensen and Meckling had designed and prepared themselves to teach a new course, "Coordination and Control," which focused explicitly on organizational problems. Concurrently, the nuts-and-bolts price theory course was resurrected, this time with more emphasis on managerial and organizational issues.

This was a time of great intellectual ferment at Rochester. Jensen and Meckling wrote the first draft of their oft-cited "Agency" paper[1] in 1973, and that paper—greatly reinforced by other publications and the overall intellectual excitement of that time and place—inspired many at Rochester to tackle new kinds of organizational problems. What ensued was an outpouring of research into agency problems associated with corporate finance and organizations, the positive theory of accounting, corporate governance, and the market for corporate control. Scholars at

Rochester and elsewhere pushed back the frontiers of knowledge and practice. Meanwhile, Jensen and Meckling introduced their new Coordination and Control course into the Rochester MBA program. It quickly became the most popular elective course in the curriculum, regularly attracting two-thirds or more of the MBA student body.

William Meckling retired from Rochester in 1983, and Jensen left for a full-time appointment at HBS in 1989. Although both Jensen and Meckling are now gone from Rochester, the intellectual legacy of the Coordination and Control course and research effort is still strong there. The course was made part of Rochester's required MBA curriculum in 1989. As Ronald Hansen, dean for academic affairs, says, "This is the one course that I will not allow students to place out of, because the course defines so much of what is special about the Simon School of Business."[2] Courses similar to CCMO are now being taught at the University of Southern California and at Chicago.

Two important traditions, both of which continue to influence the O&M group today, were established during the early Rochester experience. First, those who taught the course subscribed to the idea that *real learning leads to (and is evidenced by) changes in behavior*. This belief has remained an important philosophical underpinning of the O&M group at Harvard. We do not just teach; we are devoted to making a difference in peoples' lives. But a change in behavior almost always means giving up an associated way of thinking, and giving up a way of thinking is almost always a painful process. Providing students with an opportunity to learn material that fundamentally changes the way they see the world generates confusion, discomfort, and controversy. We have seen this phenomenon of discomfort frequently in our classrooms, both here at HBS and in the earlier incarnation of the course at Rochester.

Another tradition of the O&M group that is traceable to the earliest days at Rochester is that of bringing new faculty on board through intensive interaction with senior faculty in the context of both research and teaching. At Rochester, for example, new faculty were brought into this difficult-to-teach course through joint teaching with either Jensen or Meckling. (These individuals have included Kevin J. Murphy and James Brickley at Rochester and, later, George P. Baker, Karen H. Wruck, Carliss

Baldwin, and Malcolm Salter at Harvard.) As a part of this effort, Jensen and Meckling developed a set of "Course Notes" to help new faculty, as well as students, master the most challenging materials in the course.[3] In the same spirit, the O&M group at Harvard has established a formal teaching group—one of the few in the second year of the MBA program.

The Growth of CCMO at Harvard: 1985–1996

After spending a year as visiting professor at HBS in 1984–1985 (and teaching the first version of CCMO as a seminar for 35 MBA and doctoral students in the winter of 1985), Michael Jensen joined the HBS faculty with a half-time tenured appointment in the Control area in the fall of 1985. Three weeks before the beginning of the term, he was drafted to teach a section of first-year Control to fill a hole created by an unexpected resignation; as a result, CCMO was not taught in the fall of 1985.

During this interval, George Baker—then a Ph.D. student in the joint Business-Economics program—asked Jensen to serve as an advisor for his thesis on management buyouts. This collaboration led to Baker's helping Jensen teach CCMO to 112 students in the fall of 1986, when the course was run as a seminar, meeting once a week for three hours.[4] The enrollment of 112 students surprised everyone, but Baker and Jensen successfully taught it as a seminar anyway. Karen Wruck joined the Control area at HBS in 1987 and began teaching CCMO in 1990 when the group was still part of Control. (Wruck received her doctorate from Rochester in 1987 and had taken the Coordination and Control course while there.) Along the way in the development of the course, Mark Wolfson, on leave from Stanford, and Kevin Murphy—now a professor at USC—jointly taught the course with Jensen in 1988–1989 and 1992–1993, respectively. Carliss Baldwin joined the O&M group in the fall of 1995 from the HBS Finance faculty, and Malcolm Salter joined in the fall of 1996 from the School's Competition and Strategy group.

Figure 6.1 summarizes the history of enrollment and faculty involvement with the course from its beginning to 1996. In the third year of the course, Jensen and Baker taught one section of the course in the standard elective curriculum format to 47 students, and that grew by 1994–1995 to the current six sections (which were taught in 1996–1997 by Baldwin, Baker, Jensen, Salter, and Wruck) with total enrollment of about 600 students.

Objectives and Foundations of CCMO

CCMO, even more than most courses, is difficult to summarize briefly without that summary's sounding trivial, obvious, or even empty. The course is to a large extent *a way of thinking* that is at once obvious and simple, and also (we hope!) subtle and complex. The following para-

FIGURE 6.1   *Historical Enrollments in CCMO and Teaching Faculty for the Period 1985–1986*

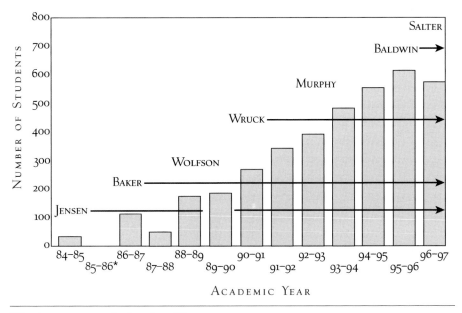

*No classes were taught in 1985–1986.

graphs are excerpts from the CCMO course description (from the School's elective curriculum catalogue) and from the course syllabus. They were written in a way that was intended to help prospective students begin to understand both the course and its "rules of the game"— a term with specific meanings, which will be described below—and therefore should be helpful to readers of this chapter. We have left the material in the voice in which we speak to our students:

CCMO takes an interdisciplinary and interfunctional approach to organizational problem-solving and value creation. The disciplines of economics and psychology are integrated and applied to problems in human resource management, labor economics, organizational behavior, finance, governance, and corporate control. Traditional economics and psychology, however, do not adequately address many topics vitally important to our understanding of organizations. This requires that we move beyond their boundaries to deal effectively with such topics.

Our objective is to develop a theory of organizations that provides a clear understanding of how organizational rules of the game affect a manager's ability to resolve problems, increase productivity, and achieve his or her objective. The course explores the choice of organizational objective function and the value implications for equity and debt holders, employees, suppliers, and society as a whole.

The viewpoint of the course is that of a general manager addressing organizational strategy with an internal rather than an external focus. The analysis emphasizes the constraints that external markets, such as capital, supplier, labor, and product markets, place on a firm's internal organizational strategy. The framework developed is analytical, but not mathematical. It provides an understanding of how organizational structure affects performance and how current economic and social forces are reshaping the role of managers, both today and in the future.

Problems analyzed include issues of motivation, information and decision-making, the allocation of decision rights, performance measurement systems, organizational and personal rewards and punishments, corporate financial policy, and governance. We apply the analysis to organizational change accomplished through restructuring, leveraged recapitalizations, leveraged buyouts, takeovers, downsizing, exit, and reengineering.

The foundation material in the first third of the course is particularly important but somewhat difficult to deal with in our [HBS] style because there are relatively few decisions to be made. The first nine sessions develop a set of "building blocks" which form the foundation on which the remainder of the course rests.

CCMO consists of three modules of approximately ten sessions each. The first module deals with the foundations of our theory of organizations, described briefly at the outset of this essay and in greater detail in the second half of this essay. The second module applies that theory to the critical task of defining the organizational rules of the game, and the third applies the theory to organizational governance and corporate control.

We concentrate here on the first foundational module of the course. This module begins with two applied cases. We then devote three days to a discussion of the nature of human beings—those unusual and complicated, self-interested and emotional creatures who populate the organizations that businesspeople seek to manage, inspire, and guide. We move on to a discussion of the critical importance of the costs of moving information between people in the economy and in organizations.

Because all information cannot be moved to a central decision maker, whether a central planner in the economy or the CEO in a firm, most "decision rights" must be delegated to those people who have the relevant information. In other words, the *cost* of moving information between people creates the necessity for decentralizing some decision rights in organizations and the economy. This decentralization creates the necessity for systems to mitigate the control problem that results from the fact that self-interested people (with their own self-control problems) who exercise decision rights as agents on the behalf of others will not behave as perfect agents. Capitalist market economies solve these control problems through the institution of alienable decision rights. (See section on alienability below.) Because organizations by definition suppress the alienability of decision rights, they must devise substitute mechanisms that perform the functions of alienability.

The remaining two modules of the course apply these concepts to a wide variety of organizations and situations. The main foundational concepts and their relations are outlined in Figure 6.2, and we discuss them in turn here.

THE DUALISTIC MODEL OF HUMAN BEHAVIOR. We devote three more or less tumultuous days to a far-ranging discussion of human physiology, human behavior, and, most important, human motivation. We begin by exploring the rational side of human behavior, which many years ago we labeled "REMM," for Resourceful, Evaluative, Maximizing Model.[5]

we labeled "REMM," for Resourceful, Evaluative, Maximizing Model.[5] (PAM, the Pain Avoidance Model, is described below.) There are many important lessons here, but among the more important are the propositions that people are inherently self-interested, that they systematically make substitutions, and that, although they may well be more or less

FIGURE 6.2   *Fundamental Conceptual Building Blocks that Form the Foundations of the CCMO Theory of Organizations*

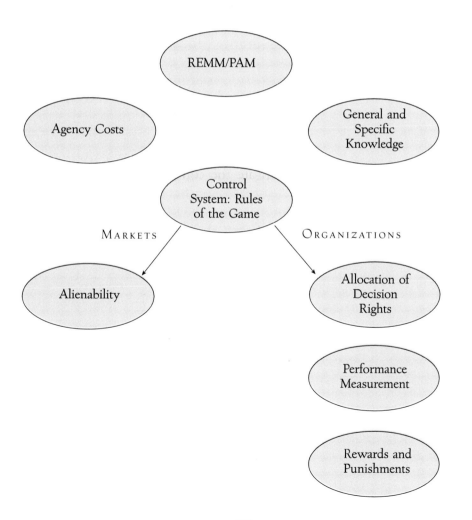

other words, no one so thoroughly embodies the preferences of another that he or she can be that person's perfect agent. Interestingly, students regularly resist this characterization of humans as too simple, yet there are enormous amounts of evidence on human behavior in the aggregate (and in the long run, even for individuals) that is consistent with it.

We then confront students with evidence from the world and from their own behavior which indicates that people frequently make decisions that make themselves worse off (in an expected-value sense) and that they learn too slowly from their own mistakes. Moreover, our evidence argues, humans often actively resist such learning, even in the face of great difficulties and pain. Ironically, this analysis and its supporting evidence commonly cause many students to rush with open arms to embrace the REMM model—a model they had vociferously rejected only the day before.

The third day in this sequence is devoted to a discussion of findings from modern neuropsychology, especially the neuroscience of emotions. This new body of scientific knowledge explains nonrational behavior as a universal condition of human behavior caused by the structure of the brain. In effect, the human brain is "flawed" because of peculiar interactions in the circuitry of the flight-or-fight response. The threat of emotional or psychic pain, as well as physical danger, can trigger the flight-or-fight response. This floods the brain (and, indeed, the whole body) with neuroactive chemicals. Once this occurs, the emotional centers of the brain take over (or at least distract) the cortex or conscious thinking part of the brain. This neural "hijacking" prevents the cortex from making the kinds of decisions that would be most likely to enhance the welfare of the decision maker. This is what we call the Pain Avoidance Model (PAM).

THE COST OF TRANSFERRING KNOWLEDGE. The second major building block is the cost of transferring knowledge between agents. Based on work in the 1940s by Nobel Laureate Friedrich von Hayek, the central proposition we put forward is that certain kinds of knowledge (which we label "specific" knowledge) are very costly to transmit. In such cases, the common managerial tactic of moving the knowledge to the decision maker is not likely to work. Instead, we must *place the decision rights for which that knowledge is valuable in the hands of the person with the knowledge.*

(This is the real economic advantage inherent in the modern empower-ment movement.) We can then also move the "general" knowledge (defined as knowledge that can be moved at lower transfer costs) to that decentralized decision maker.

The course makes the point that, because vast amounts of knowledge are specific, centralized decision making is likely to fail in most situa-tions. Moreover, we can say much about how control systems and the nature of specific knowledge and its location can change with technol-ogy, uncertainty, and so on, so that we can make substantive proposi-tions about how such decision rights should be allocated. In addition, we can simply sidestep as irrelevant the age-old debate over centraliza-tion versus decentralization. Because some bodies of specific knowledge reside at the top of the organization, while others reside in the middle or at the bottom, the real issue is *which* decision rights to decentralize, and *which* to centralize.

AGENCY COSTS. Having established the fact that a completely centralized solution will seldom, if ever, be optimal, we are then led to confront the difficulties caused by the fact that human beings are self-interested and otherwise imperfect agents. This raises the specter of agency costs and the control problem: the problem associated with limiting the costs due to conflicts of interest with others and with ourselves.

ALIENABILITY AND THE ORGANIZATIONAL RULES OF THE GAME. As noted above, the institutional device that allows a free-market capitalist system to solve the control problem is alienable decision rights. A decision right is the right to choose an action and to take an action, in a context where the police powers of the state will be used to ensure the party's ability to take the action. An *alienable* decision right is one that can be sold or exchanged by the owner, with the owner pocketing the proceeds offered in exchange. If Harry owns the alienable decision rights in a machine, for example, no one can use or sell that machine without his permission. More important, alienable decision rights enable exchange to occur. Exchange, in turn, works to ensure that those who have the specific knowledge and talents valuable to the exercise of a particular right will have a mechanism for gaining possession of that right (by peaceful means). Anyone with better information or talents regarding the use of Harry's machine can make an offer to purchase it—and if they have better information they are likely to value his machine more highly than they value Harry, and the exchange will tend to occur.

Thus alienability creates an automatic and decentralized system for partitioning and assigning decision rights to those who value them most highly. In addition, the prices that are determined in these voluntary exchanges provide an effective measure of performance of the party who owns the rights. Assuming there are no externalities, this measure incorporates the total value implications of his or her actions with the rights (to the full extent that the contracting parties can anticipate them). Continuing with our example, if Harry fails to maintain the machine and thereby reduces its present and future productivity, the sale price of the machine will be lower. Finally, because alienability allows the owner of the rights to capture the proceeds offered in the exchange, it automatically rewards and punishes the owner for his or her performance with the rights. It does so by capitalizing the entire present value of the future costs and benefits of the owner's actions onto his or her shoulders.

We call these three dimensions of system design—the allocation of decision rights, performance measurement, and rewards and punishments—the "rules of the game." They are of particular interest and importance to managers because the defining characteristic of firms is that they do not assign alienable decision rights to agents, but they reserve alienability (the right to pocket the proceeds) to the organization (or, more precisely, to the residual claimants). When General Motors delegates a decision right—say, the use of a machine—to an individual, that individual is not given the right to sell that machine to the highest bidder and capture the proceeds of the sale. If such alienability *were* granted, there would be nothing left for the residual claimants of the firm. Therefore, the alienability is held by the board of directors, and any sale price inures to the firm itself, not the individual manager. Thus firms are like lumps in cake batter: they disable the very system that so effectively solves the control and rights-assignment problems in the economy at large.

Obviously, firms must also get *benefits* from suppressing alienability, or they could not survive. These benefits come from two sources: (1) the advantages of specialized risk bearing, made possible by separating the running of an enterprise from the bearing of its risks by stockholders and bondholders; and (2) the gains that come from better coordination across units of the firm that would otherwise lead to externalities in a market solution. Put simply, this last point means that, when managers can coordinate production and commerce better than arm's-length transactions in a market, firms can create value for their owners and society.

Like a compass needle swinging to the north, the CCMO analysis now points us to a key consideration: what managers must do when they disable the important functions of alienability. The answer, we assert, is that they must provide managerial substitutes for the rules of the game. In other words, they must provide systems that (1) partition decision rights among agents so as to maximize their value; (2) measure and evaluate the performance of agents with respect to those decision rights; and (3) reward and punish agents based on their performance, in ways that motivate them to move toward efficiency in their actions.

The building blocks of the theory, simple as they are, are now complete. We spend the last two modules of the course applying these very general and powerful concepts to the analysis of management and organizational problems. We apply the concepts to all kinds of for-profit and nonprofit organizations; to large and small organizations; to partnerships and corporations; and to government and military organizations (such as the Tactical Air Command). We also apply the CCMO concepts in a wide range of management actions and activities: compensation of line workers and CEOs; financial decisions on dividends, capital, and ownership structure; leveraged buyouts; conflicts with unions; downsizing; leveraged growth; total quality management programs; decisions about the use of cost centers versus profit centers; and so on.

We conclude the course by applying these concepts to the top-level governance systems (including boards of directors) of corporate organizations, limited partnerships, and venture capital organizations. In the last class session, we use the concepts to understand the broad industrial trends of the past 40 years and the conflicts they have engendered among social classes, and between the developed and underdeveloped nations of the world.

CCMO and Controversy

CCMO has been a controversial course over its history. When Michael Jensen first arrived at HBS, he proposed to teach essentially the same version of CCMO at HBS as he had taught at Rochester. That course placed heavy emphasis on theory, logical analysis, and empirical evidence. Put simply, although it used cases, CCMO was definitely not designed as a traditional HBS case course. "You can't teach theory to Harvard MBA students," several senior colleagues cautioned Jensen in no uncertain terms. "They will throw you out of the classroom."

In fact, for many of the students in CCMO, something like the opposite turned out to be true. It emerged that many second-year students (at least among those signing up for the CCMO elective) were hungry for a general framework that they could use to structure the vast store of knowledge that they had accumulated in the case-oriented first year of the program. As one student phrased it to Jensen, "They don't teach us theory in the first year; they only teach us how to use it." The students find it useful to have CCMO's explicitly articulated theory in which to store, organize, and generalize the implicit theories they learn in the first year.

So the CCMO faculty discovered to its satisfaction that HBS students are not averse to theories and frameworks *per se*. On the other hand, HBS students, like their counterparts at Rochester before them, were far from uniformly happy with the CCMO experience. In fact, many were (and are today) often shocked, depressed, and even angry, especially during the early weeks of the course.

Why does this phenomenon occur? We think it is a natural consequence of the students' beliefs about the world running into both the theory and the evidence embodied in the material. The first third of the course, as explained above, is devoted almost entirely to the foundations of the theory. This material leads naturally to a "point of view," in the sense that the answers to important questions become not simply a matter of opinion, but hypotheses subject to logical and evidentiary rules. Students find that the logic and evidence of CCMO can be used, and *are* used, to challenge some of their deeply felt beliefs—beliefs that were often unconscious and therefore unexamined.

Many are made quite uncomfortable by this process. To cite a basic example: many students, before exposure to the logic of CCMO, would express some sympathy with the basic notion of rent control. Rent control is intended to guarantee affordable housing to people of limited means, and, many students would agree, it is therefore a "good" thing. But the logic of price theory and CCMO, when applied to the issue of rent control, forces students to recognize that rent control actually *destroys* the housing stock. In the long run, therefore, it creates exactly the opposite outcome (it reduces rather than increases the availability of housing) to what its proponents originally intended. This logic is comparably powerful when applied to managerial issues.

This gap between hoped-for outcomes and reality is disconcerting, especially when it is applied to concepts, such as the "stakeholder model," that are dear to the hearts of many of our students. Application of the analysis to the standard stakeholder model yields the conclusion that the weakness of the stakeholder model is the absence of an overall objective function that implicitly or explicitly specifies the tradeoffs from expenditures on various items, including each of the firm's stakeholders. This in turn implies that the top managers of such organizations cannot be held accountable for their decisions because, without an overall objective function, there is no way to measure and evaluate their performance. Managers are then left free to exercise their own preferences and prejudices in the allocation of the firm's resources, with no logical way to hold them accountable for their stewardship.

Gradually, however, most students become accustomed to the CCMO logical framework. They become more skilled at applying rigorous analysis to their own belief systems and more comfortable at having other people challenge them in these ways. At one point, Jensen's daughter reported back to him after spending an evening with friends who were in the course. "Dad," she told him, "the scoop on CCMO is that it is three weeks of weird, and then it gets OK." It is interesting to note that many students ascribe this transition—from discomfort to comfort—to a change in the course, rather than a change in their own thought processes and behaviors.

Some have asserted that the CCMO course deviates significantly from the time-honored teaching traditions of the Harvard Business School. We assert the opposite. It *is* true that only about a third of the course materials we use are traditional HBS cases. (Another third consists of classic academic journal articles, and the remaining third is drawn from business publications, such as *Fortune, Business Week*, and the *Wall Street Journal*.) It is also true that some of our course material is theoretical (but not mathematical) in nature and that, although the course draws heavily on the principles of economics, it is innovative in its articulation of the underlying principles of organization theory and analysis. As a result, it has had to develop a language of its own to make more precise the analysis of many formerly vague organizational issues. One inescapable result is that many people, students and faculty colleagues alike, find our language "foreign" and difficult to understand.

And though our teaching methods are definitely Socratic, they vary widely in their reliance on didactic exchange. Often, especially early in the course, the faculty member plays a stronger role than is traditional at the School. This is not heresy for heresy's sake, of course; we have found it necessary to use a variety of techniques in order to efficiently communicate and lay the theoretical groundwork for later use in case discussions. It is an inefficient use of time to do otherwise.

Our teaching approach *is* very tough-minded, especially during what Jensen's daughter dubbed the "three weeks of weird." But we are convinced that tough-mindedness is one of the proudest traditions of the School. It was brilliantly captured by the legendary marketing professor Malcolm P. McNair in a 1953 speech to participants in the Advanced Management Program:

> *William James, a great teacher of philosophy at Harvard during the early years of this century, made the useful distinction between people who are "tough-minded" and people who are "tender-minded." These terms have nothing to do with levels of ethical conduct; the "toughness" referred to is toughness of the intellectual apparatus, toughness of the spirit, not toughness of the heart. Essentially it is the attitude and the qualities and the training that enable one to seize on facts and make those facts a basis for intelligent, courageous action. The toughminded have a zest for tackling hard problems. They dare to grapple with the unfamiliar and wrest useful truth from stubborn new facts. They are not dismayed by change, for they know that change at an accelerated tempo is the pattern of living, the only pattern on which successful action can be based. Above all, the toughminded do not wall*

themselves in with comfortable illusions. They do not rely on the easy precepts of tradition or on mere conformity to regulations. They know that the answers are not in the book.[6]

Finally, we infer that the CCMO course is controversial because of the effect it has on both our students' views of the world and how they behave in the HBS community. As they begin to understand the CCMO theory (albeit imperfectly), they apply it to their environment—including all the other classrooms in which they are spending time thinking and learning. And as the old saying goes, "To a child with a new hammer, the whole world looks like a nail." To judge by the comments we receive from our faculty colleagues, on-the-fly references to CCMO are not always helpful additions to discussions in other courses.

On occasion, HBS students have perceived inconsistencies or even conflict between what they are learning in CCMO and what they are learning in another course. That is what happened in the fall of 1988, for example, when the students in both CCMO and the required Business Policy course requested that the two faculty groups meet with them in Burden Auditorium to discuss what the students perceived to be inconsistent theories being taught in CCMO and Business Policy. The specific topic in question was a BP case, Johnsonville Sausage. The issue appeared to be whether workers would behave as perfect agents, in the sense that trust between managers and workers would itself bring about an increase in performance. In fact, the issues of apparent disagreement turned on the existence of powerful but indirect controls that played a major role in the productivity increases at Johnsonville.

From today's vantage point, almost a decade later, we would not venture to assert that either faculty group "won" the "debate." (In fact, no one on the HBS faculty would knowingly engage in a shoot-out.) And although the differential emphasis in the two courses led the students to believe that there was an inconsistency, the two faculty groups in fact ended up agreeing on the analysis of the case.

Furthermore, we felt then, and still feel today, that the students are always the winners in this kind of situation. Most, if not all, courses at HBS attempt to provide students with powerful tools of analysis. It is only appropriate that students practice using those tools and call us to account when two different sets of tools appear to be taking them in contradictory directions.

Organizations and Markets: The Research Program

From its inception, the CCMO course has been intimately associated with and driven by the research interests of the Organizations and Markets (O&M) interest group.

As mentioned earlier, the overarching objective of this group is to develop a rigorous and useful theory of organizations in a market economy; although we readily recognize (as do our students) that, with only slight adjustments in the viewpoint, the material applies with equal force to families, governmental entities, and other nonmarket organizations. We focus on organizations that arise in noncoercive situations, where voluntary exchange is the principal mechanism of action. And because we focus on voluntary action and exchange, we need to understand how individuals make choices. This central theme unites many parts of our research agenda. Each interest group member has his or her own research program, and one of the challenges facing the group is to integrate our findings into a broader theory than any single person could develop alone. The research agendas of the members of the group encompass four distinct areas:

1. *The nature of human behavior.* We are working to formulate a model of human behavior that incorporates work in economics, psychology, and neuroscience to understand both rational (calculated) and non-rational (uncalculated) human behavior.

2. *Performance measurement, compensation, and career systems.* Our work on performance measurement, compensation, and career systems attempts to build an analytical framework and a body of evidence that enable managers to design and implement systems to fully utilize human resources employed in their organizations.

3. *Task structure, organizational boundaries, and technology.* We are attempting to understand how interlocking systems of organizations and markets can best exploit the inherent structures of different production technologies.

4. *Governance, corporate finance, and organizational performance.* The objective of our research in this area is to provide a theory that enables one to understand how a firm's governance structure and its relationships with its employees, managers, and suppliers of capital and materials influence strategy, internal decision making, and the creation and distribution of value. Each of these four research programs is described in detail below.

The Nature of Human Behavior

Human beings are the elementary unit of action in all organizational systems. Thus a theory of how humans behave—as individuals and in groups—is the necessary foundation for any theory of organizations (as well as any theory of markets).

Over the past 200 years, the "harder" social sciences, such as economics and political science, have made enormous progress in explaining and predicting human behavior on the basis of a *rational* view of human nature. By "a rational view" we mean a model of human behavior that assumes that humans generally make decisions designed to increase their welfare on an expected-value basis. In our lexicon, "welfare" includes not just consumption goods, but the full range of things that human beings value and make sacrifices for, including human life, family, community, and society, as well as ideals like wisdom and beauty.

More recently, psychology and sociology have made progress with models that are *nonrational.* In other words, people are assumed to make decisions that are not consistent with their own consciously held values. We have become very interested in this research. The generally acknowledged shortcomings of corporate internal control systems—combined with our own study of human beings, our discussions with other colleagues in the behavioral area, and our associations with leading neuroscientists—all lead us to the conclusion that human beings regularly make decisions that, on an expected-value basis, make themselves worse off. We have begun to study in detail why people often act in ways that they do not intend, why they don't learn from their mistakes, why they engage in self-deceptions, why they become stuck and resist learning, and why they cling to inaccurate theories. Although this behavior is nonrational, it is not random; it is highly systematic and predictable.[7] Chris Argyris has been especially helpful in aiding our research into counterproductive human behavior, and Richard Hackman has helped us understand some of its implications for group behavior.

Actions inconsistent with one's own values are triggered by unconscious circuits in the brain. Recent research has shown that these unconscious circuits lie in the emotional brain (the limbic system) and respond independently of (and often faster than) the conscious circuits of the brain. Thus one set of questions we are working on involves understanding the complexity of human behavior at a deeper level, and in a way that integrates these different aspects of humanity. Jensen, Argyris, and Hackman are particularly interested in these questions and have spent the last five years engaged with the Mind, Brain, Behavior Interfaculty Initiative at Harvard University. (Jensen has served on the MBB Steering Committee since its inception and informally co-directed the effort with Gerald Fischbach, chairman of the Division of Neuroscience, Harvard Medical School, in the first two years of the effort.) This initiative brings modern neuroscience faculty together with faculty from other Harvard schools and departments (including medicine, public health, humanities and history, social sciences, business, law, public policy and administration, and religion) to engage in constructive dialogue and research on important issues at all levels of analysis—including the brain and its circuitry, individual behavior, and the behavior of organizations and society. The objective is to better understand key managerial, organizational, and social policy issues and solutions.

As a result of these efforts, Jensen has formulated a model that incorporates both rational and nonrational (that is, calculated and uncalculated) actions into a dualistic theory of human behavior. According to this model, human beings can be said to exist in one of two regimes at any moment in time—either the rational or the nonrational regime. Dualistic behavior is rooted in the biological and neurological structure of the brain—in particular, in the brain circuitry associated with the fight-or-flight response that is so critical for survival. Because of this basic brain circuitry, no human being is free of this dualistic behavior. Fear of pain (both physical and emotional) is the trigger that causes individuals to switch from calculating to noncalculating behavior; that is, from the rational to the nonrational regime. We characterize the rational mode by the Resourceful, Evaluative, Maximizing Model (REMM) and the nonrational mode by the Pain Avoidance Model (PAM) of human behavior. Clearly, this dichotomy is an oversimplified and incomplete characterization of human behavior, and much work remains to flesh out our understanding of these issues. However, we have found that the dualistic approach provides a powerful engine of analysis that enriches the discussions and analysis of organizational and management problems, both in our research and in CCMO.

Compensation, Career Systems, and Performance Measurement

Our work on compensation, career systems, and performance measurement is contributing to an analytical framework and a body of evidence that enables managers to design and implement systems to fully use the human resources in their organizations. Research in this area has roots at HBS that go back to Roethlisberger and Mayo in Organizational Behavior and Anthony and Vancil in Control, as well as work by economists outside HBS.[8] Our work builds on these traditions, attempting to discover how the design of performance measurement, compensation, and career systems can be used to increase the potential for creativity, productivity, and efficiency in an organization.

Although the study of incentives is well established, there is still a significant gap between what standard theory prescribes and what organizations do. We are trying to understand, empirically as well as conceptually, how firms attract and retain employees, motivate them to be as productive as possible, and match their skills and talents with jobs in the organization. These four goals—attraction, retention, motivation, and matching—are at the center of the human resource management problem. An organization's ability to attract and retain employees with the appropriate capabilities is a function of its compensation system, its employee recruiting and screening systems, and the methods it uses to match employees with particular jobs. We have thus far spent more of our effort understanding the effects of the compensation system and an organization's career system (the policies and criteria for promotions and job matching) than on recruiting and screening systems. These latter issues, however, are clearly on our research horizons.

RESEARCH ON COMPENSATION. Our analysis of compensation systems goes beyond the study of "who gets paid what," and recognizes the importance of nonmonetary rewards and punishments, both because these dimensions are important in determining total compensation and because they can often be managed to provide powerful incentives to individuals in organizations. We emphasize the three basic components of compensation in our analysis: (1) the expected level of total compensation (including all sources of utility to the employee, particularly the nonpecuniary components); (2) the composition of the compensation package (its breakdown into money, fringe benefits, quality of the working environment, and so on); and (3) the functional form of compensation (the way compensation varies with various measures of performance, time, or status).

We would also like to understand how the process of distributing rewards and punishments—such things as timing and visibility—can change the efficacy of these organizational levers. We pay careful attention to the determinants of the expected level and composition of total compensation, and to its functional form—that is, the relation between changes in compensation and changes in variables such as performance, seniority, and hierarchical position.

An early paper by Baker, Jensen, and Murphy, written when Murphy was a Marvin Bower Fellow at HBS, lays out much of the research agenda for the group in this area. It has had a substantial impact on the outside profession as well.[9] In this general line of research, the work by Jensen and Murphy on the relation between CEO compensation and corporate performance has also established a small cottage industry of follow-on research into such issues. The basic finding of this work is that, contrary to claims of CEOs, compensation consultants, and compensation committees, most CEOs are paid in a way that is largely independent of firm performance.[10]

RESEARCH ON MOTIVATION AND MATCHING. The problems of motivation and matching are central research questions for the group. Motivation in an organization is significantly influenced by how the organization measures and rewards performance. Indeed, how managerial performance is measured is often more important than the form the rewards take.

George Baker's work in this area explores the characteristics of performance measures, both ideal and actual, to uncover the organizational consequences of their use. His theoretical research (with Robert Gibbons and Kevin J. Murphy) suggests, as a general proposition, that effective measurement systems must use subjective judgment and qualitative assessments in combination with objective measures. Purely objective performance measurement systems, though easy to administer, rarely solve the problems of motivating employees and coordinating their efforts. In effect, it is managers' ability to assess performance subjectively (including the quality of partial or incomplete output), in combination with a firm's reputation for honoring implicit agreements, that gives firms a competitive advantage over markets in performing tasks that do not have well-defined, easily measured direct outputs.[11]

In its barest form, the results of this work indicate that, if the performance of any individual or group in the firm can be perfectly measured by an objective standard, then there is little reason for that individual or group to be a member of the firm; arm's-length market transactions can then solve the coordination problem better than managers. Most managers would prefer to have a purely objective performance measurement system to avoid the conflicts and problems associated with subjective systems. But the Baker, Gibbons, and Murphy research indicates that such subjective performance measurement is one of the primary functions of managers and one of their major advantages over markets as a coordination mechanism.

The process of matching employees' skills and talents with the demands of the organization is one of the most complex problems in human resource management. This matching is accomplished through a wide array of systems and processes, including hiring and firing rules, career counseling and planning, formal and informal training, talent assessment, job evaluations, succession planning, and promotion contests. Organizations invariably attempt to design human resource systems so that individuals will be matched with the jobs for which they are best suited over their careers. However, such systems inevitably create incentives for individuals to thwart optimal matching or sacrifice current efficiency in order to promote personal career advancement. (Bureaucratic empire building is one example of the organization's goal of efficiency conflicting with the individual's interest in personal advancement.)

The demands of the incentive system (to reward individuals for performance in their past positions) often come into conflict with the demands of matching (to place individuals in positions in which they will be most productive in the future). The pernicious effects of this conflict in organizations where rewards come primarily in the form of promotions is one of the factors that lies behind the waste of resources that motivated the 1980s takeover wave in the United States.[12]

When promotions are the primary mode of reward for managers—as they were in the post–World War II high-growth era—growth is required to feed promotions into the managerial reward system. But in the post-oil-crisis period that began in 1979, the economy turned from a state of sustained high growth to a state of substantial excess capacity, with an attendant necessity to restructure and downsize. The managerial hunger for growth—needed to feed the promotion-based reward systems prevalent in corporate America—did not subside, however, and this led to ill-advised investment and acquisitions, which in turn led to massive waste. Jensen estimates that this waste amounted to hundreds of billions of dollars and argues that it was one of the major forces behind the hostile takeovers and leveraged buyouts of the 1970s and 1980s.

We are only beginning to understand the full implications of the conflict between incentives and matching in organizations, and the effect that recent trends in organizational redesign (reengineering and downsizing, delayering, and outsourcing) will have on the productivity and efficiency of these systems.

Task Structure, Organizational Boundaries, and Technology

One of the challenges facing organization theory is to understand how interlocking systems of organizations and markets can best exploit various productive technologies. Different technologies require different allocations of decision rights, different performance measures, and different compensation systems. For example, sequential, linear technologies (steel making or automobile assembly) give rise to different types of organizations and markets than do circular, interconnected processes (designing a new product) or modular processes (managing a stock portfolio). But there is little theory to indicate what types of organizations and what types of market transactions will best support any particular technology. This gap creates a large intellectual opportunity.

Inquiry into the relationship between the structure of organizations and markets on the one hand and technologies on the other has deep roots at the Harvard Business School. Alfred Chandler laid the foundation for this work with his analysis of the origins and evolution of the modern multidivisional corporation. The work by Carliss Baldwin and Kim Clark on these issues builds on his contributions, and also on the contributions of many who have followed in his footsteps: Robert Hayes, Joseph Bower, and William Abernathy at HBS; and Oliver Williamson, Richard Nelson, Sidney Winter, Paul Milgrom, John Roberts, and many others outside HBS. In addition, insights on task structure (the relationship of tasks to one another and of tasks to design) can be gleaned from the writings of designers working within various technical domains, including electronics, computer architecture, software, biology, mechanical design, and manufacturing systems design.

At present, the relationship of task structure to organizational design and technology is the least-developed subfield in Organizations and Markets. Carliss Baldwin's work with Kim Clark on modular systems in the computer industry is a step toward building our knowledge in this area. It promises to lay the foundation for solving what we have come to call the "chunking" problem. This problem involves finding well-developed criteria for deciding on the relative advantages of alternative ways of grouping assets, people, and materials in an organization for the purpose of defining units of the firm—whether they be departments, functions, groups, or divisions. Should such assets and people be grouped by product, by geography, by technology, by function, and if so, for what purposes are they to be grouped (that is, performance measurement, the allocation of decision rights, or compensation)?

These are questions to which we do not yet have answers, nor does anyone else. In our work and teaching, we (like others) currently take the definition of the unit as given and proceed to do the organizational analysis from there. What we know now from the work of Baldwin and Clark is that optimal groupings will depend on fundamental characteristics of the physical technology, on strategic investments in the design of products and production processes, and on the management technology that is available for coordinating the actions of people and units of the firm.

Governance, Corporate Finance, and Organizational Performance

Understanding corporate governance and financing is essential to the development of a useful theory of organizations. The objective of our research in this area is to understand how a firm's relationship with its suppliers of capital influences strategy, internal decision making, and the creation and distribution of value. Because the data required to understand these governance issues are qualitative and detailed, the field-based clinical methodologies developed at HBS are playing a critical role in the development of new knowledge in the field. For example, Baker and Wruck's study of the O. M. Scott leveraged buyout from ITT pointed the way for a new genre of published research in the Clinical Paper Section of the *Journal of Financial Economics*, edited by Richard Ruback of HBS.[13]

In the language of our theory, corporate governance sets the organizational rules of the game for top managers. More specifically, governance comprises the systems and structures by which a corporation interacts with outside holders of ownership claims. These systems include the processes adopted and developed by boards of directors to exercise the rights delegated to them by these outside claimants. Most often, rights exercised by the board include the rights to hire, fire, and set the compensation of top managers and the right to ratify decisions pivotal to the firm's future (such as major investment projects, financing decisions, or acquisitions). A firm's financial and ownership structure determines how claim holders delegate rights to boards of directors and, in turn, how directors exercise those rights. Governance has a critical impact on organizations because it strongly influences how top managers choose to set the rules of the game for everyone else.

Our work in this area follows that of HBS researchers in closely related areas, including Gordon Donaldson, Paul Lawrence, Jay Lorsch, Richard Walton, and Richard Ruback. In addition, a great deal of research on governance, financial structure, and ownership structure has been conducted in financial economics. Our work is also tied to this outside community of scholars, including Harry and Linda DeAngelo, Joe Grundfest, Steve Kaplan, John Pound, Mark Roe, Andrei Shleifer, and Rob Vishny.

Overall, financial researchers believe that firms' governance and financing choices affect firm value. However, because finance researchers view organizations from the outside, they do not carry their analysis through to look at strategy, operating decisions, or investment choices. Conversely, researchers in organizational behavior study the internal aspects of governance, such as strategy formulation, the role of headquarters, and the allocation of power within the hierarchy, but do not consider the role of capital structure nor the implications of such choices for firm value. Because these two bodies of research focus on different aspects of the phenomenon, bringing these two views together can lead to powerful new insights. For example, Jensen's work on the agency costs of free cash flow[14] has motivated researchers and practitioners to consider the importance of the conflicts between managers and shareholders over the payout of free cash flow in a very different way. Rather than thinking about managers as setting payout policies to maximize firm value, these interested parties now think about managers' reluctance to devote resources to payouts, and their preferences to spend the money instead on internal growth or acquisitions, even when that choice means destroying value.

Also in this vein, Karen Wruck's research seeks to understand how governance and decisions coupled with internal management systems can lead to shareholder value creation at all levels of an organization—all the way down to the shop floor.[15] Her work focuses on organizations in transition or crisis owing to changes in ownership and control, product market failures, failing relationships with organized labor, or regulatory changes. Her papers on the voluntary recapitalization of Sealed Air Corporation under CEO Dermot Dunphy and the KKR leveraged buyout acquisition of Safeway show how new forms of governance and financing can be used to solve the severe internal organizational problems of firms undergoing major threats in their product markets.[16] These papers, combining the best field work traditions of HBS and the principles of modern finance and organization theory, have set the standard for a new type of empirical research in our field. This approach is slowly being disseminated to and imitated by researchers at other universities across the country.

Another area of active research is the relationship between corporate governance and strategy. Malcolm Salter is particularly interested in this topic. He has been studying organizations, like GM, where the existing set of contracts (particularly contracts with unionized labor) are no longer sustainable. Research in this area analyzes bargaining and negotiations between various constituencies as they try to influence corporate strategy in ways that serve their separate and common interests. While some of these negotiations take place in corporate boardrooms, many are carried out in other settings. In fact, a flow of understandings, agreements, and "implicit contracts" are constantly being negotiated and renegotiated throughout the management hierarchy. Many such negotiations take place through the budgeting and resource allocation processes—the most tangible expression of strategic decisions. Other negotiations involve formal bargains with suppliers of capital, government officials, organized labor, and other external constituencies over critical decisions including acquisitions and divestitures, restructurings, outsourcing, plant closings, trade legislation, and environmental protection. Salter's research on the competitive advantages and disadvantages of vertical ownership of auto components suppliers, and the political dynamics surrounding changes in vertical ownership structures, characterizes some of the work in this area.

Looking Forward

From the beginning, the goal of the O&M group at the Harvard Business School has been to enrich our understanding of how organizations and markets work, and to improve the performance of all organizations. Although much has been done since John McArthur helped launch us on this journey at HBS more than a dozen years ago, we are well aware that we are still at an early stage along our road.

We look forward to major innovation and expansion of our educational programs. The development and staffing of new elective courses is an ongoing project, as is the development of doctoral courses and executive programs that extend the reach of the O&M material from young scholars to senior executives. In addition, we will continue to reach out to scholars and practitioners through seminars, conferences, and links with consultants and managers throughout the world.

We mentioned at the outset of this paper that, as early as the 1970s at Rochester, Jensen and Meckling realized that their students were often too quick to apply concepts that they had only half-mastered. The same thing has happened at HBS, sometimes to the distress of our colleagues in other courses. There are two sides to this phenomenon. On the upside, it is clear that CCMO changes students' behavior. On the downside, it is clear that, in one short semester, students can't learn enough to become masters in the exercise of their new skills. When people are learning a new skill—a tennis serve, a language, a way of thinking about organizations and markets—they are by definition *incompetent*. With continued practice and learning, they can become competent, even masterful, but there is no shortcut on this path. The time to mastery can be shortened, but mastery cannot be instantly created. It is clear that in 30 sessions over 13 weeks, the CCMO faculty can't bring about full mastery or even full competence with the analytical tools we provide. We *can* present materials more selectively, however, and give students more time to practice what they're learning. But inevitably they must achieve competence and then mastery through application of this material in their lives, including other courses here at HBS.

We also have to take responsibility for making our conceptual points more clearly and persuasively among our academic colleagues, both at HBS and elsewhere. We have to clarify why we do the things we do in the particular way we do them, so that purposeful, even provocative, pedagogical devices don't obscure our underlying ideas. For example, since first tackling the issue of the effects of emotions on decisions, we have emphasized in the course that we wish to stimulate and endow our students with both intellectual rigor and emotional rigor. By the latter we mean, first, that they must understand and be accountable for the role that their own emotions play in their lives and decisions. Second, they must understand and be accountable for the role that emotions of others will play in their reactions to business decisions and policies that they as managers will make and implement.

As an example of the confrontation of emotions with reason, we use the case of Michael Milken and Drexel. Who, we ask our students, has created more value in this century than Milken? Was Milken overcompensated for that effort (even after legal penalties) by his contract with Drexel, which gave him a $50,000 salary and approximately one-third of the profits of the division he founded at Drexel? Overcompensated according to what standard? How was Drexel's decision to break its contract with Milken different from (for example) a machine shop's refusing to honor its contract with its workers when they "make too much money"? What will each of these actions do to break the level of trust in an organization (Drexel and the machine shop) which is so necessary to its functioning? Was it Drexel's failure to take the reactions of other constituencies (such as the public's envy of Milken and others like him) into account that caused the destruction of that firm and the resulting loss of 10,000 jobs? Where was the "morality" in that sequence of management decisions, or in the attacks on Milken by competitors, government officials, and others whose wealth and power were threatened by the profound changes in capital markets that he induced?

Collectively, these questions are but one example of a kind of teaching that is designed to be counterintuitive, challenging, and rigor-provoking.

In addition, we must clarify—for the benefit of our students and academic colleagues—a point that we often assume to be obvious: that CCMO is nothing more nor less than a set of propositions about how the world behaves. It is (or tries to be) an integrated worldview that starts at a very basic level by describing the characteristics of the individuals who are actors, agents, managers, employees, and customers in a system, as well as the nature of information (its inherent scarcity and the differential cost of moving it between people); and builds a structure—describing organizations, markets, and social systems—that we think is a logical consequence.

We are honestly surprised, therefore, when we hear CCMO described as being "ideological" in some way. All of the propositions of CCMO are testable and potentially refutable. Indeed, some former underpinnings have been thrown out the window (such as the assumption that people are totally rational), and more no doubt will be in the future. At the beginning of each run of CCMO, we warn our students that, like all teachers, we will definitely be teaching them some erroneous concepts and that, if we could only figure out today which ones were wrong, we wouldn't teach them. We also tell them that it is their obligation to continually confront the learning they obtain from CCMO with the data they gather from the world as they live their personal and professional lives. And then we set about to give them a structure through which they become competent to test, challenge, and revise CCMO's and their own "theory of the world." By definition, this is a never-ending process.

But highest on our agenda, looking forward, is to continue to create and deliver ideas—in the form of books, articles, cases, and courses—that deepen and broaden the understanding of organizational problems and their solutions. We are now at work on several major books that bring together much of the intellectual effort of the past 20 years. In addition, field research, empirical analysis, and conceptual development currently under way are pushing back the frontiers of knowledge in our field and will continue to do so for years to come. In fact, if one thing characterizes both the history and the anticipated future of O&M, it is our excitement with *ideas*. We look forward to expanding the influence of the Organizations and Markets unit (and, by extension, HBS) on scholarship and practice for many years.

CHAPTER SEVEN

Service Profit Chain Research

GARY W. LOVEMAN AND JAMES L. HESKETT

I N THE WINTER OF 1988–1989, *John McArthur invited Len Schlesinger—a former colleague who was then a senior manager with a chain of French bakery cafés—to return to HBS to help teach the required General Management course. This raised the prospect for Jim Heskett and Earl Sasser of a possible longer-term relationship with Schlesinger, involving the teaching of Service*

Management, an increasingly popular second-year MBA elective. Schlesinger was excited about the prospect of working closely with Heskett and Sasser. On the other hand, he saw little logic in joining any of the School's existing areas, including Production and Operations Management, where service management scholars like Heskett and Sasser were then housed. The POM folks were bright people, working on interesting enough things, Schlesinger acknowledged. They just weren't working on things that interested him.

The recruitment process stalled. Finally, with mounting frustration, Heskett and Sasser approached Dean McArthur. It was foolish to miss the opportunity to bring

Schlesinger back, they argued, simply because no one could figure out where he should "sit" in the larger organization. Why not give them responsibility for Schlesinger's care and feeding?

McArthur immediately agreed to this proposal. Thus emboldened, Heskett and Sasser pressed on. As long as we're going to go that far, they asked, why not create a new interest group—call it the "Service Management Interest Group"—and collect a number of affiliated researchers and teachers under this new umbrella? It might not rival mighty Finance or other long-established groups, but it would be a start and might someday amount to something.

Interest groups were one of McArthur's favorite tools for innovation. In short order, the Service Management group was created, Schlesinger was rehired, and a new stream of innovation began to flow.

THE "SERVICE PROFIT CHAIN" is a concept designed to provide coherence to a set of hypotheses researched over the past 25 years by a number of scholars, at Harvard and elsewhere, and also to make the work of these scholars relevant and accessible to managers. At Harvard, much of this work has been carried out by the Service Management Unit (SMU, successor to the Service Management Interest Group), which coined the service profit chain (SPC) terminology.[1]

The service profit chain applies particularly, but not exclusively, to service-providing organizations. Put very simply, the SPC hypothesizes that profit and growth are directly linked to a number of key criteria. These include, for example, customer loyalty and satisfaction, and the amount of value provided to customers (measured in terms of the value of results provided, as well as process quality, in relation to the cost of a service to the customer and ease of access to the service). They also comprise the productivity and quality of the work of employees, employee loyalty, employee satisfaction, and the capability with which employees are able to deliver a service. ("Capability" is measured in terms of job latitude; care in selection, training, technical and other support; and results-related compensation). These relationships are diagrammed in Figure 7.1.

FIGURE 7.1   *Service Profit Chain*

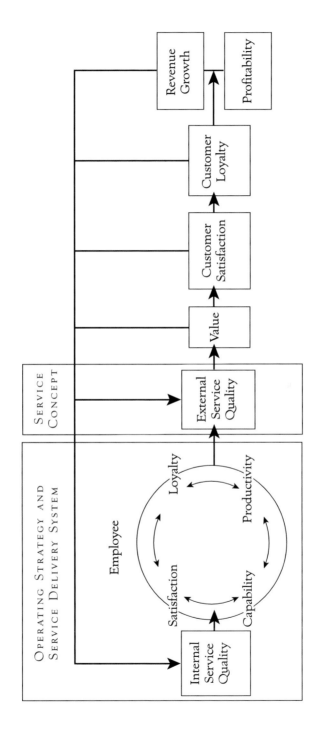

The SPC concept has fueled an effort by the SMU to conduct not only comprehensive studies of the chain's entire set of relationships, but also focused inquiries into specific links along the chain. The SPC has provided the group with a broad context for its investigations. It has also provided us with a common language and a focus for our research, course development, and teaching over the past ten years.

The cohesion derived from this set of ideas by the members of the SMU, in their various intellectual endeavors, was noticed very early in its development by then-dean John McArthur. As illustrated anecdotally above, McArthur intervened at key intervals to ensure that the SPC work would receive the support it needed. This timely support, which took many forms, allowed the group to concentrate on ideas rather than on administrative concerns.

In this chapter, the authors retrace the evolution of the service profit chain concept—an idea that argues powerfully against some long-standing ideas about management. Although this evolution may seem overly HBS-specific to the outside reader, we think it provides a necessary background for understanding the material in the second half of this chapter. That material consists of preliminary findings from a field-based and data-derived test of the key hypotheses of the SPC at PNC, a Pittsburgh-based bank holding company. These exciting results underscore the power of the SPC concept.

The Service Profit Chain Idea Trail

Ideas underlying the service profit chain can be traced back at least to the work of Bennis (1970), Lawler (1973), and Blau (1974). The ideas they set forth dealt with the organization of work and its impact on quality, productivity, and employee satisfaction. Sasser and Arbeit (1976) developed these ideas further, suggesting that success in delivering results to customers was a primary contributor to employee satisfaction, and also helped a service business attract outstanding "frontline" employees. An early empirical study by Parkington and Schneider (1979) (replicated and enhanced by Schneider and Bowen [1985a,b], Johnson and Seymour [1985], and others) not only confirmed hypotheses set forth earlier, but also extended the set of relationships to those linking employee satisfaction with customer perceptions of the quality of the service received.

An influential set of papers edited by Czepiel, Soloman, and Surprenant (1985) further documented the links between employee satisfaction and customer satisfaction. Through these and other focused studies, the stage was being set for a more comprehensive effort, aimed at identifying the broader possibilities of what would become the service profit chain.

Heskett (1986) identified several of these, but it wasn't until Heskett, Sasser, and Hart (1990) described a comprehensive "self-reinforcing service cycle" that the full potential of the SPC began to take shape. Schlesinger and Heskett (1991) then gave the chain its name and set forth what would become its basic elements, finally described in terms that the SMU currently employs in Heskett, Jones, Loveman, Sasser, and Schlesinger (1994) and Heskett, Sasser, and Schlesinger (1997).

This, then, is the bare-bones, bullet-point genealogy of the SPC. But such a summary fails to convey how several distinct streams of work were brought together to produce a whole that is greater than the sum of its parts. *Synergy* is an overworked word, but productive intellectual collaboration is a rare phenomenon. So let's look one level deeper, both to better understand the evolution of the field and to trace the complementary contributions of key individuals.

Perhaps the first of these streams to carve its own distinct channel was Earl Sasser's interest in various facets of customer satisfaction and loyalty, and the impact that these might have on an organization's profitability. A sense of intellectual context is extremely important here. The reader will recall that research in the 1970s and 1980s had suggested that market share was most prominently related to profitability. This conclusion grew in large part out of analyses from the Profit Impact of Market Share (PIMS) project, begun in the mid-1970s and originally based largely on business-unit-level data from General Electric (see Buzzell and Gale 1987). PIMS and similar analyses were highly influential. They helped fuel enthusiasm for the round of mergers and acquisitions that took place during the ensuing decade, as many firms sought to follow GE's lead and become the largest or second-largest player in their businesses.

It was against this tide that Sasser and a few others with a primary interest in the service sector were swimming. Sasser's own work culminated in a study conducted with Frederick Reichheld, a former student. This frequently cited work strongly suggested that *customer loyalty*, rather than market share, was the primary determinant of profitability in the diverse sample of service firms whose data they studied (1990). Further investigation of these ideas, resulting in the identification of reasons why loyalty is not always fully reflected in surveys of customer satisfaction levels, provided the basis for a widely read book by Reichheld (1996).

Meanwhile, on a track parallel to Sasser's work, Heskett (1986) was using a number of case studies to develop what he termed the "strategic service vision." Among other things, this conceptual framework hypothesized that what customers really bought was *results*—not products or services per se—and that results could be measured either in economic terms or in the degree to which process quality (that is, the way services were delivered) exceeded customer expectations. This became the basis for a "value equation" at the heart of the service profit chain, in which value was defined as the ratio of *results delivered to customers* plus the *process quality* with which the results were delivered, relative to *price* plus *customer costs* incurred to obtain the results.

Heskett defined the primary purpose of an organization's "operating strategy" as enhancing results for customers in relation to the costs of achieving those results. Logically, this called for the exploration of organizational structure, control, job design, incentives, and operational decision making as tools for leveraging results over costs. This, in turn, suggested important linkages between operating practices and human resources management techniques on the one hand, and the value equation on the other.

While this research was going on, many of these human resources techniques were being tested in practice by Len Schlesinger, who had left the Harvard Business School faculty to serve for several years as executive vice president of Au Bon Pain, a large chain of French bakery cafés. In his executive capacity, Schlesinger hypothesized that he and his competitors were unwittingly creating what he termed a "cycle of failure" for their managers, front-line employees, and businesses. As a group, Schlesinger felt, they were paying little attention to issues of employee selection, training, support, and job design. Minimum-wage pay scales were causing high rates of employee turnover, which in turn were creating undocumented (but presumably large) costs.

Schlesinger set out to test these ideas at Au Bon Pain through the invention of what he termed a "Partner/Manager Program." The new program gave store managers who achieved core quality objectives a great deal of latitude in running their business and also provided significant performance-based incentives that linked store managers' compensation to the success of their store. Managers were free to establish their own compensation schemes for front-line employees, including schemes incorporating aspects of their own incentive plan. Encouraged by the preliminary results of his experiments, Schlesinger continued to explore his ideas upon returning to the Harvard Business School's faculty (with Dean McArthur's encouragement) in 1990. The experiments and their results were documented in a series of papers and articles published by Schlesinger and Heskett (1991a,b,c,d).

To summarize, Sasser's concentration on customer-related elements, Heskett's focus on elements of the value equation, and Schlesinger's testing of employee-related elements of what would become the service profit chain were all occurring concurrently and more or less independently. Also going on independently in this same period was a series of ground-breaking investigations by Robert Kaplan and David Norton (1992, 1993, 1996). These studies, later referred to collectively as the "Balanced Scorecard" inquiries, reached one conclusion that was of particular interest to Sasser, Heskett, Schlesinger, and their colleagues. Kaplan and Norton argued forcefully that measurement systems should provide both historical data of past performance and indicators of future performance. Among the *pro forma* measures of performance cited by Kaplan and Norton were customer and employee satisfaction, which seemed to validate some of the emerging hypotheses of the Service Management Unit (SMU).

The formal development of the comprehensive chain of relationships that would become known as the SPC required formal support. It required, in particular, that its three principal researchers—Sasser, Heskett, and Schlesinger—be able to work intensively together and in close proximity at the School. This, in turn, required another round of interventions on the part of Dean McArthur.

Spreading the Word

The process of generating a good idea is often inseparable from the processes of testing and disseminating that idea. When a good idea (even in a preliminary form) circulates, it tends to serve as a magnet for other powerful ideas—and also for the people who have generated them. It seems worthwhile, therefore, to recount how the ideas of SPC found their way into the intellectual marketplace and to trace the positive impacts of that dissemination.

Many ideas generated at the Harvard Business School receive their first real-world scrutiny in the context of executive education, where practitioners react to the presentation of those ideas in high-level functional or general management courses. The SMU offered its first SPC-oriented executive development program, entitled "Achieving Breakthrough Service," in 1991. It was well received, and the SMU subsequently was encouraged by Dean McArthur and the leaders of the School's publishing venture to package the program on videotape for use by business organizations with on-site facilitation. To do this, the SMU had to enlist the extensive cooperation of several service organizations that were known to be practicing various aspects of what would soon be known as "service profit chain management." Among the firms that soon found themselves hosting camera crews—and otherwise participating in a unique and challenging intellectual process—were Banc One, Citibank, Intuit, ServiceMaster, Southwest Airlines, Taco Bell, and Xerox.

The tangible results of this large-scale effort included three coordinated series of videotapes, designed for top-level and front-line managers. These video series, along with their accompanying published materials, were notable for their ambitious scope. Scaled-down versions of this material were used as the basis for the School's first teleconference, viewed by more than 7,000 alumni and associates early in 1993. They also have served as illustrative teaching tools for the Achieving Breakthrough Service executive development programs now offered annually on the Harvard Business School campus, as well as in cooperation with other schools around the world, including IPADE (Mexico), Western Ontario University (Canada), and IESE (Spain). All told, more than 10,000 copies of the various videotapes on service created by the SMU were sold by the School between 1991 and 1997.

The dissemination effort just described is relevant to this essay because it influenced the direction of research into the service profit chain. Organizations participating in the production of the video materials formed the nucleus of a small group of firms that agreed to cooperate closely with the SMU over time in the collection and analysis of field data pertaining to relationships in the SPC. Thus a research partnership with rich and important data sources was established, and that partnership still flourishes today.

Also, as has been suggested above, success begets success. Between 1992 and 1994, the SMU grew in response both to the popularity of its MBA and executive courses and to the appeal of its research agenda. The SMU faculty increased both in numbers and in quality. The three key recruits were Gary Loveman, an MIT labor economist; Tom Jones, former CEO of a leading market database management firm; and Jeffrey Rayport, a member of the marketing faculty who was studying electronic distribution channels. Again, all three additions of faculty to the SMU were facilitated by Dean McArthur, who supported the unit's efforts to add colleagues with common interests, both inside and outside the School.

As a result, the stage was set for a far more comprehensive exploration of various aspects of the SPC. The story of that exploration—which is still under way today—follows.

Setting the Stage: The Doctoral Seminar

The SPC, as first presented in Heskett, Jones, Loveman, Sasser, and Schlesinger (1994), was a theory based on extensive case study evidence and a growing body of complementary scholarly research, published by authors within and outside the SMU. Members of the SMU, together with collaborators outside the group, continued to research many of the key relationships embodied in the SPC. Jones and Sasser (1995) published a detailed examination of the relationship between customer satisfaction and customer loyalty. Alan Grant and Schlesinger (1995) examined mechanisms for improving the value of customer relationships over time. These studies were preceded by John Kotter's and Heskett's examination of corporate culture and performance (1992), which offered extensive evidence in support of the importance of adaptable (rather than merely strong) cultures in achieving high, sustained performance levels. This suggested the importance of "listening posts" as a staple of successful management in the service profit chain.

But despite this kind of impressive empirical work on portions of the SPC, the full range of hypothesized relationships comprised by the SPC had not been subjected to systematic large-sample analysis. This deficit arose primarily because of the daunting data gathering and interpretation that would be required in order to link employees, customer outcomes, and financial performance at the same level of analysis. In an effort to understand what other academics and practitioners had learned from looking at components of the SPC—some of which, under other names, had been active research areas for many years—the SMU organized a doctoral seminar in the spring of 1994, entitled "Researching the Service Profit Chain." The seminar included students from several disciplines, faculty colleagues, and invited guests, all of whom focused on research relating to the hypotheses put forth by the SPC.

Although the existing empirical work was limited, most of it proved to be quite supportive of the underlying logic of the SPC. Rust and Zahorik (1991), Fornell (1992), Anderson and Sullivan (1993), and Boulding, Staelin, Kalra, and Zeithaml (1992) all reported evidence of a significant positive relationship between customer satisfaction and loyalty. Rust and Zahorik (1992) found positive correlations between customer satisfaction and profitability in health care. Anderson, Fornell, and Lehmann (1993) used data from the Swedish Customer Satisfaction Barometer to show positive relationships between customer satisfaction and return on investment in a cross-section of firms from many industries.[2] Finally, Bernhardt, Donthu, and Kennett (1994) found that, although customer satisfaction does not correlate significantly with sales or profitability in a national chain of fast food restaurants, *changes* in customer satisfaction are associated with *changes* in unit-level financial performance.

There is also mounting evidence of a positive relationship between employee satisfaction and customer satisfaction. Schlesinger and Zornitsky (1991) found such a result using data from a personal lines life insurance company, and Schneider, Parkington, and Buxton (1980) and Schneider and Bowen (1985a) showed that increased employee satisfaction initiatives enhance customer satisfaction in banking. Further support is found in Tornow and Wiley (1991) and Wiley (1991).

A central tenet of the SPC is that cost-reduction schemes, efforts to increase market share, and quality initiatives can have an ambiguous effect on profitability if they do not simultaneously address customer loyalty. Indeed, as seen in the empirical work of Anderson, Fornell, and Lehmann (1993), market share may be *negatively* correlated with profitability, as firms spend more money at the margin to attract customers who find the firm's approach to service less compelling. In many instances, excessive attention to building market share results in inadequate attention to the retention of existing customers. One contemporary example is the blizzard of efforts to promote cellular and long distance telephony in the United States, which often slight the existing customer in favor of the new account.

Results from the doctoral seminar suggested that existing evidence generally supported those relationships in the SPC, where data were available to perform the analysis. Again, however, no one had yet assembled and analyzed a database of sufficient depth and breadth to examine all (or even most) of the empirical relationships in the SPC. Indeed, few organizations collected the data necessary to conduct such analysis. In many companies where employee and customer satisfaction were measured, there were no mechanisms for correlating those two kinds of satisfaction with profitability. Furthermore, customer loyalty, where measured at all, was typically proxied by "intent to repurchase," rather than by actual purchase behavior. So, although the seminar taught the SMU's members a great deal about what had been done to examine components of the SPC, it also presented the SMU with the inescapable challenge of conducting a more comprehensive and rigorous empirical analysis of the SPC concept.

Following the doctoral seminar, therefore, SMU members began looking for organizations that could give us the data necessary to enhance existing empirical tests of the SPC. The search eventually led us to the PNC Bank, which had assembled high-quality data to help it use the SPC to better understand and manage its businesses. The PNC data offered an exciting opportunity not only to test SPC relationships, but also to develop concrete managerial interventions on the basis of the empirical relationships.

In the following section, we focus on the data that have been gathered and analyzed to date, and present some of the results that have been generated in the early stages of our analysis. And finally, we speculate about the managerial implications that seem to be associated with these results.

PNC

The PNC Bank is a Pittsburgh-based bank holding company with over $72 billion in assets. It serves more than 3 million customer households through 900 branches and 2,000 ATMs, in markets ranging from Massachusetts to Indiana to Florida. Following a series of acquisitions, PNC Bank management established customer satisfaction as its "singular goal," and in 1994 began extensive employee and customer surveys to better understand how each group viewed two things: (1) the company generally, and (2) the branch in which they worked or banked specifically. Under the auspices of this program, all PNC employees are surveyed annually, and 44,000 customers complete two-page surveys that are distributed by mail throughout the year.[3]

The data are organized at the branch level of analysis. Of the roughly 900 branches in the PNC network, data are available from 560 branches. (The remaining 340 or so branches either were recently acquired through purchase of another institution or are too small to generate meaningful branch averages.) Branch employee satisfaction results and branch customer satisfaction responses are averaged separately to create a cross-section of branch-level data. These data are combined with branch-level measures of financial performance, customer retention, and the extent to which customers purchase multiple services from the bank. On the employee side, the data also include employee tenure by job category, and also some very interesting measures of employee satisfaction with internal services they receive from various departments within the bank. In short, PNC's complement of employee, customer, and financial variables provides a unique database, useful for examining the entire SPC.

Our research, conducted in partnership with the Marketing Research group at PNC Bank, has generated two approaches to evaluating the SPC using cross-sections of branch data. The first approach groups branches into three categories according to overall customer satisfaction performance and then compares performance on several SPC criteria across the three categories. This approach has substantial appeal for internal presentation to and interpretation by management, and has been put to productive use within PNC Bank using data from 1994. The second approach is to use regressions to test the relationships hypothesized by the SPC. This latter approach is clearly more rigorous, but it has fewer intuitive interpretations. We begin by presenting the "managerial" review of the SPC at PNC Bank and follow with an overview of the cross-sectional regression results using 1995 data.

A Managerial Review

For ease of internal presentation to management, PNC data have been categorized into three cohorts of branches, based on the percentage by branch of customer satisfaction surveys that registered a 6 or 7 (high) response on overall satisfaction (Figure 7.2). The groups are defined by changes in the slope of the distribution across branches and are labeled as Tier I, II, and III. The SPC suggests that this ordinal grouping of branches in terms of customer satisfaction should be correlated with the same ordinal performance ranking on several employee, customer, and financial outcome measures. Specifically, employee satisfaction and job tenure should fall from Tier I through Tier III, as should customer retention, services purchased per household, and financial performance. The data support all of these SPC implications.

Our analysis suggests that customer satisfaction and employee satisfaction are highly positively correlated. Detailed analysis of the factors that discriminate between "highly satisfied" customers (6 or 7 on a 7-point scale) and "somewhat satisfied" customers (4 or 5 on a 7-point scale) shows that 5 of the top 6 factors are directly related to front-line service by employees.

Top Six Discriminators	High Impact by Employee
Employees you know and trust	Yes
Making it easy to do business	Yes
Providing financial advice you trust	Yes
Making financial issues easy to understand	Yes
Products and services that meet your needs	No
Handling inquiries or problems	Yes

FIGURE 7.2   *Distribution of Branches by Satisfaction with Primary Branch*

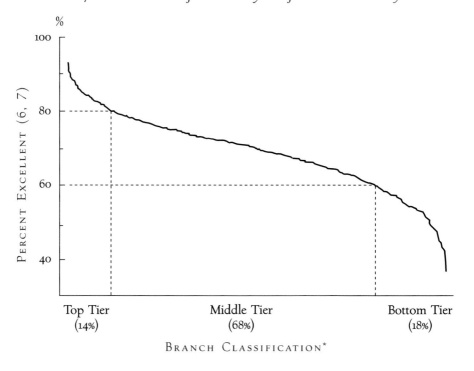

Source: 1994 Consumer Tracking. Reprinted by permission of PNC Bank.

*Includes the 498 branches with 40 or more responses during 1994.

There is also clear evidence of a positive relationship between employee tenure and customer satisfaction. Branches with high levels of satisfaction among customers tend to have more experienced managers, in terms of both time in the job and length of service with the bank.

CUSTOMER SATISFACTION	BRANCH MANAGER MONTHS IN JOB	BRANCH MANAGER MONTHS EMPLOYED
Tier 1	76.7	209.3
Tier 2	68.3	184.0
Tier 3	59.3	164.5

The effect of customer satisfaction on customer loyalty can be seen by examining three different dimensions of loyalty. Figure 7.3 shows that annual retention rates (as measured by annual retention of the household checking account) are a positive function of satisfaction. Figures 7.4 and 7.5 demonstrate that more satisfied customers also have a higher average number of relationships (such as credit cards, mortgages, car loans, checking account, CDs) and keep a larger portion of their financial assets with PNC Bank.

The financial consequences of these differences in customer behavior are significant. They result from the combination of differences in retention rates, the number of services per household (cross-sell), and percentage of assets held by the bank. PNC records revenue at the branch level and creates a rough estimate of operating profit by adjusting for staffing levels in the branch. Figure 7.6 shows that revenue per household, adjusted by the number of full-time-equivalent employees (as a proxy for operating cost), is much higher at Tier I branches than at Tier II and III branches. A simple manipulation of these figures suggests that if middle-tier branches could achieve the customer satisfaction levels achieved by the top tier, they would enjoy a 20 percent increase in branch revenue, which would represent an incremental return of $170 million for the bank.

Regression Results

Although our analysis of the PNC data is ongoing, some early regression results are available to test SPC relationships. Though much work

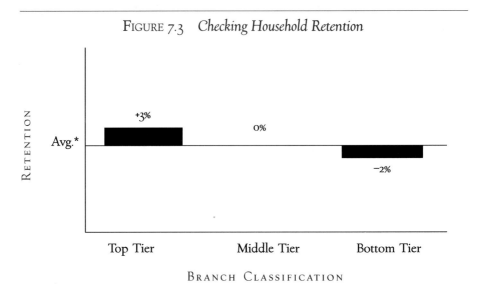

FIGURE 7.3   *Checking Household Retention*

Reprinted by permission of PNC Bank.

*Bank Average.

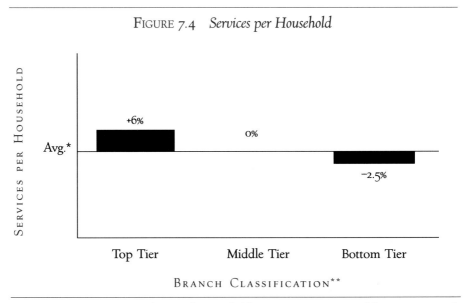

FIGURE 7.4   *Services per Household*

Source: 1994 Consumer Tracking and Household Data System. Reprinted by permission of PNC Bank.

*Bank Average.

**Includes the 498 branches with 40 or more responses during 1994.

remains to be done with these valuable data, the results so far are supportive of the SPC in at least five ways. They are as follows:

1. Customer loyalty and customer satisfaction are positively correlated with profitability.

Because it is difficult to estimate operating and overhead costs at the branch level, PNC adjusts revenue by staffing levels in the branch to generate a rough estimate of operating earnings. This estimate is further divided by the number of households served, to generate a measure of operating earnings per household. Table 7.1 shows regression results for equations linking measures of customer loyalty and satisfaction to the operating earnings per household measure.

These estimates provide mixed support for the SPC. Checking and deposit retention are unrelated to operating profits, but cross-sell (services per household) and the percentage of highly satisfied customers are posi-

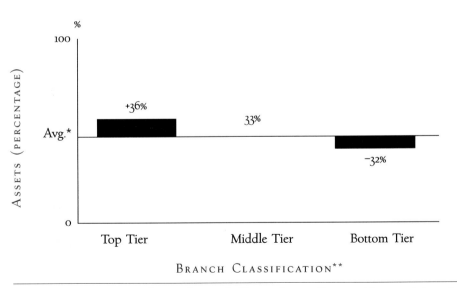

FIGURE 7.5 *Percentage of Assets with PNC Bank*

Source: 1994 Consumer Tracking and Household Data System. Reprinted by permission of PNC Bank.

*Bank average.

**Includes the 498 branches with 40 or more responses during 1994.

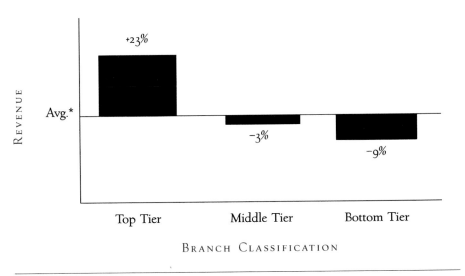

FIGURE 7.6 *Annual Revenue/FTE per Household*

Source: Reprinted by permission of PNC Bank.
*Bank average.

TABLE 7.1 *Impact of Customer Satisfaction and Loyalty on Financial Performance,* PNC Bank*

INDEPENDENT VARIABLES	DEPENDENT VARIABLES
	Operating Profit per Household
Checking Retention	−4.61
	(−0.2)
Deposit Retention	−3.05
	(−0.1)
Cross-Sell	8.84
	(1.8)
Branch Satisfaction % 6 or 7	0.40
	(4.2)

*Coefficient estimates with *t*-statistics shown in parentheses. Results derived from 1995 cross-section of 557 PNC branches. A *t*-statistic of 1.96 indicates significance at the 5 percent level.

tively correlated with operating profits at marginally statistically significant levels. Our early work with the data suggests that there is considerable cross-sectional variance in branch financial performance that is not
well captured by the gross estimate of operating profits used in this analysis. Variance in the demographic profiles of customers across branches is
also clearly important. A better test of the relationship between customer
behavior and profitability will come with the analysis of longitudinal
data, which will allow tests for the impact of *changes* in loyalty and satisfaction on *changes* in financial performance at the branch level.

2. Customer satisfaction is positively correlated with customer loyalty.

Customers are asked to report their satisfaction with their branch and
with PNC Bank overall. Table 7.2 shows that increases in the percentage of 6 and 7 (high) responses, or decreases in the percentage of 1 and
2 responses (low), are associated with increases in measures of customer
loyalty, such as retention and cross-sell.

TABLE 7.2   *Impact of Customer Satisfaction on Loyalty,* PNC Bank*

INDEPENDENT VARIABLES	DEPENDENT VARIABLES		
	Deposit Retention	*Check Retention*	*Services per Household*
Branch Satisfaction % 1 or 2	−.001 (−1.6)	−.002 (−1.6)	−.017 (−3.4)
Branch Satisfaction % 6 or 7	.001 (5.1)	.001 (2.5)	.002 (2.7)
PNC Satisfaction % 1 or 2	−.002 (−3.0)	−.002 (−1.7)	−.018 (−3.9)
PNC Satisfaction % 6 or 7	.001 (5.0)	.001 (2.9)	.002 (2.6)

*Coefficient estimates with *t*-statistics shown in parentheses. Results derived from 1995
cross-section of 557 PNC branches. A *t*-statistic of 1.96 indicates significance at the 5
percent level.

215

Low levels of satisfaction, whether with the branch or with PNC overall, are negatively related to retention and the number of services per household, and the reverse is true for high levels of satisfaction. The majority of the results are statistically significant.

3. Employee satisfaction is positively correlated with customer satisfaction.

The PNC *employee* survey asks respondents to rate their satisfaction with a wide range of issues, from ability to serve customers to authority to make decisions and the provision of sufficient training and development to improve as an individual. Table 7.3 shows a small but representative sample of the results from regressions linking employee satisfaction with customer satisfaction at the branch.

As predicted by SPC tenets, increased levels of satisfaction among branch employees—as manifested by agreements with statements such as "I am committed to PNC's growth and success"—are positively and statistically significantly related to both increased percentages of highly satisfied customers and decreased percentages of highly dissatisfied customers.

TABLE 7.3   *Impact of Employee Satisfaction on Customer Satisfaction,**
PNC Bank

INDEPENDENT VARIABLES	DEPENDENT VARIABLES	
	Branch Customer Satisfaction % 1 or 2	Branch Customer Satisfaction % 6 or 7
I am committed to PNC's growth and success	-0.33 (-3.3)	1.59 (3.3)
I am happy with the team-work in my department	-0.20 (-2.8)	0.85 (2.5)

*Coefficient estimates with *t*-statistics shown in parentheses. Results derived from 1995 cross-section of 557 PNC branches. A *t*-statistic of 1.96 indicates significance at the 5 percent level.

4. Employee satisfaction is positively correlated with employee tenure.

Human resource records have been merged with employee satisfaction data and are available by job category at the branch level. Table 7.4 displays regression results linking three representative measures of employee satisfaction with teller and "platform staff" (such as account representatives and customer service representatives) job tenure, measured in months. Months of service with the bank are used as the tenure measure for managers, because they are more likely to have been promoted through other jobs.

Here the statistical results are mixed. Having resources to satisfy customers and being empowered to make decisions are significantly positively correlated with tenure for teller and platform employees. Training and rewards for job performance are not correlated with tenure for these two jobs. Managers, on the other hand, show a less significant

TABLE 7.4 *Impact of Employee Satisfaction on Employee Tenure,* PNC Bank*

INDEPENDENT VARIABLES	DEPENDENT VARIABLES		
	Teller Job Tenure	Platform Staff Job Tenure	Manager Tenure at Bank
I have resources to satisfy customers	2.32 (2.1)	2.87 (2.6)	−1.10 (−0.2)
I have training that helps me grow and advance	−0.23 (−0.2)	−0.56 (−0.4)	12.9 (1.9)
I have authority to make decisions about how to do my job	3.22 (2.7)	2.80 (2.4)	−6.94 (−1.0)
I am rewarded for good job performance	0.24 (0.2)	0.54 (0.4)	−10.4 (−1.4)

*Coefficient estimates with *t*-statistics shown in parentheses. Results derived from 1995 cross-section of 557 PNC branches. A *t*-statistic of 1.96 indicates significance at the 5 percent level.

impact of their reported satisfaction levels on their tenure with the bank. Training is positively correlated and nearly significant at the 5 percent level, but the other satisfaction factors are largely unrelated to tenure. The employee survey includes at least 50 different detailed questions, and our analysis of these data is still in the early stages. It nonetheless appears likely that the relationship between satisfaction and tenure is different for teller and platform employees than for managers, even though there are positive correlations for all three groups.

5. Internal service quality is positively correlated with employee satisfaction.

In addition to its broad coverage of variables at the branch level, one of the most useful aspects of the PNC data is the availability of employee ratings of the services they receive from the three internal departments (or "Service Partner Groups" in PNC terminology) on which they rely most. The SPC predicts that internal service quality is positively correlated with employee satisfaction, but most data sets do not include the variables necessary to test this proposition. Table 7.5 shows that four key measures of employee satisfaction are significantly positively correlated with employee ratings of the quality of service they receive from their three most important internal service providers. Thus, being well served enhances an employee's level of satisfaction—and this, as has been shown, leads to rewarding results for both the customers and the bank.

In summary, the PNC Bank data support nearly all of the relationships posited by the SPC. Internal and external service value measurements remain to be included in the analysis, and the regression modeling sketched out above has only just begun. Much more careful multivariate approaches clearly are required, and the development of these more rigorous approaches is ongoing. Of course, none of the results speaks to causality; indeed, cross-sectional data rarely are informative on causal linkages. But as longitudinal data are collected at PNC Bank, we will be able to consider the more powerful test of relationships between changes in SPC components—for example, the effect of increased customer satisfaction on customer loyalty and profitability at the branch level.

The SPC: Summarizing a Work in Progress

We have presented results from an intensive study of field data sets as a way of illustrating the manner in which the Service Management Unit has been systematically investigating various aspects of the Service Profit Chain construct, and we have suggested some of the managerial implications of our preliminary findings.

The work to date has required a certain amount of elapsed time to develop close working relationships with the organizations that have supplied the data. In some cases, we have helped these organizations to restructure the way performance is measured, in order both to assist in improving management decisions and to gain access to information about variables in the SPC.

Nearly all of our cooperating organizations have been willing to share their information for both educational and research purposes. Just as importantly, several have provided case materials and other resources for our course offerings. In a sense, this small circle of companies has formed what we have come to regard as a research "club," providing a

TABLE 7.5   *Impact of Internal Service Quality on Employee Satisfaction,** *PNC Bank*

INDEPENDENT VARIABLES	DEPENDENT VARIABLES			
	I have resources to satisfy customers	I have information I need to do my job	I know how to satisfy customers	I am committed to PNC's growth and success
Overall quality of service received from three most important internal service providers	.337 (2.6)	.539 (3.9)	.495 (2.4)	.409 (2.1)

*Coefficient estimates with *t*-statistics shown in parentheses. Results derived from 1995 cross-section of 557 PNC branches. A *t*-statistic of 1.96 indicates significance at the 5 percent level.

wealth of information that constantly challenges our hypotheses. In more than one case, managements have adopted the SPC concepts as an important element of strategy, the starting point of policy formulation, a key determinant of performance measures, or even a rationale for organizing themselves in certain ways. A more rigorous test of this work lies ahead, as we collect longitudinal data that will allow us to identify causes and effects among elements of the chain. But even today, the preponderance of evidence suggests that our cooperating institutions have found our work valuable—and we take this to be a very important "real-world" validation of our preliminary findings.

Finally, we should underscore the fact that, entirely aside from the talents of those involved in this work, there are very few places in the world where it could be carried out. Work such as we've been doing requires a foundation of trust—between the School and cooperating business organizations—which can only be built up over years and decades. It requires great institutional patience (on the part of both the School and our corporate "partners") and a willingness to support research that may have only a long-term payoff. It requires patrons and colleagues who are willing to place bets, sometimes on little more than faith, that the outcomes will be useful and important. And finally, it requires a strong dose of leadership at the top of the institution, as evidenced by the kinds of carefully timed and calibrated interventions that make all things possible in a complex educational setting. We in the Service Management Unit have indeed been fortunate to have all of these advantages.

CHAPTER EIGHT

Ethics, Organizations, and Business Schools

LYNN SHARP PAINE AND THOMAS R. PIPER

O N MARCH 30, 1987, at a formal dinner sponsored by the HBS Club of New York City, John McArthur announced the creation of a $30 million endowment in support of ethics and leadership at the Harvard Business School. Much of the funding was to come from John S. R. Shad, a prominent investment banker and member of the MBA Class of 1949, who—as chairman of the Securities and Exchange Commission from 1981 to 1987—had been shocked by the misdeeds of graduates of leading professional schools, including HBS.

By 1987, discussions between Shad and McArthur had been going on for six years, and Shad's decision to create the endowment was not a complete surprise (although the ultimate size of the gift astounded McArthur). But the timetable for the announcement was accelerated when Shad's wife was diagnosed with terminal cancer. The Shad family and McArthur agreed that he should ask the New York club's permission to speak at its already-scheduled dinner.

Reaction to the speech was positive, but McArthur was apprehensive. For under-standable reasons, he had broken one of his own cardinal rules for managing his faculty: Never announce an initiative before that proposed scheme has a faculty champion. Now, arriving at HBS the day after the announcement, he was on the hook to find such a champion. As he made his way in from the parking lot to his office, he was stopped by a long-time colleague and friend on the faculty, Professor Thomas Piper. "I don't know if you have someone in mind for this already, John," said Piper, "but I'd love to be involved in it."

Business schools have historically regarded teaching and research on ethics as marginal, if not irrelevant, to their educational mission. But by the late 1980s, a variety of factors converged to create a fertile environment for intensified efforts to address business ethics. As is so often the case, practice led theory. The Watergate-era excesses led to dramatic new legislative actions, such as the Foreign Corrupt Practices Act in 1977, and U.S. businesses spent the ensuing half-decade trying to build new internal structures to conform to this and other new laws and regulations. Critics from the left and the right challenged corporations for their inattention to the environment, to consumers, to employees, and to shareholders.

At the same time, of course, American companies were struggling to remain competitive in the international economy. They often found themselves competing against non-U.S. companies that played by very different rules. Then came the merger-and-takeover binge of the 1980s, lubricated by a surging junk-bond market. The SEC, under the leadership of John S. R. Shad, launched high-profile actions against insider traders. Public regard for business seemed to reach a new low. Tom Wolfe's *Bonfire of the Vanities* came to epitomize and define what the 1980s were about. It was not a definition in which many Americans took pride or comfort.

The decline in trust had been gradual, but nonetheless dramatic. In 1968 Yankelovich and Skelly reported that 70 percent of the American people believed that business tried to strike a balance between profits and the public interest; but only 15 percent believed so 10 years later.[1]

Naturally enough, Americans began to ask how things had gotten to this state, and one of the first places they asked this question was at the nation's leading business schools. Had these schools—which for many years had claimed, proudly and accurately, to be turning out the nation's business elite—somehow devalued issues of purpose, principle, and responsibility? Had they focused too narrowly on tools and techniques, and abandoned the high ground of leadership, vision, imagination, values, and courage?

The Harvard Business School was only one of many schools to respond to these tough questions—and the answer was an explicit "yes." With support and prodding from the School's dean, John McArthur, and several prominent alumni (most notably, John Shad), the School introduced a broad program of mutually reinforcing initiatives in an effort to integrate issues of leadership and ethics into the MBA experience. These included a required nine-session module in the first year, discussion of ethical issues in other first-year courses, a selection of electives in the second year, and efforts to surround the curriculum with opportunities to reflect on and discuss issues and dilemmas with moral consequences. The product of long discussion, debate, and a studied consideration of antecedent efforts, both at Harvard and elsewhere, the initiative was guided by eight underlying beliefs. During the past decade, we have tested these beliefs and have become increasingly convinced that they are valid and effective guidelines.

BELIEF 1. Ethics is several things combined: an attitude and aspiration, as well as a set of skills and knowledge. All are needed. In the absence of a philosophy of management, skills in ethical reasoning and stakeholder analysis will almost certainly remain dormant or stunted. Beliefs, in other words, are the wellsprings of action. But skills are equally important. Ethical aspirations can easily misfire, and even produce harm, in the absence of the requisite understanding, knowledge, and skills.

BELIEF 2. Throughout the course of instruction, the School should emphasize outstanding leaders, organizations, and practice. Surely it is useful to understand the pathologies of misconduct, so that students can avoid pitfalls. But it is more important to place before students compelling examples of principled business practice.

BELIEF 3. The focus of instruction should be on decision making in a real-world context—with all of its attendant complexity and ambiguity—rather than on issues of ethics or social responsibility in isolation. The real world lends immediacy and urgency. Immersion in the real world (or a reasonable approximation thereof) forces the student to recognize that ethics is rarely about angels and archvillains; it is about ordinary people facing tough decisions that have no easy answers. And practically speaking, a focus on the real world helps keep ethics in the mainstream of the faculty, as opposed to a curiosity pursued by an isolated Ethics Department.

BELIEF 4. Students should engage the issues of ethics and organizations from the very moment they begin the MBA program. This is the juncture when students stand at the boundary of the organization and are most receptive to cues from the environment. They are anxious, under competitive pressure, eager to fit in and to succeed, and concerned about the moral center of this institution to which they are committing so much of their time, energy, and money. As a result, students watch very carefully in their first days at business school to gauge exactly how important faculty members believe leadership, ethics, and corporate responsibility to be. If these topics are *not* legitimized and addressed effectively, students will conclude—rightly or wrongly—that these matters are unimportant in this new culture they are joining.

BELIEF 5. Sustained ethical discussion is essential to success. Students need regular opportunities to examine assumptions and beliefs, to challenge ideology, and to reformulate purpose. No single pedagogical approach has proven effective in placing leadership, ethics, and corporate responsibility at the center of the business school experience. This means we must teach ethics in the context of a dedicated and required course, in the context of our elective courses, and in the context of our required functional courses (for example, marketing and finance).

BELIEF 6. Faculty encouragement and development are as important as student development. The teaching of leadership, ethics, and corporate responsibility should be a concern of the faculty at large, not the domain of a few specialists. All must support the program, an many must actively participate in it. This belief reflects an educational reality: that all teachers carry an eraser. When we decide not to talk about leadership ethics and corporate responsibility, we undermine the progress that other people have made in this critical area. Our silence is heard as a statement that these issues are unimportant and unworthy of discussion.

BELIEF 7. On a consistent basis, the faculty, administration, and staff of the School must "walk the talk." The beliefs and attitudes that sustain our courses and our teaching, the conduct that is encouraged and rewarded within the community, the criteria that are applied to hiring and promotion decisions, the qualities that characterize our actions and relationships—all must be consistent with the ethics initiative. If we are going to advocate certain behavior, our own standards must provide reinforcement.

BELIEF 8. This is an extension of the previous belief: strong, visible, sustained commitment to the initiative on the part of the dean is essential to its success. The Harvard Business School, more than many institutions, is a potential victim of its own success. As students of organizations know full well, it is extremely difficult to adjust an institutional strategy when that strategy is (or seems to be) meeting challenges effectively. In such cases, leadership from the top is critical. The dean and his or her key faculty resources must sketch out a compelling picture of how the future will be better, and how the proposed changes don't jeopardize ongoing institutional strengths.

In the following pages, we provide background on the wellsprings of these beliefs and their implications for management education.

Antecedents and Attitudes

In their landmark 1959 report on management education, Robert Gordon and James Howell argued that "business education must be concerned not only with competence but also with responsibility, not only with skills but also with the attitudes of businessmen" and that "business schools have an obligation to do what they can to develop a 'sense of social responsibility' and a high standard of business ethics in their graduates."[2]

Professor Frank Pierson, in an influential report for the Carnegie Corporation in the same year, wrote of "the increasing attention being given to the social responsibilities of business enterprises." He underscored the community's expectation that business fulfill the informal as well as the formal obligations inherent in its relationships with "government, unions, suppliers, stockholders, rival firms, and the like."[3]

Unfortunately, despite these and other exhortations over subsequent decades, the intersection of leadership, ethics, and corporate responsibility has remained at best a peripheral concern at most business schools. To be sure, "shared purpose" and "values" are now almost universally recognized as critical contributors to organizational effectiveness. But a meaningful discussion of *what* purpose, and *which* values, has been sparse, muted, and mostly unproductive.

We recognize that there have been individual and institutional efforts in these areas, many of them quite courageous. The number of Business Ethics and Business and Society courses steadily increases, as do the numbers of books and conferences related to ethics and leadership. All too often, however, these activities remain remote from the traditional intellectual center of gravity of business education. As then–Harvard President Derek Bok observed in 1986:

> [F]ew influential voices from our schools of management speak out on issues of corporate responsibility or the role of free enterprise, even though many prominent executives believe that public attitudes about the corporation's place in society will have a decisive influence on the future of American business. Corporate leaders sometimes complain that academic critics have a bias against business, citing authors such as John Kenneth Galbraith, Charles Lindblom, and Robert Heil-

broner. Yet the wonder is not that critics exist, but that so few members of the leading management faculties are willing or able to contribute significantly to the debate.[4]

Through the "air time" that we devote to various topics—in and outside of the classroom—we in management education risk making serious errors of omission. We are conspicuously silent on matters of ethics and corporate responsibility, but we elaborate with skill and enthusiasm on economic and market theories. By so doing, we risk implying that shareholders are the only stakeholders of consequence. We risk suggesting to our students that corporate purpose can be fully defined in terms of shareholder wealth maximization, and that a combination of the law and market mechanisms somehow will serve as full and complete guides to conduct.

Such implications must be challenged. This is especially important when we consider the starting point of our students. The young men and women who enter the leading business schools are for the most part outstanding individuals.[5] In her research at the Harvard Business School and elsewhere, Sharon Daloz Parks found that these talented, highly motivated students have a strong sense of personal accountability—of the need to be trustworthy—in immediate face-to-face situations with colleagues and superiors.

This is a solid foundation, but it is far from a complete ethical structure. While many of our students aspire to build or lead important companies, few are fully aware of the responsibilities that go with these positions of leadership. Few completely grasp the broad impact that their decisions are likely to have. Their knowledge of the social and ethical systems in which they will be acting is understandably scant, and few understand the limitations of their own mental models and decision-making processes. Most are surprised to learn that, as business leaders, they will be responsible not only for themselves, but also for the behavior of other people in their organizations. If they are as successful as they hope to be, they will have the power to shape the culture and values of the companies they build. Yet few have pondered which particular values might contribute to personal, organizational, and social excellence. Even fewer have wrestled with difficult conflicts among important values and responsibilities.

In short, most MBA students are ill prepared for the full panoply of business leadership. In part, of course, this unpreparedness results from their relative youth. Ethical development, like cognitive development, occurs over time, with increasing maturity, knowledge, and experience. But this lack of preparation also stems in part from the success our students have already enjoyed. Most are graduates of the best undergraduate schools. After college, many were recruited and trained by prestigious commercial and financial institutions. Upon graduation from Harvard's MBA program, many will earn starting salaries that will place them in the top few percent nationwide. Our society seems to work for them.

Clearly, these young adults are privileged. Yet their very histories of success, as Parks has noted, raise troubling questions about their potential as future managers and leaders. Precisely because they have been in the flow of success, many have had less occasion than others their age to reflect on the world around them, and their place within it. Most are good at critical thinking and can apply their powerful intellects effectively to the analysis of a specific set of circumstances. But in the absence of significant adversity or cross-cultural dissonance, few have given much thought to the conditions (social, cultural, political, and economic) that are the inescapable backdrop to their success. To a surprising degree, they are captives of conventional thinking and unexamined assumptions.

Consider the cynicism that business school students tend to display for government and other large institutions. This attitude is intended to signify a sophisticated understanding of how society's institutions *really* work. (It also conveys, less intentionally, the cynical individual's sense of powerlessness in relation to such institutions.) Many have grave doubts that their own ethical frameworks can survive in the context of a large corporation. They are confident about their own personal futures; but paradoxically, few have a vision for effecting significant positive change in the organizations and communities to which they belong.

Another manifestation of the standoffish ethos of many of these young adults is their view of business as a "game." Pervasive in some segments of the business world, the game metaphor serves not only to insulate players from responsibility for the rules that govern the game, but also to locate their actions within a special circumscribed playing field, far removed from the expectations and judgments of the larger society. In other words, the game orientation insulates potential decision makers from the consequences of their actions in the real world and allows them to rationalize ethically dubious choices as simply "part of the business game."

In sum, we work with outstanding young adults, but they are often individuals who have yet to develop the gravitas—the skills, knowledge, concepts, and experience—that will enable them to engage the kinds of complex ethical questions that they will inevitably face in their business careers. Many lack any compelling purpose in their professional lives beyond the vague goal of personal success. Most secure in their past successes, fearful of appearing naive, they are quite comfortable operating "within the system." They do not expect to tackle tough issues that might call into question the design and evolution of the system itself.

The Responsibility of Management Education

Is it the responsibility of management education to address these issues? Some say no. They argue that the requisite faculty training is slim to nonexistent, that ethics is just another subject being crammed into an already overcrowded curriculum, that the values of management students are already fully formed, and that values don't lend themselves to review or revision in the classroom.

These arguments are useful in portraying the challenges, but they are unconvincing in their implications. Unless business schools help students understand, anticipate, and address the ethical *and* economic dimensions of business, they are shortchanging their students, the companies that employ them, and the societies they serve.

Business education should be an enterprise of both the intellect and the spirit. It should be an endeavor that engages one's character and values, spurs one's imagination and sense of meaning, stimulates a sense of responsibility and purpose, and elicits a desire to lead and create. Management education must be more than the transfer of skills and knowledge. It should also be a passing on, from one generation to the next, of a kind of wisdom about what is worthy of one's commitment and what is not. Faculty at professional schools have an opportunity to help students connect their capacity for high achievement to a sense of purpose. They can help their students forge a connection between self and social issues, thereby strengthening the ethical underpinnings essential for effective leadership.

The joining of career to purpose and principle provides graduates with a sense of excitement and worth in their professional lives as business leaders. Not to do so would be a tragedy and a fundamental failure of education. Theodore Roosevelt put it negatively: "To educate a [person] in mind but not in morals," he commented, "is to educate a menace to society." At Harvard, we have tried to phrase it more positively: To educate a person in mind and morals is to create a great resource for society.

A Field of Questions

The field of ethics is at once frustrating and fascinating, exhilarating and exasperating, profound and confounding. It forces us to raise many more questions than the wisest of us can answer with certainty—today, tomorrow, or in many lifetimes. For example: Can ethics be taught? What is the best way to do so? In the field of management and management education, more specific but equally challenging questions cry out to be answered: What constitutes "responsible" management? Whose definition deserves our respect?

This essay attempts to provide at least preliminary answers to these and other challenging questions. Some of our answers are personal, provisional, and even idiosyncratic. But many of the concepts we will present have been developed as part of the Harvard Business School initiative on Leadership, Ethics, and Corporate Responsibility, which was launched in 1987. They therefore reflect the contributions of numerous faculty members who have been involved in this effort, and whose efforts we gladly acknowledge.

Let us define our terms, and then perhaps broaden them. We will then consider the implications of this broader definition of ethics for management.

Broadening the Definition of Ethics

The word *ethics* has been defined in many ways. At the most general level, it is the system of values by which human beings live their lives. These values provide a sense of meaning and purpose in life and regulate our relationships with one another. An ethical framework is important at both the individual and the societal level. Without an internal moral compass, individuals can lose not just their bearings, but their very identity. Without a common ethical framework, societies cannot develop the trust and cooperation they need to flourish.

These ideas are not new, of course. The seventeenth-century philosopher Thomas Hobbes warned that, in the absence of a shared ethical framework, life was likely to be "poore, nasty, brutish, and short."[6] Hobbes's description of a world populated by hostile individuals, responsible only to themselves, is worth recalling:

> In such condition, there is no place for Industry; because the fruit thereof is uncertain; and consequently no Culture of the Earth; no Navigation, nor use of the commodities that may be imported by Sea; no commodious Building; no Instruments of moving, and removing such things as require much force; no Knowledge of the face of the Earth; no account of Time; no Arts; no Letters; no Society; and which is worst of all, continual fear and danger of violent death.[7]

Hobbes cautions us, in other words, that ethics is not a luxury, an overlay, or an afterthought, but rather an essential precondition for productive economic interactions. In our own time, the Harvard political scientist Robert Putnam has reached similar conclusions through his studies of the reasons for very different patterns of regional development within Italy. "A society that relies on generalized reciprocity," writes Putnam, "is more efficient than a distrustful society."[8]

Ethics is sometimes conceived of as a set of precepts for conduct—comprehensive, immutable, and fundamentally outside of one's self. (The Ten Commandments, graven in stone and derived from the ultimate authority, are perhaps the most obvious example.) But it may also be thought of as a *way of thinking*, especially in relation to others. This puts onto the shoulders of the individual a measure of responsibility for defining and advancing the group's needs. It obligates the individual to help reinterpret the group's ethical framework when the context changes dramatically. When all bets are off, how can the group's collective sense of responsibilities be carried forward?

Clearly, those in positions of power and authority have a compelling obligation to embrace these ways of thinking. Managers in particular must make their business decisions within a social and normative context. They must think ethically as they search for opportunities, as they identify organizational problems, and as they design and implement plans of action.

Some 20 years ago, the Nobel laureate in economics Kenneth Arrow observed that, because we "cannot mediate all our responsibilities to others through prices," this makes it "essential in the running of society that we have what might be called 'conscience,' a feeling of responsibility for the effect of one's actions on others."[9]

Ethics and Organizational Effectiveness

A sense of responsibility is no less important for the running of organizations. Like individuals and societies, organizations need clear ethical premises if they are to flourish. Most observers agree that outstanding organizational performance requires the confidence and cooperation of all the organization's constituencies. The most important of these constituencies, most would further agree, are the employees and others who do the day-to-day work of the organization. In order for companies to thrive and grow in a rapidly changing environment, employees must be willing to commit to the enterprise not only their energies, but also their ideas, their goodwill, and their loyalty. They must be prepared—even eager—to go beyond the letter of the job description or the employment contract, if their organization is to have a good chance of adapting quickly to new demands and opportunities.

But few members of organizations are willing to take risks, share ideas, and work together to solve problems unless they trust the people they work with. Seen in this light, the importance of ethics to organizations comes into sharp focus. A set of shared principles (that is, ethics) is essential to maintaining a sense of trust and engagement among employees across functional, divisional, and other organizational boundaries. As the late management consultant W. Edwards Deming once observed,

> All of the components—research and development, sales, manufacturing, etc.—are interdependent and must work together to produce products and services that accomplish the aim of the system. Trust is mandatory for optimization of a system. Without trust there cannot be cooperation between people, teams, departments, divisions. Without trust, each component will protect its own immediate interests to its own long-term detriment, and to the detriment of the entire system.[10]

In many business settings, firm-specific knowledge provides the critical competitive edge. But most employees are reluctant to invest in developing firm-specific knowledge and capabilities unless they can expect to be treated fairly in return.[11] People tend to do their best and most creative work in an environment of trust, responsibility, and high aspirations.[12] Such an environment can be built only around basic ethical principles, including candor, fairness, respect, and reliability.

An ethical orientation helps companies build their reputations and relationships with other important stakeholders.[13] Most customers want low prices, but many want much more than that. Increasing numbers of customers are interested not only in the products and services they buy, but also in the behavior of the companies that produce them.[14] Many customers look for companies that are honest, reliable, and fair, and whose products meet their expectations for quality, safety, suitability, and effectiveness. The era of *caveat emptor* is long since over, and most high-performance companies increasingly recognize that building buyer confidence is the most effective way to approach the marketplace.[15]

Similarly, other stakeholder groups have a set of concerns that often extend beyond the purely financial. High-quality suppliers are apt to favor customers that treat them fairly, pay on time, and offer opportunities for joint learning and development. (These concerns are particularly important in supply chains that are knit together by mutual investments in technology or other shared resources.) Communities, for their part, want to attract industry—but most want enterprises that are prepared to obey the law, uphold and strengthen the social fabric, and respect the natural environment.

We contend, in short, that pressure for ethical corporate behavior comes naturally from *all* of the constituencies essential to a company's success: its customers, suppliers, investors, and the general public. Unless these constituencies enjoy high levels of confidence in the company, feel they are treated fairly by it, and benefit from their involvement, they will not participate with enthusiasm in the affairs of the enterprise. They are likely to withdraw their support altogether if and when more attractive options become available.

Our argument is not that ethics always "pays," or that unethical actions always fail financially. It is obvious that fraud, broken promises, inadequate disclosures, overreaching, and abuses of power often can be perpetrated "successfully," at least in the short run. Such abuses can succeed when they go undiscovered, when their victims are powerless, or when no powerful third party is willing and able to intercede. But business strategies that hinge on unethical behavior are difficult to sustain in free-enterprise economies where information is free-flowing, business transactions are voluntary, economic power is constantly shifting, and laws are enforced. In open societies, companies involved in wrongful or socially harmful behavior always run the risk of being targeted in a variety of forums, from the press to the courtroom.

The critical question for business leaders, however, is not whether such behavior is possible or profitable. Rather, the question is: Can it serve as standard operating procedure for a company that hopes to create value for its constituencies and prosper over time? We think not. We think that, year after year, the companies that are most admired in our culture are those that create superior value—in both economic and noneconomic forms—for their diverse constituencies. According to the annual surveys conducted by business publications, the ethical stances of companies are of great importance to the American public. They are not sufficient in themselves, of course; growth, financial performance, the ability to innovate, and other measures are also critical. But given two companies with equivalent financial performance but divergent ethical standards, the company with higher ethical standards—the one that treats people fairly, contributes to employees' personal development, and respects the environment—is held in higher esteem than the one that does not. Surely this affects the customer's purchasing decision and, by extension, the companies' relative competitive positions over time.

Profits and Principles

What, then, is "responsible" management?

Throughout the twentieth century, multiple perspectives have been brought to bear on this question. Two perspectives in particular have been invoked at regular intervals: the economist's and the ethicist's. All too often, these two views have been seen as unrelated at best, or mutually exclusive at worst. The economist, as noted earlier, entrusts perhaps too much to market mechanisms, and the ethicist perhaps too little.

There is an equivalent debate among practitioners. Among those with front-line responsibility for earnings, the ethical perspective is often perceived as "nice to have," but only after more pressing real-world needs have been attended to. "First we meet payroll," says the hard-bitten realist, "then we worry about the niceties."

Based on a decade of research, teaching, and reflection about the field of leadership, ethics, and responsibility, we advocate not dichotomy, but consensus and synthesis. It is clear to us that economists and ethicists, and realists and idealists, provide perspectives that a company needs to perform successfully in today's world. We therefore need to move beyond an either-or construction of the world to a both-and construction. We need to follow the lead of those practicing managers who have seized upon ideas from both economics and ethics because they are essential in creative combinations.

We submit that the debate between economic imperatives and ethical dictates is wrongheaded. The experience of managers around the

235

world has taught us this: to favor one over the other on a selective basis is risky, and to do so systematically can be disastrous. Like fractious but affectionate siblings, ethical and economic thought need each other: they are deeply intertwined and interdependent. Ultimately, we are convinced, the best prospects for sustainable long-term profit and growth lie in the zone where ethics and economics overlap.

The importance of profitability can hardly be overestimated. It is a measure of a firm's viability and a prerequisite for access to capital. Without access to capital, companies can achieve their primary mission only with great difficulty. If they are to produce goods and services, provide jobs, innovate, take risks, and—through this sustained process—contribute to the well-being of the population at large, access to capital is imperative. Managers who fail to keep vigilant watch over profitability deserve moral praise from no one.

While strong profitability is clearly necessary, adopting a narrow focus on profits and profitability without paying explicit attention to ethics can be equally dangerous and self-defeating in the long run.

Profit is why owners risk their capital. It is the reward for bearing risk and for deferring consumption. The shareholders' expectation of return lends great discipline to the marketplace and enhances allocative efficiency. But a company's motivational system must add up to more than the priorities of its investors. If a company can be fairly described as a network of necessary and interdependent members assembled to meet a need in the marketplace, then the leader's role is to inspire and motivate those members to work toward the company's aims.[16] For understandable reasons, managers identify closely with the owners and tend to give priority to their profit objectives. But the sophisticated manager knows that neglecting the motivations of an organization's other members can undermine that organization's ability to create value and, paradoxically, to reach its full profit potential.[17]

When managers focus solely on phrases like "profit maximization" and "maximizing shareholder wealth," they are often not providing appropriate motivation to the workforce. At best, these phrases are abstract and sterile prescriptions, awaiting translation into concrete programs of action.[18] At worst, they signal to multiple constituencies that the company is now focused on the interests of a single, elite constituency: its owners. They are phrases that, in the ears of many, seem to sanction and legitimize harm to the nonowning stakeholders.

Many scholars have pointed out that language has the power—subtly, but relentlessly—to direct how the mind values, organizes, and structures the information it comes across. Because phrases like "maximizing shareholder wealth" validate only the interests of a single set of stakeholders, they necessarily numb us to the whole spectrum of *other* consequences to our actions, across the whole range of affected parties. They sometimes blind us to the rights, needs, and interests of those other parties.

Such an outcome is made more likely by the deep and peculiarly American faith in the power and purity of markets. Adam Smith was a Scot, but the most fervent acolytes of the invisible hand are Americans. Americans are philosophically inclined to believe that the well-being of the whole results automatically from the individual pursuit of pecuniary goals. We, however, contend that a focus on maximizing along only one objective function can lead to a deadened imagination and a foreshortened measure of empathy. And this, in turn, is a poor basis for strategic calculation in business.[19] How can one adequately weigh the costs and benefits of alternative actions if one remains resolutely unaware of the full impact of each alternative?

A narrow focus on economic considerations and market signals can also place a company in conflict with societal expectations, which in turn contributes to adversarialism and cynicism. What economists call "market imperfections"—such as externalities, information asymmetries, and insufficient competition—can put companies at cross-purposes with society. For example, when negative externalities are involved, companies can profit from transactions that are on the whole more harmful than beneficial, as long as they are not required to bear the full costs of the harm caused. (Should the cost of a diesel engine reflect the societal costs of the pollutants it emits? Should the cost of a fertilizer reflect the cost of counteracting algal bloom in a pond?) Similarly, when information asymmetries are present, the better informed party can profit from transactions that are less than optimal for, and may well be detrimental to, the less knowledgeable party. But such exchanges are not only sub-optimal for one of the involved parties. From the larger, societal point of view, they also lead to a misallocation of resources and a breakdown of trust.

Business, for better or worse, is our society's dominant institution. This situation creates immense opportunities, but huge responsibilities as well. Either those responsibilities will be assumed voluntarily, or they will be taken on under legal duress. The great legal historian James Willard Hurst has argued that the legitimacy of corporations in the United States has depended on their ability to satisfy both the economic and the ethical expectations of society.[20] This tradition is only reinforced by the historical tendency of Americans to blame big business for any dissatisfaction they may feel with the performance of the social system. The 1930s were only the most obvious example of this tendency. In times of social stress, there is almost always a politician to be found who is willing to play on populist, antibusiness sentiment—especially when that sentiment is partially justified. Sooner or later, people awaken to hurtful and unfair excesses, and force change on the institutions that are responsible for those excesses. When managers ignore negative social consequences of their behavior, flout the law, or otherwise violate broadly held ethical standards, they bring to the surface the public's latent inclination to blame—and punish—business.

The desire to punish, unfortunately, does not necessarily lead to wise public policy. When legislators and regulators come under intense political pressures, they are likely to act quickly, and often to misunderstand the root causes of the problems being addressed. They are also likely to pay insufficient attention to the consequences of their proposed solutions. What results is a patchwork of ad hoc measures, sometimes mutually contradictory, sometimes transparently irrelevant to the real problems at hand, and sometimes very likely to create outcomes that are worse than the precipitating circumstances. As a result, serious problems remain unaddressed, while moral energy is dissipated both in bashing and in defending business. The net outcome, in many cases, is a further erosion of the social capital on which business fundamentally depends.[21]

Ethics and Management Education

We have argued that living within a strong ethical framework is essential to a healthy organization and that trusting the marketplace—or adhering strictly to the law—is necessary, but an insufficient substitute for systematically ethical behavior. These facts, among others, lead us to assert that ethical instruction must be part of a business curriculum. That is the challenge to which the Harvard Business School initiative on Leadership, Ethics, and Corporate Responsibility has been trying to respond since 1987.

Is It Too Late?

Some observers, including some of our colleagues at Harvard, assert that it is too late to explore questions of values, ethics, and corporate purpose with students who are in their twenties or thirties. They argue that such students are fully formed, unchangeable, and constant. Ethics, they assert, is learned in early childhood—often at the proverbial mother's knee. After that, it is too late.

Emphatically, we reject this assertion. Empirical evidence demonstrating the importance of moral education for young adults has been charted by numerous researchers.[22] This work, together with insights from constructive-developmental learning theory and our own study at Harvard Business School,[23] strongly suggests that moral development can continue into adulthood. We are convinced that particularly dramatic changes can occur in young adulthood in the context of professional school education.

Indeed, there is no juncture that is more critical for shaping the norms and the vision that will guide the future manager. Students in graduate school are at a critical stage in the development of their perceptions about capitalism, organizational excellence, business practice, corporate purpose, leadership, and the appropriate resolution of ethical dilemmas in business. They need time to sort through preconceptions, internalize analytical frameworks, develop sufficient strength to acknowledge the presence of ethical dilemmas, imagine what could be, and recognize in explicit terms avoidable and unavoidable harms. They need time to develop into tough-minded individuals with the courage to act in the face of sometimes-conflicting responsibilities. And despite our crowded curriculum and sometimes frantic pace, time is one thing we can offer to our students.

The typical matriculating student in the nation's best MBA programs is particularly suited for ethical reflection. Those from privileged backgrounds may have contended with relatively few high-stakes ethical dilemmas in their lives. Even those who are ethically mature are unlikely to have wrestled with the full range of ethical challenges they will face in their careers as managers and leaders of companies. None learned about the responsibilities of corporate executives at their mother's knee. When it comes to professional responsibility, *we* are mother's knee.

The responsibilities of management educators are therefore enormous. The question we must ask is not whether, but what and how.

Questions for Management Education

Our admonition to place leadership, ethics, and corporate responsibility at the center of management education is not a call for a heavy-handed moralism or indoctrination in the classroom. Instead, it is a recommendation to ground management education in a more robust conception of the role and responsibilities of the manager. It is a call for our educational programs to be informed by a deeper sense of purpose, a broader sense of responsibility and accountability, a more active spirit, and a more encompassing set of questions, rigorously reasoned. Such questions might include:

- What are the preconditions for the effective functioning of democratic capitalism? What are the appropriate roles for markets, government, the law, and management?

- What is the corporation's purpose, and to whom is it responsible? What is the basis of its legitimacy and authority?

- What responsibilities does management have to the stakeholders who constitute the corporate community? What are the legitimate rights, interests, and expectations of each of these parties?

- Can business leaders work with other organizations and sectors of society to strengthen the social fabric while at the same time fulfilling their responsibilities to their core constituencies? If so, how?

- What are the characteristics and values of outstanding organizations and their leaders? How can managers create an organizational context to support decisions that are ethically and economically sound? How do choices of systems, structures, processes, and leadership shape the decisions and actions of the organization's members?

- What are the blind spots in our commonly used decision frameworks and management models? Do they give due attention to issues of ethics?

- How do our implicit assumptions about human nature inform and shape our decisions? To what extent do they vary—across cultures, countries, companies, and individuals?

- How should an individual decision maker assess the impact of alternative strategies, actions, or processes on the various stakeholders? How should competing claims be weighed? How can conflicting positions be understood and articulated?

- How can managers develop action plans that are competitively, organizationally, economically, and ethically sound?

These are difficult and troubling questions. They may seem only to complicate the already complex and overfilled lives of business school students, and of corporate leaders. But they must be asked and answered if we are to address the challenges that lie before us.

Unfinished Business

We are far from impartial, but we believe that the accomplishments of the Harvard Business School Initiative in Leadership, Ethics, and Corporate Responsibility during the past eight years have been significant. We believe that, collectively, we have developed both a distinctive perspective on ethics and a distinctive approach to ethics education. We now understand the requirements for successful integration of ethical issues into the mainstream of the MBA program. In the 1995–1996 school year, we introduced a second new ethics module, Society and Enterprise, into the required curriculum. In the context of this module, students explore the responsibilities of business leaders to their communities and consider the challenges and possibilities for effective community involvement. An effort is under way to strengthen the linkages between this introductory ethics module and the other required first-year courses—particularly the general management course. We are broadening our scope to include international and cross-cultural ethical issues. With our active encouragement, course heads have begun to integrate issues of ethics and corporate responsibility into every nook and cranny of the first-year curriculum, and the second-year curriculum now includes a number of successful ethics-related electives.

In the course of these and related activities, our colleagues have created valuable intellectual capital, which has been disseminated to good effect. Over the past eight years, members of the core ethics faculty have published 28 articles, 5 books, more than 100 cases, 12 classroom notes, and 42 teaching notes. They have also made more than 100 presentations outside Harvard and to Harvard alumni reunions and associations.

But it would be premature to claim victory or to assume that these accomplishments and this progress are safely institutionalized. In a sense, we have just lived through the easy time. This eight-year period has been devoted to the introduction and expansion of a challenging and exciting program. Participants have seen themselves as pioneers and, like most pioneers, have been able to point to clear signs of progress. We have ourselves been highly motivated, and we have received enthusiastic encouragement from most of our colleagues, from the School's alumni, from other educators, and from society in general.

But history suggests that sustaining such a program will be much more challenging than launching it. Educational institutions are subject to influences that can work against the perpetuation of an ethics initiative: the rapid turnover of faculty and leadership; the steady barrage of new ideas and major themes that vie for faculty attention and institutional resources; and the tendency for the hard to drive out the soft. Perhaps most challenging, over the long run, are the excessively full agendas of junior faculty. They come to us fresh from very demanding doctoral programs into which ethical issues are not likely to have been integrated. They must grapple with the School's ethical agenda at the same time they are developing strong teaching skills, devising and executing fruitful research projects, cultivating an international perspective, and figuring out the research and teaching implications of information technology. This is a daunting agenda!

As we continue along our challenging road, a number of programmatic efforts will be needed to further strengthen the larger initiative, to broaden faculty involvement and support, and to counter the tendency for attention to drift away from the familiar toward the new. Linkages between the introductory ethics module and other required courses will need further strengthening, to assure that students are exposed to the wide array of ethical issues that managers face. New opportunities for students to develop the essential competencies they will need for responsible management in tomorrow's environment will have to be invented, extended, and reinforced. And we must expand our current commitment to research and course development in this field, to keep our ideas current and vital.

Just as fundamental to the long-term success of our efforts are the experiences of our young graduates as they join and make their careers with business organizations. The mores of those organizations quickly challenge the ethical framework of the professional school. The workplace becomes the classroom, and senior managers serve as the real world's professors. Once again, the signals of the initiation phase—intended and unintended—are critical.

All of these experiences will feed back to HBS and other professional schools. We can be certain that recent MBA graduates will effectively enlighten those who are coming after them about what really matters in the corporate world. This real-world feedback will directly influence the faculty, whom we hope to engage in thoughtful discussion of leadership, ethics, and corporate responsibility. Past a certain point, in other words, our effort can't succeed as a purely "local" effort. It will have to be validated in the marketplace to have any chance of long-term health. If companies take up this challenge—if they work in partnership with schools to foster a broad approach to leadership, ethics, and corporate responsibility—then our efforts will certainly succeed. If they do not, our initiative will surely fail.

This is a challenge worthy of our deepest commitment and our finest intellectual effort.

CHAPTER NINE

Business History

THOMAS K. MCCRAW, NANCY F. KOEHN,
AND H. V. NELLES

I N THE FALL OF 1984, John McArthur sent an unusual letter to Alfred D. Chandler, Jr., the School's Isidor Straus Professor of Business History and the most influential business historian in the world. Chandler's scheduled retirement was then five years away, but he was proposing to leave early. Then at work on a complicated and demanding book, he believed that he could not also continue teaching in the MBA program and attending the numerous meetings that are part of the normal schedule of a good citizen of the School. But McArthur wrote Chandler that MBA classes and routine meetings should not be troubling him. He urged Chandler to stop worrying about teaching and to concentrate instead on his research and writing. Astonished at having received such a letter, Chandler agreed to stay on until his scheduled retirement date.

Few deans find themselves urging senior faculty members not to retire. McArthur's reasoning was that business history at the School was in the midst of exceptional intellectual growth and that Chandler's continued presence could only benefit that process.

He also wanted to underscore the overall importance of research at the School. He mentioned in his letter that Chandler was a model for the entire faculty of the dedication necessary for sustained excellence as a scholar.

To be excused from the classroom for several years to write and do research was (and is) quite uncommon at Soldiers Field. But the episode symbolized McArthur's long-term blueprint for building the Business History group into a robust asset for the School. At the end of McArthur's deanship, there were seven historians at the School: five full-time faculty members, one postdoctoral research fellow, and by-now-emeritus professor Chandler.[1]

T HE FOUNDERS of the School saw history as a big part of professional education. The first dean, Edwin Gay, was an economic historian by training, and he believed that the art of management could be refined through the analysis of both history and contemporary case studies. Wallace Donham, who succeeded Gay, and who in the 1920s apparently coined the phrase "business history," argued for the creation of a research professorship whose holder would study "specific situations as they came to business men and their communities in the past," and compare "these situations with current conditions."[2]

Both deans were enamored of an inductive pedagogy that was based on the Harvard Law School's "case method." Donham, a graduate of that school, was particularly convinced of the pedagogy's power. He and his colleagues called it the "problem method," because it concerned particular business problems. The label didn't stick, but the pedagogy did.

As for business history, the creation of the Isidor Straus Chair in the late 1920s did not make it indispensable, but did make it unavoidable. One way or another, there would always be a business historian at the School who would have to teach—something. In 1927 the first incumbent of the Straus chair, N. S. B. Gras, articulated a challenge that others have felt down through seven decades:

Teaching history to a group of professional students just a few months before they expect to enter practical affairs is an exceedingly difficult task. I am not sure I will suc-

ceed, but I do sympathize with the motive behind the experiment, that is, to give the students a cultural background for their work and a perspective to their training.[3]

One feels sympathy for Gras. But one also empathizes with the deans and other colleagues who had to deal with Gras and his successors. In many respects, history is an awkward subject to have around at an institution dedicated to providing practical problem-solving techniques to students who are relentlessly (and appropriately) future oriented. History is, after all, the burden of the past. It is the impediment to change that a school of business is training people to overcome.

Obviously, one can learn from the past. But exactly what is to be learned? The lessons of history are never unequivocal, or without asterisks. History is messy and sometimes short on theory. Worst of all, it is exasperating. It keeps reminding us that there really is nothing new under the sun. When we think we have detected such a thing, some historian pops up to chide us that our memories are too short.

Most other American business schools, for all of these reasons as well as budgetary constraints, have simply dispensed with history. This was particularly true from about the start of the twentieth century through the 1960s. Then came the 1970s, when business schools came under fire for their overly short-term, technical, and blinkered approach to issues. (This was the inevitable reaction to some of the excesses of the 1960s, when business schools struggled to respond to the Ford and Carnegie Foundation reports that criticized the schools' lack of rigor and quantitative competence.) Now, critics were arguing that narrowly defined vocational training was insufficient. Suddenly the value of an MBA lay in its cultivation of leadership, communication, and integrative problem-solving skills, which in turn depended on a broad, multidisciplinary kind of training.

The Harvard Business School was well prepared for this challenge. One of its responses in the 1970s was the invention and refinement of a multidisciplinary course called Business, Government, and the International Economy (BGIE). BGIE became a required part of the MBA curriculum, and some of Harvard's business historians played a role in its evolution.

The roots of the BGIE effort first took hold a few years before John McArthur became dean. At that time, a small group of professors in what was then the General Management Area inaugurated an unusual course organized around the idea of national economic strategy.[4] The group was led by Bruce Scott, who had been co-author with McArthur of a book on "indicative" industrial planning by the government of France.[5]

Scott and his colleagues prepared a series of complex cases on France, Japan, Britain, and other countries. These "country" cases, which traced the evolution of the macroeconomic, political, and cultural environments of business, were something new in management education. They were informed by notions of corporate strategy, which were adapted to the study of entire countries. The authors of these cases accomplished a successful fusion of strategy-related ideas derived from a number of scholars, many of them from HBS.[6] Most importantly, the country cases were comparative, across time within each country and across numerous countries: France compared with Britain, Japan with Germany, Brazil with Mexico, and so on. Through some noteworthy innovations in teaching, the group made these new materials work well in the classroom.

The whole BGIE effort was well ahead of its time. It was begun in the middle and late 1970s, in advance of the emphasis on the international economy that is evident today at other schools. The word *globalization* had barely been coined, much less become a buzzword of business scholarship and journalism. In large measure because BGIE was such a pioneering effort, it became an established and often an honored element of the required curriculum in the School's programs.

The business historians were involved in the BGIE enterprise from the start. During the McArthur years, there was always at least one historian teaching and writing cases for BGIE. The average number was two; the maximum, three. For 9 of the 15 years of John's deanship, the BGIE course head was an historian (Thomas McCraw, for 4 years; Richard Vietor, for 5). All of the School's historians have taught the course, and the five historians on the active faculty today are members of a larger group called the BGIE Unit. This 17-person unit is a cross-disciplinary group composed of economists, historians, political scientists, and scholars whose doctoral degrees are in business administration. Members of the group are united by their interest in such topics as economic growth and development, business-government relations, and business history.

Cross-disciplinary groups are rare in academic life, and successful ones are rarer still. Most prevailing trends within universities work against their formation and survival. These include the balkanization of disciplines and the reluctance of members of one field to listen to those of another; specialization within disciplines and the focusing of inquiry on ever-narrower topics; the dominance since the 1960s of economics over the other social sciences; and what seems to be an academywide aversion to cross-national comparisons. Our group at Harvard has had what in retrospect can only be called remarkable success in going against these academic trends.

There was another important factor contributing to the success of business history in this period, as well as in earlier decades. The case method—the School's organizing pedagogy—is an historical approach to the study of business. Many cases are stories gleaned from actual business experience, and these kinds of true stories are, by definition, little histories.

The curriculum is not primarily about the past, of course, but about the present and the future, and a heavy dose of theory is embedded in the design of every successful course. But even the best types of theory derive largely from observation. Scientists, physicians, and many others—lawyers, explorers, police officers—are constantly recording case histories and interpreting them as they go along. Good theory comes from blending induction with deduction, from seeing patterns in case histories and distilling broader models through rigorous reasoning and projection.

Alfred Chandler and the Evolution of Business History

Another stream in the evolution of Business History at HBS originated from the work of Alfred D. Chandler, Jr. Chandler's career is described in detail in Thomas McCraw's introduction to *The Essential Alfred Chan-*

dler: Essays Toward a Historical Theory of Big Business, which appeared in 1988; what follows is a necessarily abbreviated summary.[7]

In 1971, almost 10 years before John McArthur became dean, Chandler accepted the School's offer of the Straus Chair in Business History. He was 52 years old at the time, and he had spent his career in university departments of history, first at MIT, then at Johns Hopkins. He had written numerous articles and had edited several volumes of the papers of two presidents: Theodore Roosevelt and Dwight D. Eisenhower. He had also published biographies of Henry Varnum Poor and Pierre S. du Pont, and—most importantly—the pioneering *Strategy and Structure: Chapters in the History of the American Industrial Enterprise*, which appeared in 1962.[8]

During the late 1950s and early 1960s, Chandler had begun to reshape the field of business history. Although some good books had been written earlier, including several by N. S. B. Gras, Henrietta Larson, and Ralph Hidy, his predecessors in business history at the School, Chandler's scholarship was of a different order. Before his intervention, many business histories tended to be morality plays. Perhaps 80 percent were company histories or biographies of executives, and in much of this work, the company was either heroic or damnable, the executive either all saint or all sinner. Chandler redirected the field toward dispassionate and penetrating analysis of the anatomy of business.

He was able to transcend the old tradition for at least three reasons. First, because of his family connections in Delaware, he had grown up knowing some of the leading figures in American business, such as Pierre and Irénée du Pont, Walter Carpenter, and Donaldson Brown (principal author of the Du Pont ROI formula). Later in his life, Chandler served as adviser to Alfred P. Sloan, Jr., in the preparation of *My Years with General Motors,* the most important autobiography ever written by a businessperson.[9] Having known the du Ponts, Sloan, and other such figures personally, Chandler found it difficult to think of them as either heroes or villains. He had a good instinct for the dramatic event and the colorful character, but he nevertheless tended toward an approach that aimed at value-neutral social science.

This choice of method was reinforced during his experience as a graduate student, when he was most powerfully influenced not by any historian, but by Talcott Parsons, the eminent Harvard sociologist. Parsonian sociology emphasized social structures, the development of organizations and professions, and the evolution of roles within bureaucracies.[10] Parsons had an enduring impact on his young protégé, and it is not too much to say that the structuralist approach in general came to define Chandler's way of writing business history.

The third reason why Chandler took a new path derived from his decision to write as his dissertation a biography of his great-grandfather, Henry Varnum Poor. Poor was a business journalist, and in effect one of the first professional securities analysts in the United States; his name lives on today as part of Standard & Poor's. At the moment when the young Chandler discovered a trove of his great-grandfather's papers and decided to write an analytical biography based on the functions that Poor had performed, the course of business history took a decisive turn.[11]

In almost all of his work, from the Poor biography down to the present time, Chandler has addressed a series of apparently simple questions: How were things done at a particular point in the history of business? What forces operated to propel changes in the way things were done? How were they then done afterward? Who led the movement for change, and why? How did roles within the organization shift, and how did the organization's own function evolve? Why did particular changes come in some types of industries but not in others? These questions, among their other virtues, comprised an almost perfect fit with the Harvard Business School's curriculum as it was evolving in the 1960s and 1970s.

In *Strategy and Structure*, published in 1962, Chandler showed how four large firms (Du Pont, General Motors, Standard Oil, and Sears, Roebuck) developed the multidivisional corporate structure during the 1920s.[12] To establish the morphology of this crucial development in the evolution of big business, Chandler read and digested reams of material from company histories, corporate archives, annual reports, trade publications, and business memoirs. He followed the same pattern in writing his next big book, *The Visible Hand: The Managerial Revolution in American Business*. Published in 1977 by Harvard University Press, *The Visible Hand* is a dense, 500-page analysis of the rise of big business in America. Its theme is the absorption by single corporations of some of the functions usually accomplished by external markets. Altogether, it is probably the most important work of business history ever published. It won the Pulitzer Prize, the Bancroft Prize, and the Thomas Newcomen Book Award.

In *Scale and Scope: The Dynamics of Industrial Capitalism* (1990, also Harvard University Press), Chandler took his story forward in time to the 1940s. He also extended it internationally, examining the evolution of big business not only in the United States, but in Great Britain and Germany as well. This book, even longer than *Strategy and Structure* and *The Visible Hand*, builds on the insights they contain, and the cumulative nature of Chandler's work is one of its most powerful attributes.

Like the work of all great scholars, Chandler's books have inspired detractors as well as emulators. Within the United States, his critics have argued that, by focusing attention on big business, he implicitly celebrates it. They contend that Chandler strikes a value-neutral pose, but in fact glorifies big business as the fountainhead of economic growth. Meanwhile, they argue, he ignores such important topics as finance, labor relations, small business, and public policy.[13] Outside the United States, a good deal of criticism has come from British scholars. Many of these critics believe that Chandler has portrayed British business, which he characterizes as "family capitalism," as being deficient in professionalism. They regard this judgment as harsh and sometimes wrong-headed.[14]

No amount of criticism, however, can gainsay the scholarly triumphs that Chandler has attained. His achievement is especially striking when one considers how much of it he accomplished while working almost alone. The field was so underdeveloped when he began his work that his accomplishment can hardly be exaggerated.

What Business Historians Do at HBS

The preceding review of the evolution of business history at the School, and of the impact that Chandler's work has had, leads to additional questions: What do historians do today at HBS, and how do they avoid the awkwardness of history mentioned earlier?

We have already begun to provide the answer to these questions with the discussion of the BGIE unit, in which historians play an important role. A second answer is our research and writing, both as individuals and in groups, which is summarized at the end of this chapter through a list of our books. In addition to BGIE and our books, there are four other major activities, which we will now consider in turn.

Teaching "The Coming of Managerial Capitalism"

In one form or other, this elective course has been offered at the School since the 1920s. In the late 1960s and early '70s, it was attracting between 20 and 40 students per year. Since the late 1980s, it has typically enrolled between 300 and 400 students annually.[15] This dramatic increase began in the early and middle 1980s, when Chandler and Richard Tedlow remodeled the course. They sharpened its focus, gave it a compelling intellectual structure, and made it much more useful to students. Later on, when Thomas McCraw and Nancy Koehn began to teach it along with Tedlow, The Coming of Managerial Capitalism became one of the School's most heavily subscribed electives.

The course is predicated on the proposition that a sophisticated knowledge of the history of business can inform managers' decision making for the present and the future. Thus it is not only about yesterday, but about today and tomorrow as well. Historians try to look forward imaginatively from the past, not just backward from the present, and the course instills in students a sense of how to use the past to think about the future. Within that general mindset, the course addresses three large questions:

1. Once, not very long ago, there was no such thing as professional business management. What happened to make it necessary, and how did it develop?

2. What was the impact of the rise of big business and professional management on the American workforce, and vice versa?

3. What was their impact on American government, and vice versa?

The course begins in the eighteenth century with Benjamin Franklin and Alexander Hamilton. These two Founding Fathers had significant business experience themselves, and they helped to shape the American economy's delicate balance between political stability and widespread entrepreneurial opportunity.

After a look at the birth of the factory system, the course moves to the rise of the railroads. Here management first appeared in its modern form, as salaried executives without major equity stakes began making the key decisions for their companies. The railroads were far larger than any business enterprises that had gone before. Whereas the biggest factories in America had employed several hundred persons, some individual railroads employed several thousand by the 1850s, and by the 1890s over 100,000.

The railroads' requirements for immense amounts of capital stimulated the development of securities markets, and in effect created modern Wall Street. As the industry grew, finance and other issues seemed almost overwhelming, and these issues were remarkably diverse: route structures, labor relations, engineering design and manufacturing, cost accounting and pricing, safety, and the industry's relationships to all levels of government. The question of safety was particularly difficult, because railroads were killing several thousand people every year: pedestrians, horseback and buggy riders, passengers in rail cars, and— not least—their own employees. The challenge of managing this unprecedented mix of problems, along with the opportunity to make a fortune, began to attract some of the country's most talented persons, many of whose names became famous: Cornelius Vanderbilt, Jay Gould, Edward H. Harriman.

Big business soon appeared outside railroading, in industries such as iron and steel, machinery, and branded packaged goods. This trend got under way in the 1870s and blossomed in the 1880s. One result was the birth of numerous companies that are still prominent today: Eastman Kodak; Johnson & Johnson; Coca-Cola; Westinghouse; Sears, Roebuck; Avon Products; Hershey Foods; and many others, all founded in the 1880s. More of today's *Fortune* 500 firms were founded in the 1880s than in any other decade except the 1920s. Almost half of the entire 500 were founded in the 50-year time frame between 1880 and

1930. To put it another way, half of all *Fortune* 500 companies were created during a period that comprises less than one-fourth of America's national history and only about one-eighth of its overall history since the first European settlers arrived.[16]

In The Coming of Managerial Capitalism, we therefore spend a substantial amount of time on the period from 1880 to 1930. We examine the careers and the companies of the railroad pioneers already mentioned, as well as such industrial and financial titans as Andrew Carnegie, John D. Rockefeller, James B. Duke, J. Pierpont Morgan, and Pierre S. du Pont. We trace the origins of cost accounting, investment banking, and management consulting. We devote a lot of attention to the development of such concepts as return on investment. We look at such innovations as the multiproduct strategy and the multidivisional corporate structure. We show who pioneered these innovations and how.

We do not teach a "great person" theory of history. Instead, we emphasize the opportunities that changing markets and technologies offered to entrepreneurs, and the necessary relationship between business strategy and corporate structure. These are "Chandlerian" themes, and much of The Coming of Managerial Capitalism represents the payoff of an exceptional collaboration between Chandler and Tedlow. Chandler's contribution was primarily conceptual, but he also wrote a large number of cases. Tedlow wrote most of the others, added vivid illustrative materials (including two documentary films that he developed), and shaped the overall structure of the course. The teaching manual he prepared is a masterpiece of the genre, a service to those who taught the course after he did. Most important, Tedlow infused the course's pedagogy with ideas from the entire MBA curriculum. This step presupposed a detailed knowledge by the history instructors of what was going on in the rest of the School. Tedlow brought to this effort his own experience in having taught first-year Marketing, and he and other teachers of The Coming of Managerial Capitalism have also taught the BGIE course.

The instructors' familiarity with the first-year curriculum is vital not only in those parts of The Coming of Managerial Capitalism that deal with business alone, but also in the course's components on the American workforce and on government. Particular themes run from the rise and fall of slavery to the development of organized labor; then on to antitrust and the evolution of the mixed economy; and finally into topics such as the LBO movement of the 1980s, the checkered career of Michael Milken, and the future of American capitalism.

All of this constitutes an imposing intellectual agenda. The faculty members involved in The Coming of Managerial Capitalism see their role as instructors not only of business history, but also as creators of an integrative course, one that provides students with the opportunity to use almost everything they have learned in their MBA education.

Offering the Research Seminar in Business History

Like the MBA elective just discussed, a seminar in business history had been offered at the School for many years before John McArthur became dean. Also like the elective, it underwent a radical change during John's deanship. Beginning in 1984, it was converted by Thomas McCraw from a conventional doctoral seminar into a faculty/student research symposium, and weekly attendance increased from about 10 to about 30. During the period from 1984 to 1995, there were 160 seminars in all, each with at least one formal presenter and two discussants.

The occasion for changing the seminar's organization in 1984 was the preparation of two books: *Scale and Scope*, written by Chandler with the assistance of Takashi Hikino,[17] and *America versus Japan: A Comparative Study of Business-Government Relations, Conducted at the Harvard Business School*, edited by McCraw and written by him and 12 other authors from five different disciplines.[18] During the academic year 1984–1985, drafts of every chapter from both books were presented in two-hour seminars. Each chapter received a formal critique from invited discussants, some from other universities, some from the School's own faculty. Doctoral students participated in these discussions as well, and wrote major research papers of their own.[19]

In the years since 1984, the Business History seminar has continued in the tradition begun at that time. Almost every book by a historian at the School has been subjected, in whole or in part, to the formal criticism of the seminar's participants. In every year for the first six years and for most years since, each of the School's historians has presented an original research paper. The whole enterprise has functioned as an occasion for vetting work in progress, not only by the historians but by many others at the School as well.

The seminar's intellectual vitality has derived from several sources: its cross-disciplinary and often cross-national approach; the faithful attendance and active participation of a dedicated core of students and faculty from several units of the School; and the common assumption that their criticisms really would affect the final shape of the published work. Another assumption was that academic one-upmanship would be held to a minimum. Work in progress would be presented with minimal risk to the presenter, and nonconstructive criticism would be discouraged. These ground rules have held for more than a decade, with results advantageous to almost all participants. If there is such a thing in academic life as a community of scholars, the Business History seminar is an authentic embodiment of it.

The seminar was not designed solely for the benefit of the School's students and business historians. A large number of projects by other members of the faculty, both inside and outside the BGIE unit, have also been presented and discussed. Faculty members from every unit or interest group at the School have taken part, either as presenters or discussants. Dozens of participants from other universities around the nation and the world, many of them distinguished scholars, have done the same.

Well over 100 doctoral students have written papers for the seminar. This work, in revised form, has often found its way into the first chapters of the students' dissertations, as historical background for the chosen topic. Adaptations of several papers have been published as articles or chapters in books.[20]

Teaching about Business, Government, and Regulation

In addition to the international concerns of BGIE, several of the historians were at the center of the School's research and course development in business and government during the McArthur years. Thomas McCraw was originally recruited to help lead these efforts. He in turn recruited Richard Vietor, and both have devoted most of their research to books and articles on business-government relations.

This kind of work requires implicit comparisons of the public and the private sectors—a challenge even if a scholar is working with only one country. When the comparisons become cross-national, the difficulties multiply. Research tends to be expensive and time-consuming. It often necessitates a lot of travel. It demands foreign language skills of a high order, or access to research associates with those skills. It presents a constant risk of superficial analyses, unsophisticated judgments, and naive conclusions. Perhaps most important of all, cross-national and cross-disciplinary comparative work is almost impossible for a lone scholar to do well. It often requires long-term collaborations.

The BGIE unit as a whole is particularly strong on regulatory topics, and the initial approach to this subject, beginning in the late 1970s and early 1980s, was historical as well as economic. Research and course development typically focused on the origins of regulation, and on the evolving strategies of government officials and business managers operating under regulatory constraints. A new elective course entitled Managing in the Regulated Environment was begun by McCraw, intensively developed by Vietor, and later passed on to the young economists in the BGIE unit, first Willis Emmons, then Alexander Dyck.[21] This course has changed as regulation itself has changed, and it now includes substantial segments on deregulation and privatization. It typically attracts not only MBAs, but also a number of students from the Kennedy School and other parts of Harvard.

A sequence similar to that of the course on regulation was followed for the important environmental initiative at the School. Vietor began to do research in this area in the late 1980s, then in the early 1990s cotaught a seminar with Forest Reinhardt, another young economist. This collaboration produced an MBA elective course and an important casebook.

Neither the regulation course nor the environmental one was primarily an effort in business history per se. But they were shaped in part by the historical approaches of McCraw and Vietor, as both placed great stress on the evolutionary and institutional nature of business-government relations as well as on static economic analysis.

Perhaps most significantly, the course has served as a platform for influential research. McCraw's book *Prophets of Regulation*, which won both the Pulitzer Prize and the Thomas Newcomen Book Award, grew in part out of his early work on the course. Similarly, most of the chapters in Vietor's outstanding study of deregulation, entitled *Contrived Competition*, were tested in the classroom and revised repeatedly prior to the book's publication.

Sponsoring the Business History Review *and Research Fellowships*

The *Business History Review* is an international quarterly journal sponsored by the School. Addressed primarily to the community of business historians, it has been published at Soldiers Field for six decades. Most subscribers, among them a fair number of corporations, are located in the United States, but the journal is mailed to addressees in 51 other countries as well. The editor of the *Review* has always been one of the School's business historians.[22] The advisory board includes the other historians at Soldiers Field, plus 17 distinguished scholars based elsewhere.

The editors of the *Review* have long followed two policies in keeping with our international and cross-disciplinary orientations. We have maintained the international scope of the *Review*, and we have reached out to invite articles from fields other than history. About one-third of our authors come from disciplines such as economics and business administration, and several members of the HBS faculty who are not historians—including the School's current dean, Kim Clark—have contributed articles.[23]

The *Review* publishes about 15 articles per year, chosen in a double-blind refereeing process. Occasionally we bring out a special issue with a cluster of articles around a single theme, such as the international automobile industry or small business in America. In addition to articles, the journal annually publishes about 80 book reviews, again written by scholars from all over the world. The *Review*'s administrative staff of two persons maintains a database of about 950 historians, economists, and students of business administration, on which it draws for names of suitable referees and reviewers. The Harvard-Newcomen Postdoctoral Research Fellow in Business History also serves as an assistant editor of the journal.

That postdoctoral fellowship, jointly sponsored by the Newcomen Society and the School, has been awarded annually since 1949. The recipient comes from history or a related discipline and is chosen by the School's business history faculty in an international competition. The winner spends a year in residence working on his or her research projects and devoting up to half time to the School's various activities in business history. Many scholars who now rank among the world's leading business historians have held this fellowship: Louis Galambos, Merritt Roe Smith, Mark Fruin, Tony Freyer, William Lazonick, Steven Tolliday—plus three members of the School's own faculty, Thomas McCraw, Richard Vietor, and Richard Tedlow, and one member of Harvard's History Department, Sven Beckert. Other leading historians, such as Robert Cuff, Leslie Hannah, David Hounshell, and Joseph Pratt, have spent one or more years as visiting professors or fellows.

Since 1991 the School has also administered the Alfred D. Chandler, Jr., Traveling Fellowships. Under this program, graduate students in history or related disciplines come to Harvard, and Harvard students go elsewhere, for research in business history or institutional economic history. Our definitions of these fields have been broad, in order to encourage a wide range of research. About six fellowships are awarded each year, and recipients are chosen in consultation with members of Harvard's Departments of History and Economics. The program was designed by the historians at the School and made possible by a generous gift to Harvard by Professor Chandler himself, who was persuaded by his colleagues that the attachment of his name to the program was not inappropriate.

Inventing and Teaching the Business History Foundations Course

In the reorganization of the Harvard MBA program that was planned during the last years of John McArthur's deanship, the School's faculty developed a special introductory curriculum. The idea was to give entering students a better intellectual background for the rigors they were about to encounter. They would receive a series of brief but intense courses on ethics, quantitative methods, project management, and other topics.

Business history was one of the topics chosen for this "Foundations" curriculum. Here the faculty's idea, as first proposed by Senior Associate Dean Leonard Schlesinger to Thomas McCraw, was that students at every professional school should know the roots of their chosen field—where it came from, how it developed, and how its activities differed from one country to another. In other words, they should be exposed to the Big Picture as early as possible. McCraw saw this challenge as a difficult one, but he believed that, given enough time, the Business History group could create a course of real distinction.

When he, Nancy Koehn, and other members of the group set to work in the spring of 1994, their first decision was to make the course cross-national. This choice reflected their conviction that Harvard MBA students should have as international an education as the faculty was able to deliver. Early in their planning, they divided the course into four equal parts on the business histories of Britain, Germany, the United States, and Japan, the countries they regarded as offering the most important historical models of doing business.

McCraw, Koehn, and the others then decided that, in contrast to the BGIE course, this new offering would take companies and entrepreneurs as its preferred units of analysis. Whereas fewer than one in ten BGIE cases takes an individual company or business manager as its analytical focus, two-thirds of the cases in the Foundations course do so. In its final form, the course has a relatively simple and symmetrical design: 4 country cases as background, then 8 company cases (2 from each country), for a total of 12. Every company case has at least one memorable entrepreneur, and most have two or three. The name of the course, and of the book that grew out of it, is "Creating Modern Capitalism."

Beyond the design of the course, the hardest task for the authors involved in the project was to compress the entire business history of the countries and companies into documents of conventional case length. A few examples follow.

In Nancy Koehn's story of Josiah Wedgwood, which takes place in the 1760s, should she emphasize the supply side of the first Industrial Revolution; that is, the development of technology and the building of national infrastructures? Or should the focus be on the demand side—Wedgwood's strikingly modern techniques for building markets through early forms of inertia selling, celebrity sanctions, money-back guarantees, and brand imaging?

In David Moss's story of the Deutsche Bank, how much space should he devote to the general phenomenon of universal banking? How much should be allocated to the period of hyperinflation in the early 1920s, which created almost intractable administrative problems for German banks? to the horrors of the Nazi era? to the postwar Occupation? to the Deutsche Bank's recent expansion into international markets?

In the chapter entitled "IBM and the two Thomas J. Watsons," how should author Rowena Olegario tell the story? (Olegario was a Research Associate and a doctoral candidate in Harvard's Department of History.) Should she emphasize the dramatic "bet the company" decision of the 1960s to develop the System/360, with an investment of $5 billion, three times the company's annual revenues? Should she focus on IBM's long tenure at or near the top of America's most admired companies? Or should she spend more space on the company's relative decline in the face of challenges from Intel and Microsoft, whose rise IBM's own management decisions facilitated?

In writing about Toyota, how much of the case could author Jeffrey Bernstein afford to spend on the Toyoda Automatic Loom Company, the original family business built up by Sakichi Toyoda, a contemporary of Thomas Edison and one of Japan's preeminent inventors? Should he emphasize the origins and spread of the Toyota Production System to numerous industries throughout the world? Should he feature the role of the Japanese government in the company's growth, or instead tell the story as one of vigorous interfirm competition with Nissan and other producers?

In all, 8 authors participated in writing the 12 cases. Thomas McCraw wrote "American Capitalism" and (in collaboration with Richard Tedlow) "Henry Ford, Alfred Sloan, and the Three Phases of Marketing." McCraw also edited all of the other cases and wrote the introductory and concluding chapters for the book in which they eventually appeared. Jeffrey Bernstein, a Research Associate at the School and a doctoral candidate in Business Economics, wrote "Japanese Capitalism" and "7-Eleven in America and Japan" in addition to the case on Toyoda/Toyota. Bernstein's Japanese language skills facilitated his interviews and his research in Japanese materials. Professor Jeffrey Fear of the University of Pennsylvania, a specialist in German business history who was the Harvard-Newcomen postdoctoral research fellow in 1994–1995, wrote "German Capitalism" and "August Thyssen and German Steel." Peter Botticelli, a Research Associate who holds a Ph.D. in modern European history, wrote "British Capitalism" and "Rolls-Royce and the Rise of High-Technology Industry." In all, the development of the Foundations material exemplified the tradition of collaborative scholarship among the historians at the School. It may not be too much to say that it could have been done nowhere else.

After two years of preparation, the Foundations business history course was taught for the first time in January 1996 and was received by students with enthusiasm and a good deal of excitement. Our own view (hardly unbiased, of course), is that we have given beginning MBAs a genuine professional "foundation": an understanding of the roots of capitalism and a sense of the possibilities open to individuals not only to build a business, but occasionally even to affect the course of a country's history. We believe the "Creating Modern Capitalism" project to be one of the most important contributions to the School that the business historians have made in recent years.

Writing Books, 1980–1995

During John McArthur's deanship, the School's historians wrote a great deal of material. Collectively they turned out hundreds of articles, cases, and reviews. Their preferred metier, like that of most other historians, was the book, and they published no fewer than 24 during or just after the McArthur years. This is an exceptionally large output for a small group of scholars, and perhaps the most vivid way to communicate the range of the group's interests is merely to list the titles of the books.

(They are enumerated in the appendix at the close of this chapter.) As eclectic as those interests are, some common threads are evident. In several of the books, the BGIE unit's propensities for comparative approaches are evident in the coverage of Japan, Germany, and Britain as well as the United States. It is also noteworthy how many of the books pertain to public policy, another major concern of the BGIE unit.

Besides the breadth of coverage exemplified by these books, the close relationship between work done for teaching and work done for research is also conspicuous. Many of the books came out of courses, and others directly influenced courses. This kind of synergy derives from the School's long tradition of creating its own teaching materials.

As a rule, historians are trained to work in isolation, and most seem to prefer solitary research and writing. But the HBS historians have worked closely together, year in and year out. We have collaborated with each other and with scholars from other disciplines as well. As the list of books suggests, it has been our good fortune not only to have contemplated doing a lot of collaborative work, but actually to have done it.

We could not have done it without the steadfast support of John McArthur. Both before and during his deanship, John paid special attention to the Business History group. He has a deep affinity for history. As a young doctoral student in business administration, McArthur had written his own dissertation (on the evolution of oil pipelines) primarily under the direction of the School's historians. To this day, he probably reads more history than do many professional historians.

What Business Historians Have Learned at HBS

The writing of our books, in combination with our collective investment in the Foundations course, has yielded some unexpected benefits. Classroom time in the required (first-year) curriculum is a precious commodity, and it must be used efficiently. Foundations forced the School's historians to be absolutely clear about the lessons we have learned from our research and to state those lessons as succinctly as possible.

In the following paragraphs, we present a shorthand version of seven of these lessons. Of course, any such list can only be a point of departure for debate. Other scholars, no doubt including some of our colleagues at the School, would substitute or add others. Still other scholars may find fault with some or all of the seven we have included. But, as we were reminded while we were developing the Foundations course, informed debate can be the most purifying of fires, and we welcome it.

CAPITALISM COMES IN SEVERAL FLAVORS. There is no one "right" road to economic development. The construction of the course Creating Modern Capitalism around the British, German, U.S., and Japanese experiences makes that point. It is a message that flows directly from the work of Chandler on the United States, Great Britain, and Germany; from the work of McCraw on the competition between the United States and Japan; and from the whole approach of the BGIE course. Creating Modern Capitalism (and other Business History activities) is a conscious assault on nationalism and on the unconscious American exceptionalism that many incoming students bring with them to our classrooms.

GOVERNMENT HAS LEGITIMACY AS A DEVELOPER AND REGULATOR. At different times in the past, and in many different ways, governments have played key roles in stimulating economic development. This role can be as minimal as providing permissive context, but more often it involves the use of state power to promote private endeavors, or to support them through the process of infrastructural capital formation. Government is not always the problem, and it should not be assumed to be so. The work of McCraw, Vietor, Koehn, and Moss argues against the demonization of government so prevalent in contemporary cant. When we assess economic regulation, for example, we are critical of governmental mistakes and excesses; but we also stress that, in many cases, regulation of the economy has been not only constructive but also essential in the maintenance of economic balance. The problem of regulation is not in its existence, but rather in its frequent failure to stay in harmony with evolving technology and business organization.

SOCIAL EQUILIBRIUM SHOULD NOT BE ASSUMED. The secrets of capitalism's success are not to be found exclusively within narrow economic confines. Like other systems of thought, capitalism depends in large part on the existence of broadly shared societal values that are at least conducive to, and at best supportive of, that economic system. Economic development depends in complex ways on the surrounding social matrix. A shared ethical perspective, for example, is likely to help a coexistent economic theory succeed. Some degree of social harmony, or at least social stability, is essential.

Conversely, all the social and economic good that has been built up painstakingly over years and decades can be lost in a twinkling if the socioeconomic system goes wildly askew—as it did, for example, in 1930s Germany. The lesson, of course, is that business ought to be profoundly concerned about the maintenance of some kind of social harmony and ought to invest in creating and sustaining that harmony. Business is not a world apart.

STRUCTURAL CHANGE IMPOSES SOCIAL COSTS. In many of the cases in the course Creating Modern Capitalism, students are asked to reflect on both the winners and the losers in the process of economic development and to assess whether the losses justify the gains. The answer in most cases turns out to be "yes," but not without heavy qualification. The simple act of asking such a question instills in students' minds the hypothesis that there are some changes that could not pass this test.

Spinners, handloom weavers, artisans, and craftspeople—as well as samurai and peasants, in other contexts—were all muscled aside by more efficient economic players. One result was the relegation of skilled individuals to repetition and tedium on the assembly line. Breaking the mold, in other words, almost always means breaking people. Schumpeter's "perennial gale of creative destruction" exacts a dreadful human toll.[24] To the extent that Harvard's MBA graduates will help shape the future of business, the business historians want those graduates to be sensitive to this key lesson from the past.

BUSINESS REQUIRES MORAL CHOICE. This lesson grows naturally out of the previous one. Running a business is obviously not a matter of debits and credits alone. At intervals that cannot be predicted, momentous moral choices must be made, such as those that faced the directors of the Deutsche Bank in the 1930s, as they capitulated to Nazi pressures. But moral choice is also embedded in other, less dramatic situations, such as competitive practices, labor relations, and policies that bear on the distribution of wealth. We live in a relativistic universe, but there are still some absolutes that must not be traded off.

CHAMPIONS ARE DRIVEN. Strip away all the structural and contextual forces behind a critical economic development, and you will probably find a champion of change. This person is very likely to be, for lack of a better word, *driven*.

With the notable exception of BGIE, as explained above, historians at HBS have chosen to use companies and entrepreneurs as the units of analysis. Among its other merits, this choice provides the opportunity for telling great stories. But the colorful genius in these stories is rarely well adjusted, or even housebroken. Think of Henry Royce, the engineering virtuoso of Rolls-Royce, who was so difficult a personality that his office had to be moved off site (to his own home, and at times to the French Riviera), lest he further disrupt the company's operations; August Thyssen, whose devotion to the quality of his steel led to scandalous neglect of his family; Henry Ford, who not only was anti-Semitic, but also followed such demented management practices that he almost killed the company that bore his name; and Sakichi Toyoda, whose marriage, like August Thyssen's, broke up over his monomaniacal devotion to business. It is stubborn, aggressive, driven people who break molds, and who can be an invaluable service to society. But their kind of single-mindedness often is not pretty when examined close up.

BUSINESS MUST VALUE BOTH THE INDIVIDUAL AND THE INSTITUTION. Over the long run, the health of business organizations depends on harmonizing the destabilizing influence of entrepreneurial genius with the power of effective organization. Founding visions can become confining; organizations can become sclerotic. The design of appropriate structures to realize business strategies is a big part of the value managers add to the process of wealth creation. Sometimes these conflicting forces can be reconciled only over several generations of a company's life.

To summarize, business history tries to provide a critical evaluation of capitalist development. It seeks to help create students with open minds, a willingness to reflect on and challenge assumptions, and the skills and courage to make reasoned arguments based in part on historical evidence.

Business history is not a world of simple solutions or unqualified lawgiving. The heart of our work lies in that misty realm in which the university was born, in which the liberal arts were invented, and in which complexity was a commodity to be savored. The Harvard Business School prides itself on accounting for the messiness of reality. We assert that it is history that makes messiness unavoidable.

Business History and Its Prospects

Toward the close of the twentieth century, the profession of business history included perhaps 2,000 active practitioners worldwide. These numbers reflect a remarkable record of growth beginning in the 1970s—coincidentally a period during which the broader discipline of history stagnated—and continuing to the present.[25]

The relationship of business history to two other subdisciplines provides some clues concerning its possible future. For about the past two decades, certain kinds of business history have been moving toward the history of technology, and vice versa. Historians of technology are becoming less narrowly engineering oriented and less concerned with hardware. They have been moving toward such subjects as the interactions among engineers and businesspeople, and between both of these groups on the one hand and the larger social context on the other. Some of the best historians of technology are outstanding historians of business as well. Exchange between the two subdisciplines surely would strengthen both. At Soldiers Field, to cite only one example, the historians have been helped in their understanding of technology by the advice of Professor Richard Rosenbloom, a regular participant in the Business History Seminar.

Another subdiscipline of special interest for business historians is economic history. Several decades ago, the border dividing these two fields was highly porous. Then, beginning in the 1960s, the leading figures in economic history began to come from departments of economics rather than history. Whereas the authorship of articles in *The Journal of Economic History* had long been fairly well balanced between historians and economists, with historians having the edge, economists began to dominate in the 1960s. By the 1980s, they had all but ousted the historians. Within economic history, meanwhile, articles (as opposed to books) became the preferred medium of publication. Today, most economic historians think of themselves as economists, rather than historians.[26]

The practitioners of the "new economic history," as it began to be called in the 1960s, insisted on sharp specification of topic and high standards of proof. They made intensive use of mathematical notation and routinely employed computers. Rigorous logic became not only a necessary standard, but often a sufficient one. Because of these methodological priorities, the scope of inquiry was necessarily narrowed. The equation began to displace the well-turned phrase. Literary grace was devalued.[27]

Despite this recent trajectory, the subfields of economic history and business history hold the potential to complement each other very well. The economist's rigor is an invaluable tool, and business historians should be comfortable using it.

And for their part, the authors propose, economic historians should try on for size the business historians' broader, more institutionally oriented approach. When business historians write about business enterprises, they are most often interested in all aspects of the subject: the performance of the company, its strategy, the makeup of its workforce, the sources of its technology, the method of its operation, the structure of its organization, its place within its industry, its relationship to government, and its role in the larger society. Business historians want to know about the mechanics of change. They are less interested in comparative statics than in the evolution of institutions. They sense that the process of change is to be found in small increments, punctuated occasionally by dramatic departures.

Like other historians, they often wish to tell stories, in addition to answering well-specified questions. They sometimes seek audiences outside the academy as well as within it. They are tolerant of ambiguity, if not altogether comfortable with it. They are often willing for readers to draw independent conclusions from the stories they tell, the data they present, the arguments they make.

They don't wish to fuzz things up. Neither do they insist on bright arrows that lead from cause to effect with absolute certainty. If they were painters, they would not be abstract expressionists. But, assuming a high reliability in the data, they might accept an impressionism in which all the colors are present on the canvas, but are not necessarily premixed on the palette of the artist.

Why? Because they know that a good deal of the fusion of particular colors and facts must take place within the mind of the beholder and the reader. They are convinced that the impact of the story might be stronger and more lasting because of the reader's active participation in the enterprise. They sense that life is complicated and that ultimate answers of total certainty are not vouchsafed to humankind. Once they accept the inevitability of this circumstance, they are happy to practice their craft in accordance with it.

Appendix

Books published by members of the Business History group during or just after John McArthur's deanship, listed chronologically.

Richard H. K. Vietor. *Environmental Politics and the Coal Coalition*. College Station: Texas A&M University Press, 1980. 285 pages.

Alfred D. Chandler, Jr., and Herman Daems, eds. *Managerial Hierarchies: Comparative Perspectives on the Rise of the Modern Industrial Enterprise*. Cambridge, Mass.: Harvard University Press, 1980. 237 pages.

Thomas K. McCraw, ed. *Regulation in Perspective: Historical Essays*. Boston: Harvard University Graduate School of Business Administration, 1981. 246 pages.

Richard H. K. Vietor. *Energy Policy in America Since 1945: A Study of Business Government Relations.* Cambridge, Eng.: Cambridge University Press, 1984. 363 pages.

Thomas K. McCraw. *Prophets of Regulation: Charles Francis Adams, Louis D. Brandeis, James M. Landis, Alfred E. Kahn.* Cambridge, Mass.: Harvard University Press, 1984. 387 pages.

Alfred D. Chandler, Jr., and Richard S. Tedlow. *The Coming of Managerial Capitalism: A Casebook on the History of American Economic Institutions.* Chicago: Irwin, 1985. 877 pages.

Richard S. Tedlow and Richard R. John, Jr., eds. *Managing Big Business: Essays from the Business History Review.* Boston: Harvard Business School Press, 1986. 425 pages.

Thomas K. McCraw, ed. *America Versus Japan: A Comparative Study of Business-Government Relations.* Boston: Harvard Business School Press, 1986. 463 pages. Translated into Japanese and published in Japan by TBS-Brittanica.

Richard H. K. Vietor and Davis Dyer, eds. *Telecommunications in Taransition.* Boston: Division of Research Harvard Business School, 1986. 221 pages.

Steven S. Tolliday. *Business, Banking, and Politics: The Case of British Steel,* 1918-1939. Cambridge, Mass.: Harvard University Press, 1987. 433 pages.

Thomas K. McCraw, ed. *The Essential Alfred Chandler: Essays Toward a Historical Theory of Big Business.* Boston: Harvard Business School Press, 1988. 538 pages. Translated into Portuguese and published in Brazil by Fundaçao Getulio Vargas.

Richard H. K. Vietor. *Strategic Management in the Regulatory Environment: Cases and Industry Notes.* Englewood Cliffs, N.J.: Prentice-Hall, 1989. 445 pages.

Richard S. Tedlow. *New and Improved: The Story of Mass Marketing in America.* New York: Basic Books, 1990, and Boston: Harvard Business School Press, 1996. 481 pages. Translated into Japanese and published in Japan by Minerva Shobo.

Alfred D. Chandler, Jr., with the assistance of Takashi Hikino. *Scale and Scope: The Dynamics of Industrial Capitalism.* Cambridge, Mass: Belknap Press of Harvard University Press, 1990. 860 pages. Translated into Italian, Japanese, and Spanish.

Richard S. Tedlow. *The Rise of the American Business Corporation.* Chur, Switzerland: Harwood Academic Publishers, 1991. 71 pages.

Richard S. Tedlow and Geoffrey Jones, eds. *The Rise and Fall of Mass Marketing.* London: Routledge, 1993. 239 pages.

Richard H. K. Vietor. *Contrived Competition: Regulation and Deregulation in America.*

Cambridge, Mass: Belknap Press of Harvard University Press, 1994. 439 pages.

Nancy F. Koehn. *The Power of Commerce: Economy and Governance in the First British Empire*. Ithaca, N.Y.: Cornell University Press, 1994. 239 pages.

Richard H. K. Vietor and Forest Reinhardt. *Business Management and the Natural Environment: Cases and Text*. Cincinnati, Ohio: South-Western, 1996. 662 pages.

Alfred D. Chandler, Jr., Thomas K. McCraw, and Richard S. Tedlow. *Management Past and Present: A Casebook on the History of American Business*. Cincinnati, Ohio: South-Western, 1996. 552 pages.

David A. Moss. *Socializing Security: Progressive-Era Economists and the Origins of American Social Policy*. Cambridge, Mass: Harvard University Press, 1996. 264 pages.

Thomas K. McCraw, ed. *The Economy*. Vol. III of *Encyclopedia of the United States in the Twentieth Century*, editor-in-chief Stanley I. Kutler. New York: Simon & Schuster, 1996. 419 pages.

Alfred D. Chandler, Jr., Franco Amatori, and Takashi Hikino, eds. *Big Business and the Wealth of Nations*. Cambridge, Eng.: Cambridge University Press, 1997. 596 pages.

Thomas K. McCraw, ed. *Creating Modern Capitalism: How Entrepreneurs, Companies, and Countries Triumphed in Three Industrial Revolutions*. Cambridge, Mass.: Harvard University Press, 1997. 711 pages.

Appendices

Senior Associate Deans (Faculty)

During his deanship, John McArthur was assisted by talented people from all walks of life, both at Soldiers Field and elsewhere. No complete list of these individuals is practicable here, because it would number in the hundreds of faculty and staff members, and the thousands if involved alumni and students were included. But the following brief list does recognize the vital administrative contributions of those faculty members who held the title of Senior Associate Dean.

Bower, Joseph L.	External Relations 1985–1989
Bradley, Stephen P.	Faculty Development 1993–1995
Corey, E. Raymond	Research 1980–1983
Crane, Dwight B.	Faculty Development 1990–1993
	Research 1995
Donaldson, Gordon	Faculty Development 1980–1987
Fox, J. Ronald	Faculty Development 1987–1990
Hayes, Robert H.	Faculty Planning 1992–1995
Heskett, James L.	Educational Programs 1980–1983
Light, Jay O.	Faculty Planning and Development 1988–1992
Lorsch, Jay W.	Research 1987–1991
McFarlan, F. Warren	Research 1991–1995
Piper, Thomas R.	Educational Programs 1983–1995
Sahlman, William A.	Publications Activities 1991–1995
Salmon, Walter J.	External Relations 1989–1994
Sasser, W. Earl, Jr.	Executive Education 1995
Schlesinger, Leonard A.	External Relations 1994–1995
Shapiro, Benson P.	Publications 1988–1991
Stevenson, Howard H.	Financial and Information Systems 1991–1994
Uyterhoeven, Hugo E. R.	External Relations 1980–1985
	Executive Education 1985–1988

The Global Financial System Research Initiatives

As part of the GFS program, we have identified four substantive areas that are the subjects of ongoing research. These four projects deal intimately with the question of the measurement, control, and allocation of risk. In particular, we are studying (1) the risks faced by pensioners and the private and public entities that may be called upon to support them; (2) the risks to be shed and assumed by corporations; (3) the measurement, allocation, and management of risk and capital by financial institutions; and (4) the restructuring of catastrophic risk bearing in the global economy.

Beyond these four explicit GFS project areas, there is a large body of work being conducted by the Finance faculty at HBS that examines closely how the institutional structures for delivering various functions are affected by the structure of those organizations and industries, and in particular how managerial incentives and transaction costs affect the decisions and performance of financial entities.

This brief snapshot cannot possibly do justice to all of the research being carried out in the finance area at HBS. However, we hope that it gives a flavor of the financial issues being studied today and their relation to the GFS project.

Equally, we hope that, like the financial system, our research will dynamically evolve over time. What is represented below is merely a snapshot of our efforts as of late 1996. However, consistent with our belief in the functional perspective, we seek to keep our research focused on fundamental economic problems, whose resolution is likely to have a large impact on the practice of managers and regulators.

(See Appendix C for full citations of the references in this appendix.)

THE RISKS FACED BY PENSIONERS

In most industrialized countries, there is mounting pressure on pension plans stemming from the aging of their populations. Employers are also seeking to lower the risk and regulatory burden they face with defined benefit plans; that is, plans in which future benefits are both guaranteed and tied to future salary. The result is a shift toward defined contribution plans, such as 401(k) plans in the United States. This approach transfers the investment decision making and risk to individuals, raising the possibility of inadequate retirement income. Our research agenda in this area is three-pronged. First, we seek to understand how individuals make investment decisions when they are in control of their private portfolios. Second, we aim to understand what might constitute "optimal" portfolio decisions. Third, we aim to propose a new form of defined contribution plan to solve the needs of households as well as of governments and corporations.

On the first of these topics, we are studying the asset allocation and security selection decisions of households in two projects. Zvi Bodie and Dwight Crane (1997) analyze a unique database to examine the asset allocation choices of 4,000 individuals. These results can inform optimal financial product design, especially in the retirement phase of the life cycle. Peter Tufano and co-author Erik Sirri (currently chief economist of the Securities and Exchange Commission) study how mutual fund buyers respond to both past performance and fund marketing activities (Sirri and Tufano 1998).

There are numerous projects under way that attempt to understand the optimal investment practices that households and institutions should follow. A recent paper by Zvi Bodie challenges the conventional wisdom that stocks are less risky in the long run (Bodie 1995). Jay Light, with co-authors Mark Kritzman and Don Rich, has studied optimal investment strategies for endowment funds facing both absolute and relative performance targets (Kritzman, Light, and Rich 1996). Sanjiv Das, with co-author Raman Uppal, has examined optimal portfolio choice decisions when investors are faced with assets whose returns are systematically correlated (Das and Uppal 1996). Kenneth Froot and André Perold address the issue of optimal currency hedging policies for investors (Froot 1993, Froot and Perold 1993).

Finally, many projects are trying to examine the returns available to investors in particular instruments and investment strategies: Froot has studied the returns to investing in commodities (Froot 1995b); Paul Gompers, with co-authors Alon Brav and Chris Geczy, has been studying the returns earned by investors in initial and seasoned equity offerings (Brav and Gompers 1996, Brav, Geczy, and Gompers 1995); Stuart Gilson has studied investments in distressed securities (1995); Lisa Meulbroek, with co-author Paul Asquith, is studying the abnormal patterns of returns to investment strategies stratified on the size of short-sale interest (Asquith and Meulbroek 1995); and Peter Tufano (1996a) is studying returns to investors in innovative financial instruments. Many of these studies, such as Gompers's and Meulbroek's work, might seem to document investment anomalies, but the focus of the work is to explain whether other salient institutional features, such as the characteristics of investors, the information structure of markets, or institutional rigidities, making short sales difficult to execute, can explain the observed results.

We are also conducting research on the design of a new pension plan model. The objective is to design a defined contribution plan that retains as many features as possible of the traditional defined benefit plans. For example, employers or employees might contribute a percentage of salary to a financial intermediary that would guarantee some level of retirement income, reducing the investment and mortality risk to which employees were exposed. The primary faculty involved in this project are Dwight Crane and Zvi Bodie.

THE RISKS FACED BY CORPORATIONS

Although capital markets have developed a wide range of tools to allow firms to manage risk, we feel there is much work to be done in helping nonfinancial corporations measure exposures, determine which risks to manage, implement risk management strategies, and evaluate and motivate risk managers. This work is both descriptive and prescriptive, aiming to describe current practice as well as to prescribe improvements to that practice.

To understand how corporate risk management is conducted by firms, we have closely examined a number of firms' activities; this field research is contained in a large body of cases.[1] These case studies have inspired large-scale statistical research in a variety of areas. For example, a case on hedging by a North American gold-mining firm (Tufano and Serbin 1993) was the stimulus for two papers on risk management in this area. The first examines which firms hedge, relating the extent to which managers choose to hedge gold price risk to both firm characteristics and managerial concerns (Tufano 1996c). A second study examines the determinants of gold price exposure for mining firms, to understand how much effect risk management programs, as implemented, seem to have on a firm's total exposures (Tufano 1998b). A case on risk management by an active acquirer of banks (Esty, Tufano, and Headley 1994) was the basis for an empirical project that looks at the impact of interest rates and interest rate hedging on the market for mergers in the banking industry (Esty, Narasimhan, and Tufano 1998).

The more prescriptive work of this project aims to provide practitioners and educators with frameworks for approaching the corporate risk management decisions. Kenneth Froot, along with co-authors Jeremy Stein and David Scharfstein of MIT, has written a widely cited piece that lays out a framework for cash-flow hedging, where firms hedge so as to continue positive net-present-value projects in the face of costly external financing (Froot, Scharfstein, and Stein 1993, 1994a,b). Peter Tufano (1998a) has written about the potential dangers of risk management programs, in that they can unwisely insulate managers from the valuable discipline of the capital markets. A third project looks at the ways corporations can use financial engineering, not merely to reduce the risks of their existing businesses, but rather to advance their firm's business strategy. Drawing on field research on firms like ECT and TVA, Tufano (1996b) argues that financial engineering allows firms to assume strategic risks (from customers, employers, and suppliers), thereby allowing them to run their firms in new ways. This material is the basis for the Corporate Financial Engineering elective offered in the MBA program and executive education (Focused Financial Management Series) at HBS.

The Distribution of Insurance Risk

Risks that originate with natural disasters, such as hurricanes, earthquakes, and floods, are large enough to exhaust the capital and surplus of insurers and reinsurers many times over. In spite of significant advances in the efficiency of risk allocation in the financial system, however, these catastrophic risks are still largely allocated through brokered insurance and reinsurance agreements.

GFS faculty working on this project (Kenneth Froot and Sanjiv Das) are studying the institutional arrangements for distributing catastrophic risks, including comparisons of public and private mechanisms for risk distribution and an analysis of various securities designed to aid in the allocation or hedging of catastrophic risk. In addition, an empirical project on the pricing of catastrophic exposures is under way. This work will indicate the historical returns that reinsurers have received for writing catastrophic risks and will provide a base for testing hypotheses about the formulation of catastrophic cover prices (Froot 1995a). In conjunction with the National Bureau of Economic Research, Kenneth Froot organized a conference for academics and practitioners that examined current developments in the allocation of property and casualty risk, and served as the editor of this book, which will appear in a forthcoming University of Chicago book, *The Financing of Catastrophe Risks*.

Risk Capital and Capital Allocation in Financial Services Firms

In order to meet the needs of households and corporations, it is likely that financial services firms will increasingly be called upon to manage more complex risks within their own firms. As a general proposition, we believe that achieving simplicity for end users typically results in greater complexity for producers. For example, in the software business, early operating systems, such as DOS, were relatively complicated for users, but simple for developers. In contrast, the more user-friendly graphic interfaces in operating systems like Windows 95 require a much larger effort by the programmers designing this operating system. Likewise, as users of the financial system seek "simpler" solutions, providers of financial services will be pressured to manage more complicated business and to control more risks.

Because of the credit-sensitive and opaque nature of principal financial firms, proper risk control is imperative. In addition, capital allocation impacts a number of decisions, such as accounting for the profitability of individual businesses, entering or divesting businesses, determining profit-related employee compensation, choosing from among alternative organizational forms, and managing the overall risk of the firm. Historically, within financial firms, these issues have been the concern principally of the CFO/treasurer, in a top-down fashion. However, as off–balance sheet (derivatives) positions have grown in importance, these issues have also fallen squarely in the domain of the "risk manager," mostly from a bottom-up perspective. Of central importance is the need for a unifying framework that can reconcile these two perspectives and be applied on a firmwide basis. In consultation with the GFS sponsors, we deemed these issues to be of very high priority.

A major focus of our work is the study of the determinants of the costs of risk capital, as well as an exploration of the possible approaches to measuring and allocating these costs to the individual businesses that comprise the firm. The faculty are pursuing alternative approaches to this problem, with the ensuing debate likely to help clarify these issues. The primary faculty researchers for this project are André Perold, Kenneth Froot, and Robert C. Merton.

In addition to the question of risk management and capital allocation at the firm level within financial services firms, the faculty is also studying the risk management and portfolio pricing decisions made within financial services firms. An important goal of this research is to provide more accurate and tractable models to value derivative securities. Robert Merton's (1973) research, along with Myron Scholes and Fischer Black's (1973) contributions, provided the seminal work in this area. Sanjiv Das's work continues this tradition, with a focus on the valuation and hedging of fixed-income instruments, especially credit risk derivatives, credit-linked instruments, and fixed-income instruments subject to systematic jump risk.[2]

INSTITUTIONAL STRUCTURE AND PERFORMANCE

Beyond the work that is narrowly under the four GFS project areas, there is an ongoing and varied research agenda of the Finance faculty that looks at how institutional structures in place in the financial services sector affect the incentives and decisions of managers of investment banks, venture capital pools, savings and loans, and banks.

Samuel Hayes's work on the Islamic financial system, which he has undertaken with Professor Frank E. Vogel of the Harvard Law School, is a wide-ranging examination of law and financial structures in the Islamic world, and how the financial system operates under the mandates of the Koran. This work, published in a book entitled *Islamic Law and Finance: Religion, Risk, and Return* (1998), illustrates that financial systems innovate to deliver fundamental functions to their users, even when working under relatively restrictive constraints.

Islam prohibits the payment of interest on bank deposits, thus creating a special relationship between Islamic banks and their depositors, who are entitled only to a share of profits the bank earns on its assets. Because these banks are similarly not allowed to make loans with an interest rate attached, they must invest their assets through such outlets as the purchase and installment resale (with a markup) of goods to both businesses and retail consumers, the financing of work-in-process=projects, and the leasing of all kinds of plant and equipment. The flip side of this set of constraints is that, although Islamic businesses cannot finance themselves with interest-paying loans, there are other means by which they create some financial leverage. These include inventory financing, construction advances, and plant and equipment leases extended to them either by Islamic banks or by conventional Western financial intermediaries who make the contracts conform to religious principles.

Joshua Lerner and Paul Gompers have examined the institutional structure and incentives of venture capitalists from a variety of perspectives, ranging from how reputational concerns of venture capitalists affect the timing of bringing companies to market via IPOs, the way in which profits are divided between general partners and limited partners, the establishment of covenants in venture capital documents, the distribution of shares from limited partnerships, and the staging of investment.[3] Their research agenda focuses on each of the institutional stages of the venture capital business, from raising funds, structuring the limited partnership agreement, making investments, liquidating those investments, and distributing the proceeds. In each case the research attempts to discern how implicit and explicit incentives affect the decisions of venture capitalists, investors, and entrepreneurs. This work has also served as the basis for Lerner's HBS course, Venture Capital and Private Equity; HBS executive education offerings; and a related MBA course developed by Gompers while at the University of Chicago.

Benjamin Esty's work on savings and loan associations examines related issues, while in a different institutional setting. His work on depository institutions examines how organizational form, capital structure, and ownership structure affect managerial incentives, particularly with regard to risk taking (Esty 1997a,b). A companion piece examines bankers' investment and capitalization decisions in the early twentieth century at a time when shareholders were not protected by limited liability (Esty 1998). Peter Tufano and Matthew Sevick's (1997) work on mutual fund boards examines how the structure of these boards is related to their decisions that set the fees faced by investors in the funds.

One of the six core functions in the GFS classification scheme is the role of security markets in providing information to help firms, households, financial institutions, and governments make decisions. Two research projects investigate the empirical evidence for the effectiveness of the U.S. stock market in serving this function. Lisa Meulbroek (Meulbroek and Hart 1996, 1997) investigates whether illegal insider trading impedes the market for corporate control by increasing the premium a bidder must pay for a target. Her previous research (Meulbroek 1992) shows that illegal insider trading has a material impact on stock prices, leading to the incorporation of the nonpublic information into the stock price. This paper tests whether managerial investment decisions about the price to bid for acquisitions are influenced by this stock price impact. The other project, conducted by Meulbroek and Robert Merton (with co-author Mark Mitchell of the University of Chicago), studies the potential role of the market in managerial decision making, asking how accurately the stock market immediately evaluates managers' investment decisions. The forecasting accuracy of this stock price response should provide some guidance to managers on how much attention to devote to it. A secondary focus of the project is an analysis of how managers actually respond to the stock price reactions to investment announcements.

Sanjiv Das's work with Ashish Nanda (of the General Management Unit at HBS) on banking structure examines the social costs of the legal divisions of banks into commercial and investment banks. Their theory shows that this division emanates from a functional source: the degree of information asymmetry and output verifiability of the banking service provided. The model they develop can help explain bank syndication, universal banking, and strategic incentives in the financial services industry (Das and Nanda 1996).

Das and colleague George Chacko have studied the problem of how and when mutual funds should spend money on acquiring timing versus stock selection information. They provide several interesting theoretical results which form a framework for understanding and managing a mutual fund's information-gathering activities (Chacko and Das 1996).

Finally, Stuart Gilson's extensive work on corporate reorganization addresses the impact of transaction costs and agency conflicts on the organization and performance of firms. For example, in a recent empirical paper, he argues that a careful consideration of transaction costs can explain the financial decisions and performance of firms emerging from financial distress (Gilson 1997). His field work, on nonfinancial and financial firms in the United States, Canada, and Europe, examines the financial and organizational structures of reorganized firms, with an eye to understanding what factors affect the path of reorganization and how the form of reorganization in turn affects the subsequent performance of the firm. This research also serves as the basis for the MBA and Executive Education courses on Creating Value through Corporate Restructuring.

The Global Financial System Project References

Asquith, Paul, and Lisa Meulbroek. 1995. "An Empirical Investigation of Short Interest." Harvard Business School Working Paper.

Balduzzi, Pierluigi, Sanjiv R. Das, and Silverio Foresi. 1995. "The Central Tendency: A Second Factor in Bond Yields." *The Review of Economics and Statistics*, forthcoming.

Bernstein, P. 1992. *Capital Ideas: The Improbable Origins of Modern Wall Street.* New York: Free Press.

Black, F., and M. S. Scholes. 1973. "The Pricing of Options and Corporate Liabilities." *Journal of Political Economy* 81: 637–659.

Bodie, Zvi. 1995. "On the Risk of Stocks in the Long Run." *Financial Analysts Journal* (May–June): 18–22.

Bodie, Zvi, and Dwight B. Crane. 1997. "Personal Investing: Advice, Theory, and Evidence." *Financial Analysts Journal*: 13–23.

Bodie, Zvi, and Robert C. Merton. 1992. "Pension Reform and Privatization in International Perspective: The Case of Israel." *The Economics Quarterly*: 152.

———. 1993. "Pension Benefit Guarantees in the United States: A Functional Analysis." In *The Future of Pensions in the United States*, edited by R. Schmitt. Philadelphia: University of Pennsylvania Press.

Brav, Alon, Chris Geczy, and Paul Gompers. 1995. "The Long-Run Underperformance of Seasoned Equity Offerings Revisited." Harvard Business School Working Paper.

Brav, Alon, and Paul Gompers. 1996. "Myth or Reality? The Long-Run Underperformance of Initial Public Offerings: Evidence from Venture and Nonventure-backed Companies." Harvard Business School Working Paper.

Chacko, George, and Sanjiv Das. 1996. "A Theory of Optimal Timing and Selectivity." *Journal of Economic Dynamics and Control*, forthcoming.

Crane, Dwight B., and Zvi Bodie. 1996. "Form Follows Function: The Transformation of Banking." *Harvard Business Review* (March/April): 109–117.

Crane, Dwight B., Kenneth A. Froot, Scott P. Mason, André F. Perold, Robert C. Merton, Zvi Bodie, Erik R. Sirri, and Peter Tufano. 1995. *The Global Financial System: A Functional Perspective.* Boston: Harvard Business School Press.

Darby, M. 1994. "OTC Derivatives and Systemic Risk." National Bureau of Economic Research Working Paper 4801, Cambridge, Mass.

Das, Sanjiv R. 1994. "Poisson-Gaussian Processes and the Bond Markets." Harvard Business School Working Paper.

———. 1995a. "Credit Risk Derivatives." *Journal of Derivatives*: 7–21.

———. 1995b. "A Direct Discrete-Time Approach to Poisson-Gaussian Bond Option Pricing in the Heath-Jarrow-Morton Model." *Journal of Economic Dynamics and Control*, forthcoming.

———. 1997. "Discrete-Time Bond and Option Pricing for Jump-Diffusion Processes." *Review of Derivatives Research* 1 (3): 211–244.

Das, Sanjiv R., and Jamil Baz. 1996. "Analytical Approximations of the Term Structure for Jump-diffusion Processes: A Numerical Analysis." *Journal of Fixed Income* 6 (1):78–86.

Das, Sanjiv R., and Silverio Foresi. 1996. "Exact Solutions for Bond and Options Prices with Systematic Jump Risk." *Review of Derivatives Research* 1 (1): 7–24.

Das, Sanjiv R., and Ashish Nanda. 1996. "A Theory of Banking Structure." Harvard Business School Working Paper.

Das, Sanjiv R., and Peter Tufano. 1996. "Pricing Credit Sensitive Debt When Interest Rates, Credit Ratings and Credit Spreads Are Stochastic." *Journal of Financial Engineering* 5 (June): 161–198.

Das, Sanjiv R., and Raman Uppal. 1996. "Shock Therapy: Global Asset Allocation with Large Market Movements." Harvard Business School Working Paper.

de la Vega, J. 1688. *Confusion de Confusiones*. Translated by H. Kallenbenz. The Kress Library Series of Publications, no. 13. Cambridge, Mass.: Harvard University, 1957.

Esty, Benjamin C. 1997a. "A Case Study of Organizational Form and Risk Shifting in Savings and Loan Industry." *Journal of Financial Economics* 44: 57–76.

———. 1997b. "Organizational Form and Asset Risk in the Savings and Loan Industry." *Journal of Financial Economics* 44: 25–55.

———. 1998. "The Impact of Contingent Liability on Commercial Bank Risk Taking," *Journal of Financial Economics* 47: 189–218.

Esty, Benjamin, Bhanu Narasimhan, and Peter Tufano. 1998. "Interest Rate Exposure and Bank Mergers: A Preliminary Empirical Analysis." *Journal of Banking and Finance*, forthcoming.

Esty, Benjamin, Peter Tufano, and Jonathan Headley. 1994. "Banc One Corporation: Asset and Liability Management." *Journal of Applied Corporate Finance* 7 (Fall): 33–51, with "Commentary," 63–65.

Finnerty, J. D. 1988. "Financial Engineering in Corporate Finance: An Overview." *Financial Management* 17 (Winter): 14–33.

———. 1992. "An Overview of Corporate Securities Innovation." *Journal of Applied Corporate Finance* 4 (Winter): 23–39.

Froot, Kenneth. 1993. "Currency Hedging Over Long Horizons." Harvard, April. NBER Working Paper 4355, May. Featured in *NBER Digest,* October.

———. 1995a. "The Emerging Asset Class: Insurance Risk." With B. Murphy, A. Stern, and S. Usher. *Special Report from Guy Carpenter and Company, Inc.* July. Reprinted in *Viewpoint* 24(3): 19–28.

———. 1995b. "Hedging Portfolios with Real Assets." *Journal of Portfolio Management* (Summer): 60–77.

Froot, Kenneth, and André Perold. 1993. "Determinants of Optimal Currency Hedging." Harvard Business School Working Paper, June.

Froot, Kenneth A., David Scharfstein, and Jeremy Stein. 1993. "Risk Management: Coordinating Corporate Investment and Financing Decisions." *Journal of Finance* 48 (December): 1629–1658.

———. 1994a,b. "A Framework for Risk Management." With D. Scharfstein and J. Stein. *Harvard Business Review* 72 (November/December): 91–102. Reprinted in *Journal of Applied Corporate Finance* 7 (Fall): 22–32.

Froot, Kenneth A., and Jeremy Stein. 1998. "Risk Management, Capital Budgeting and Capital Structure Policy for Financial Institutions: An Integrated Approach." *Journal of Financial Economics* 47 (January): 55–82.

Gammill, J., and André Perold. 1989. "The Changing Character of Stock Market Liquidity." *Journal of Portfolio Management* 13 (Spring): 13–17.

Gilson, Stuart C. 1995. "Investing in Distressed Situations: A Market Survey." *Financial Analysts Journal* (November/December): 8–27.

———. 1997. "Transactions Costs and Capital Structure Choice: Evidence from Financially Distressed Firms." *Journal of Finance* 52: 161–196.

Gilson, Stuart C., and Jerold Warner. 1997. "Junk Bonds, Bank Debt, and Financing Corporate Growth." Harvard Business School Working Paper.

Gompers, Paul. 1994. "The Rise of Venture Capital." *Business and Economic History* 23 (Winter): 1–24.

———. 1995. "Optimal Investment, Monitoring, and the Staging of Venture Capital." *Journal of Finance* (December): 1461–1490.

———. 1996a. "A Clinical Examination of Convertible Securities in Venture Capital." Harvard Business School Working Paper, June.

———. 1996b. "Grandstanding in the Venture Capital Industry." *Journal of Financial Economics* (July): 133–156.

———. 1996c. "Resource Allocation, Incentives, and Control: The Importance of Venture Capital in Financing Entrepreneurial Firms." *Entrepreneurship, SMEs, and the Macroeconomy*, forthcoming.

Gompers, Paul, and Joshua Lerner. 1996. "The Use of Covenants: An Analysis of Venture Partnership Agreements." *Journal of Law and Economics* 39 (October).

———. 1998a. "An Analysis of Compensation in the U.S. Venture Capital Partnership." *Journal of Financial Economics*, forthcoming.

———. 1998b. "Venture Capital Distributions: Short-Run and Long-Run Reactions." *Journal of Finance*, forthcoming.

Grossman, S. J., and O. D. Hart. 1982. "Corporate Financial Structure and Managerial Incentives." In *The Economics of Information and Uncertainty*, edited by J.J. McCall. Chicago: University of Chicago Press.

Hendershott, Patric H., and James D. Shilling. 1989. "The Impact of Agencies on Conventional Fixed-Rate Mortgage Yields." *Journal of Real Estate Finance and Economics* 2: 101–115.

Hindy, Ayman. 1995. "Elements of Quantitative Risk Management." In *Risk Management: Problems and Solutions*, edited by William H. Beaver and George Parker. New York: McGraw-Hill.

Homer, S. 1977. *A History of Interest Rates*. 2d ed. New Brunswick, N.J.: Rutgers University Press.

Hubbard, R. G. 1994. *Money, the Financial System, and the Economy*. Reading, Mass: Addison-Wesley.

Jameson, Mel, S. Dewan, and C. F. Sirmans. 1992. "Measuring Welfare Effects of 'Unbundling' Financial Innovations: The Case of Collateralized Mortgage Obligations." *Journal of Urban Economics* 31: 1–13.

Jensen, M. C. 1986. "The Agency Costs of Free Cash Flow: Corporate Finance and Takeovers." *American Economic Review* 76 (May): 323–329.

Kohn, M. 1994. *Financial Institutions and Markets*. New York: McGraw-Hill.

Kritzman, Mark, Jay Light, and Don Rich. 1996. "Risk Containment Strategies for

Endowments with Absolute and Relative Targets." Harvard Business School Working Paper, January.

Lerner, Joshua. 1994a. "The Syndication of Venture Capital Investments." *Financial Management* 23 (Autumn): 16–27.

———. 1994b. "Venture Capitalists and the Decision to Go Public." *Journal of Financial Economics* 35 (June): 293–316.

———. 1995. "Venture Capitalists and the Oversight of Private Firms." *Journal of Finance* 50 (March): 301–318.

———. 1998. "The Government as Venture Capitalist: The Long-Run Impact of the SBIR Program." Harvard Business School Working Paper.

Luehrman, T., and P. Tufano. 1994. "MW Petroleum Corp. (B)." Harvard Business School Case 295–045.

Mason, Scott, Robert C. Merton, André Perold, and Peter Tufano. 1995. *Cases in Financial Engineering: Applied Studies of Financial Innovation.* Englewood Cliffs, N.J.: Prentice Hall.

Merton, Robert C. 1973. "Theory of Rational Option Pricing." *Bell Journal of Economics and Management Science* 4: 141–183.

———. 1989. "On the Application of the Continuous-Time Theory of Finance to Financial Intermediation and Insurance." *The Geneva Papers on Risk and Insurance* 14 (July): 225–262.

———. 1990. "The Financial System and Economic Performance." *Journal of Financial Services Research* 4 (December): 263–300.

———. 1992a. *Continuous-Time Finance.* rev. ed. Oxford: Basil Blackwell.

———. 1992b. "Financial Innovation and Economic Performance." *Journal of Applied Corporate Finance* 4 (Winter): 12–22.

———. 1993. "Operation and Regulation in Financial Intermediation: A Functional Perspective." In *Operation and Regulation of Financial Markets,* edited by P. Englund. Stockholm: The Economic Council.

———. 1994. "Influence of Mathematical Models in Finance on Practice: Past, Present and Future." *Philosophical Transactions of the Royal Society of London* 347 (June): 451–463.

———. 1995. "Financial Innovation and the Management and Regulation of Financial Institutions." *Journal of Banking and Finance* 19 (January): 461–481.

———. 1997. "A Model of Contract Guarantees for Credit-Sensitive, Opaque Financial Intermediaries." *European Finance Review* 1 (1): 1–13.

———. 1998. "Applications of Option-Pricing Theory: Twenty-Five Years Later." *Les Prix Nobel* 1997. Stockholm: Nobel Foundation.

Merton, Robert C., and Zvi Bodie. 1992a. "A Framework for Analyzing the Financial System." Harvard Business School Working Paper.

———. 1992b. "On the Management of Financial Guarantees." *Financial Management* 22 (Winter): 87–109.

———. 1993. "Deposit Insurance Reform: A Functional Approach." In *Carnegie-Rochester Conference Series on Public Policy,* vol. 38, edited by A. Meltzer and C. Plosser.

Merton, Robert C. and Alberto Moel. 1997. "Smith Breeden Associates: The Equity Plus Fund." Harvard Business School Case 297-089.

Merton, Robert C., and André F. Perold, 1993. "Theory of Risk Capital in Financial Firms," *Journal of Applied Corporate Finance* 5 (Fall): 16–32.

Meulbroek, Lisa. 1992. "An Empirical Analysis of Illegal Insider Trading." *Journal of Finance* 47: 1661–1700.

Meulbroek, Lisa, and C. Hart. 1996. "An Exploratory Analysis of the Effect of Insider Trading on the Market for Corporate Control." Harvard Business School Working Paper.

———. 1997. "The Effect of Illegal Insider Trading on Takeover Premia." *European Finance Review* 1 (1): 51–80.

Miller, M. 1992. "Financial Innovation: Achievements and Prospects." *Journal of Applied Corporate Finance* 4 (Winter): 4–11.

Modigliani, Franco, and Merton Miller. 1958. "The Cost of Capital, Corporation Finance and the Theory of Investment." *American Economic Review* 48: 261–297.

North, D. C. 1994. "Economic Performance Through Time." *American Economic Review* 84 (June): 359–368.

Norton, J., and P. Spellman, eds. 1991. *Asset Securitization: International Financial and Legal Perspectives.* Oxford: Basil Blackwell.

Perold, A. F. 1992. "B.E.A. Associates: Enhanced Equity Index Funds." Harvard Business School Case 293-024.

Pierce, J. L. 1993. "The Functional Approach to Deposit Insurance and Regulation." In *Safeguarding the Banking System in an Environment of Financial Cycles,* edited by R. E. Randall. Proceedings of a Symposium of the Federal Reserve Bank of Boston, November, 11–130.

Rose, P. S. 1994. *Money and Capital Markets: The Financial System in an Increasingly Global Economy.* 5th ed. Burr Ridge, Ill.: Irwin.

Sanford, C. S., Jr. 1993. "Financial Markets in 2020." *Federal Reserve Bank of Kansas City Economic Symposium,* 20 August.

Scholes, M. S. 1994. "Financial Infrastructure and Economic Growth." Conference on Growth and Development: The Economics of the 21st Century, Center for Economic Policy Research, Stanford University, June.

Sirmans, C. F., and John D. Benjamin. 1990. "Pricing Fixed Rate Mortgages: Some Empirical Evidence." *Journal of Financial Services Research* 4:191–202.

Sirri, Erik R., and Peter Tufano. 1998. "Costly Search and Mutual Fund Flows." *Journal of Finance,* forthcoming..

Smith, Clifford W., and René Stulz. 1985. "The Determinants of Firms' Hedging Policies." *Journal of Financial and Quantitative Analysis* 20: 391–405.

Stulz, René. 1984. "Optimal Hedging Policies." *Journal of Financial and Quantitative Analysis* 19: 127–140.

———. 1990. "Managerial Discretion and Optimal Financing Policies." *Journal of Financial Economics* 26: 3–28.

Tufano, Peter. 1995. "Securities Innovations: A Historical and Functional Perspective." *Journal of Applied Corporate Finance* 7 (Winter): 90–103.

———. 1996a. "Do Fools Rush In? Rewards to Buying and Selling the Newest Financial Products." Harvard Business School Working Paper, July.

———. 1996b. "How Financial Engineering Can Advance Corporate Strategy." *Harvard Business Review* (January/February): 136–146.

———. 1996c. "Who Manages Risk? An Empirical Examination of Risk Management Practices in the Gold Mining Industry." *Journal of Finance* (September): 1097–1137.

———. 1998a. "Agency Costs of Corporate Risk Management." *Financial Management* 27 (Spring): 67–77.

———. 1998b. "The Determinants of Stock Price Exposure: Financial Engineering and the Gold Mining Industry." *Journal of Finance* 53 (June): 1015–1052.

Tufano, Peter, and Cameron Poetzscher. 1996. "Tennessee Valley Authority: Option Purchase Agreements." Harvard Business School Case 296–038.

Tufano, Peter, and Matthew Sevick. 1997. "Board Structure and Fee-Setting in the U.S. Mutual Fund Industry." *Journal of Financial Economics* 46 (December): 321–356.

Tufano, P., and J. Serbin. 1993. "American Barrick Resources Corp.: Managing Gold Price Risk." Harvard Business School Case 293–128.

Vogel, Frank E., and Samuel L. Hayes. 1998. *Islamic Law and Finance: Religion, Risk, and Return.* Boston, Mass.: Kluwer Law International.

Williamson, O. E. 1985. *The Economic Institutions of Capitalism.* New York: The Free Press.

———. 1988. "Corporate Finance and Corporate Governance." *Journal of Finance* 43 (July): 567–591.

Zweig, P. L., ed. 1989. *The Asset Securitization Handbook.* Homewood, Ill.: Dow Jones-Irwin.

Organizations and Markets References

Baker, George P. "Pay for Performance: Causes and Consequences." *The Journal of Applied Corporate Finance* 3, no. 3 (Fall 1990).

Baker, George P., Robert Gibbons, and Kevin J. Murphy. "Relational Contracts and the Theory of the Firm." Harvard Business School Working Paper, December 1997.

Baker, George P., Michael C. Jensen, and Kevin J. Murphy. "Compensation and Incentives: Practice vs. Theory." *Journal of Finance* (July 1988).

Baker, George P., and Karen H. Wruck. "Organizational Changes and Value Creation in Leveraged Buyouts: The Case of O. M. Scott & Sons Company." *Journal of Financial Economics* 25 (1990): 163–190.

Brickley, James A., Clifford W. Smith, Jr., and Jerold L. Zimmerman. *Managerial Economics and Organizational Architecture.* Homewood, Ill: Irwin, 1997.

Jensen, Michael C., "The Agency Costs of Free Cash Flow: Corporate Finance and Takeovers." *American Economic Review* 76, no. 2 (May 1986).

———. "The Takeover Controversy: Analysis and Evidence." *The Midland Corporate Finance Journal* (Summer 1986). Also appears in *Knights, Raiders, and Targets: The Impact of the Hostile Takeover*, edited by John Coffee, Jr., Louis Lowenstein, and Susan Rose-Ackerman. New York: Oxford University Press, 1988, and *Corporate Restructuring and Executive Compensation*, edited by Joel M. Stern, G. Bennett Stewart III, and Donald H. Chew, Jr. Cambridge, Mass.: Ballinger Publishing, 1989.

———. "Takeovers: Their Causes and Consequences." *Journal of Economic Perspectives* 2, no. 1 (Winter 1998).

———. "Self Interest, Altruism, Incentives, and Agency Theory." *The Journal of Applied Corporate Finance* (Summer 1994): 40–45.

Jensen, Michael C., and William H. Meckling. "Theory of the Firm: Managerial Behavior, Agency Costs and Ownership Structure." *Journal of Financial Economics* 3, no. 4 (1976).

———. "The Nature of Man." *The Journal of Applied Corporate Finance* (Summer 1994): 4–19.

Jensen, Michael C., and Kevin J. Murphy. "Performance Pay and Top Management Incentives." *Journal of Political Economy* (April 1990): 225–265.

———. "A New Survey of Executive Compensation," Full Survey and Technical Appendix to "CEO Incentives—It's Not How Much You Pay, But How." *Harvard Business Review* (May/June 1990): 150–153.

Jensen, Michael C., and Richard S. Ruback. "The Market for Corporate Control: The Scientific Evidence." *Journal of Financial Economics* 11, nos. 1–4 (April 1983).

McNair, Malcolm P. "Tough-Mindedness and the Case Method," in *The Case Method at the Harvard Business School: Papers by Present and Past Members of the Faculty and Staff*, edited by Malcom P. McNair, 15–24. New York: McGraw-Hill, 1954. Adapted from an address given 25 February 1953, at the first meeting of the executives registered for the 23rd Advanced Management Program at the Harvard Business School.

Tversky, A., and D. Kahneman. "The Framing of Decisions and the Psychology of Choice." *Science* 211 (1981): 453–458.

———. "Rational Choice and the Framing of Decisions." *Journal of Business* 59 (1986): S251–S278.

Wruck, Karen H. "Financial Policy, Internal Control, and Performance: Sealed Air Corporation's Leveraged Special Dividend." *Journal of Financial Economics* 36 (1994): 157–192.

Wruck, Karen H., and Michael C. Jensen. "Science, Specific Knowledge and Total Quality Management." *Journal of Accounting and Economics* 18 (1994): 247–287.

Wruck, Karen H., and Sherry P. Roper. "Sink or Swim? Cytec Industries' Spin-Off (A)." Harvard Business School Case 9-897-053 (9/18/96).

———. "Sink or Swim? Cytec Industries' Spin-Off (B)." Harvard Business School Case 9-897-054 (9/18/96).

Wruck, Karen H., and Steve-Anna Stephens. "Safeway, Inc.'s Leveraged Buyout (A)." Harvard Business School Case 9-294-139 (6/2/94).

———. "Safeway, Inc.'s Leveraged Buyout (B)." Harvard Business School Case 9-294-140 (6/2/94).

———. "Safeway, Inc.'s Leveraged Buyout (C), Media Response." Harvard Business School Case 9-294-141 (6/2/94).

Service Profit Chain Research References

Anderson, Eugene W., Claes Fornell, and Donald R. Lehmann. 1993. "Customer Satisfaction Market Share and Profitability: Findings from Sweden. "Working paper, December.

Anderson, Eugene W. L., and Mary Sullivan. 1993. "The Antecedents and Consequences of Customer Satisfaction and Repurchase Likelihood." *Marketing Letters.*

Bennis, Warren G. 1970. "Beyond Bureaucracy." In *American Bureaucracy,* edited by Warren G. Bennis, Chicago: Aldine Publishing Company. 3-17.

Bernhardt, K., N. Donthu, and P. Kennett. 1994. "The Relationship Among Customer Satisfaction, Employee Satisfaction, and Profitability: A Longitudinal Analysis." Working paper, Georgia State University, January.

Blau, Peter M. 1974. *On The Nature of Organizations,* 80-84. New York: Wiley.

Boulding, William, Richard Staelin, Ajay Kalra, and Valerie Zeithaml. 1992. "Conceptualizing and Testing a Dynamic Process Model of Service Quality." Technical Working Paper 92-121, Marketing Science Institute, August.

Buzzell, Robert D., and Bradley T. Gale. 1987. *The PIMS Principles: Linking Strategy to Performance.* New York: The Free Press.

Czepiel, John A., Michael R. Soloman, and Carol F. Suprenant, eds. 1985. *The Service Encounter: Managing Employee/Customer Interaction in Service Businesses.* Lexington, Mass.: D. C. Heath.

Fornell, Claes. 1992. "A National Customer Satisfaction Barometer: The Swedish Experience." *Journal of Marketing* (January): 1-21.

Grant, Alan W. H., and Leonard A. Schlesinger. 1995. "Realize Your Customers' Full Profit Potential." *Harvard Business Review* (September/October): 59-72.

Heskett, James L. *Managing in the Service Economy.* 1986. Boston: Harvard Business School Press.

Heskett, James L., Thomas O. Jones, Gary W. Loveman, W. Earl Sasser, Jr., and Leonard A. Schlesinger. 1994. "Putting the Service-Profit Chain to Work." *Harvard Business Review* (March/April): 164-174.

Heskett, James L., W. Earl Sasser, Jr., and. 1990. *Service Breakthroughs: Changing the Rules of the Game.* New York: The Free Press.

Heskett, James L., W. Earl Sasser, Jr., and Leonard A. Schlesinger. 1997. *The Service Profit Chain: How leading Companies Link Profit and Growth to Loyalty, Satisfaction, and Value.* New York: The Free Press.

Johnson, E. M., and D. T. Seymour. 1985. "The Impact of Cross-Selling on the Service Encounter in Retail Banking." In *The Service Encounter: Managing Employee/Customer Interaction in Service Businesses,* edited by John A. Czepiel, Michael R. Soloman, and Carol F. Suprenant, 225-239. Lexington, Mass.: D. C. Heath.

Jones, Thomas O., and W. Earl Sasser, Jr. 1995. "Why Satisfied Customers Defect." *Harvard Business Review* (November/December): 88-99.

Kaplan, Robert S., and David P. Norton. 1992. "The Balanced Scorecard— Measures that Drive Performance." *Harvard Business Review* (January/February): 71-79.

        . 1993. "Putting the Balanced Scorecard to Work." *Harvard Business Review* (September/October): 134-147.

        . 1996. *The Balanced Scorecard: Translating Strategy into Action.* Boston: Harvard Business School Press.

Kotter, John P., and James L. Heskett. 1992. *Corporate Culture and Performance.* New York: The Free Press.

Lawler, E. E., III. 1973. *Motivation in Work Organizations,* 153-165. Monterrey, Calif.: Brooks/Cole.

Parkington, J. J., and Benjamin Schneider. 1979. "Some Correlates of Experienced Job Stress: A Boundary Role Study." *Academy of Management Journal.* 22: 270-281.

Reichheld, Frederick F. 1996. *The Loyalty Effect: The Hidden Force Behind Growth, Profits, and Lasting Value.* Boston: Harvard Business School Press.

Reichheld, Frederick F., and Keith Aspenall. 1993-1994. "Building High Loyalty Business Systems." *Journal of Retail Banking* (Winter): 21-29.

Reichheld, Frederick F., and W. Earl Sasser, Jr. 1990. "Zero Defections: Quality Comes to Services." *Harvard Business Review* (September/October): 105-111.

Rust, Roland L., and Anthony Zahorik.1991 "The Value of Customer Satisfaction." Working paper, Vanderbilt University, June.

        . 1992. "A Model of the Impact of Customer Satisfaction on Profitability: Application to a Health Service Provider." Working paper, Vanderbilt University.

Sasser, W. Earl, Jr., and Stephen P. Arbeit. 1976. "Selling Jobs in the Service Sector." *Business Horizons* (June): 61-65.

Schlesinger, Leonard A., and James L. Heskett. 1991a "Breaking the Cycle of Failure in Services." *Sloan Management Review* (Spring): 17-28.

.1991b. "Customer Satisfaction Is Rooted in Employee Satisfaction." *Harvard Business Review*(November/December): 148-149.

.1991c. "Enfranchisement of Service Workers." *California Management Review* (Summer): 83-100.

. 1991d. "The Service-Driven Service Company." *Harvard Business Review* (September/October): 71-81.

Schlesinger, Leonard A., and Jeffrey Zornitsky. 1991. "Job Satisfaction, Service Capability, and Customer Satisfaction: An Examination of Linkages and Management Implications." *Human Resource Planning* 14: 141-149.

Schneider, Benjamin, and David E. Bowen. 1995a. "Employee and Customer Perceptions of Service in Banks: Replication and Extension." *Journal of Applied Psychology* 70: 23-433.

. 1985b. "New Services Design, Development, and Implementation and the Employee." In *New Services*, edited by W. R. George and C. Marshall, 82-101. Chicago: American Marketing Association.

Schneider, Benjamin, J. J. Parkington, and V. M. Buxton. 1980."Employee and Customer Perceptions of Service in Banks." *Administrative Science Quarterly*, June.

Tornow, Walter W., and Jack W. Wiley. 1991. "Service Quality and Management Practices: A Look at Employee Attitudes, Customer Satisfaction, and Bottom-Line Consequences." *Human Resource Planning* 14: 105-115.

Wiley, Jack W. 1991."Customer Satisfaction: A Supportive Work Environment and Its Financial Costs." *Human Resource Planning* 14: 117-127.

Notes

1. From McArthur's address at the AMP graduation ceremony, 15 December 1983.

2. McArthur had been a professor of finance, and the financial model he adopted for the School would warrant an essay of its own. Simply put, it relied on roughly equal contributions from three sources: MBA tuition, executive programs, and publications. Gifts from alumni and other friends of the School would constitute a fourth important income stream, and one that would finance much of the School's most innovative work.

   During McArthur's tenure, contributions from the MBA program, executive programs, and publications all increased about fourfold in nominal terms, to $35 million, $35 million, and $55 million, respectively. Annual giving grew from $8 million to $30 million, and the number of chaired professorships increased from 50 to 87. The market value of the School's share of the Harvard endowment multiplied sixfold, from $100 million to $600 million (again in nominal terms)—with considerable help from a bull market. Despite this success, McArthur wasn't particularly interested in piling up surpluses without a purpose. "I am persuaded," he told one of the School's governing boards in 1992, "that a big endowment is a strategic error for a professional school. We have to live by our wits, and do. We should not make *any* next generation feel at all comfortable."

3. Fred I. Greenstein, *The Hidden-Hand Presidency: Eisenhower as Leader* (New York: Basic Books, 1982), 233.

4. These numbers were a regular feature of McArthur's writings and speeches in the early part of his deanship. See, for example, his introduction to the School's 1979–1980 "annual report" to contributors. McArthur predicted that there would be a shakeout in the industry and that two groups of schools were best prepared to survive that shakeout: the dozen "national, research-oriented schools" like HBS, and local schools that were thoroughly attuned to the needs of their constituents.

5. A celebrated *Fortune* article from 1974 had dubbed the Harvard MBA Class of 1949 "the class the dollars fell on." This same class later became the subject

of a book—*The Big Time: The Harvard Business School's Most Successful Class and How It Shaped America* (New York: Harper & Row, 1986)—by the journalist Laurence Shames.

6. Fouraker is also credited for effecting necessary economies in the operation of the School, for beginning a major and overdue restoration of the campus, for braking growth in the size of the faculty, and for imposing strict quality controls on executive education. For a summary of Fouraker's perspective on the state of the School as he had left it, see his interview in the March/April 1981 issue of the *Harvard Business School Bulletin*, 24.

7. McArthur interview with one of the authors, 10 June 1997.

8. Unless otherwise noted, the quoted materials from the subsequent section are from the 29 August 1979 letter from John McArthur to Derek Bok.

9. This elaboration is borrowed from McArthur's talk to HBS alumni on 10 October 1980.

10. Each of the authors heard McArthur make this comment more than once.

11. McArthur interview with one of the authors, 10 June 1997.

12. Ibid.

13. From McArthur's 1 October 1988 speech to the 25th and 30th reunion classes.

14. There was a stealthy antecedent to this love affair. Throughout the Fouraker deanship, an informal arrangement was set up whereby exotic trees that had to be "outsourced" by Harvard's Arnold Arboretum were quietly transplanted to the Business School, where they were sure to be well cared for. These trees—along with the School's rare stand of lovingly maintained American elms—make the campus a remarkable arboreal setting.

15. McArthur told this story to many colleagues and visitors, including two of the authors.

16. From McArthur's memo submitted to the 17 June 1992 University Academic and Planning Process and Retreat.

17. The source of this story is Professor Richard S. Tedlow.

18. From McArthur's annual report for 1981–1982.

19. Chester Barnard, *The Functions of the Executive* (Cambridge, Mass.: Harvard University Press, 1938), 194. Barnard, not given to excessive use of italics, italicized this entire sentence. The colleague who came to McArthur's office was Professor Charles Christenson.

20. From McArthur's comments at the 3 June 1989 Alumni Awards program.

21. McArthur interview with one of the authors, 10 June 1997.

22. From McArthur's January 1981 annual report.

23. From McArthur's comments to a 5 June 1989 faculty workshop.

24. See, for example, McArthur's notes for the 7 February 1984 meeting of his "coordinating group."

25. From McArthur's notes for his comments on 7 March 1990 to the Council of Deans.

26. From McArthur's notes for his 10 March 1990 comments to the School's Visiting Committee.

27. From McArthur's January 1980 speech to the faculty.

28. From McArthur's speech to the 17 April 1980 International Dinner of the HBS Club of New York City.

29. From McArthur's talk to the 25th and 30th reunion classes, 10 October 1980.

30. McArthur interview with one of the authors, 10 June 1997.

31. The three were Michael Porter (Competition and Strategy), Howard Stevenson (Entrepreneurship), and Thomas McCraw (Business and Government).

32. From a 27 September 1983 internal memo.

33. From McArthur's notes for his comments to the Visiting Committee on 11 March 1994.

34. From McArthur's speech to the 25th reunion class, 10 October 1986. He attributed the "kiss of death" idea to his colleague Warren McFarlan.

35. From McArthur's notes for his talk to an "IBM lunch," 15 April 1988.

36. Warren McFarlan interview with Jeffrey L. Cruikshank, Summer 1995.

37. Earl Sasser interview with Jeffrey L. Cruikshank, Summer 1995.

38. McArthur interview with one of the authors, 10 June 1997.

39. From McArthur's notes on his comments to the Board of Directors of the Associates, 24 February 1989.

40. From McArthur's talking points for the meeting of the Visiting Committee, 13 March 1993.

41. From McArthur's undated memo to Derek Bok, from early Spring 1985.

42. "And when things *didn't* work out," McArthur recently commented, "Derek never threw those things back at me. He was fantastic in that way. He'd push you hard, and after the fact, support you wherever things came off the track."

43. One of the authors of this essay heard Bok's comment about the "most managed" part of Harvard during the 1980s, in the context of discussing McArthur's deanship. McArthur's comment about Bok is from an interview with another of the authors, 8 October 1997.

44. From McArthur's comments to the final session of the "Breaking New Ground" symposium at HBS, 11 October 1996.

45. From McArthur's memo prepared for the University Academic and Planning Process and Retreat, 17 June 1992.

46. From McArthur's notes on his comments to the Board of Directors of the Associates, 27 March 1993.

2 TECHNOLOGY AND OPERATIONS MANAGEMENT

1. The authors would like to stress at the outset that the speculative passages in this chapter—although derived in part through years of collaboration with their colleagues in TOM and other units—represent only their own view of the world and in no way constitute a formal "agenda" of the TOM group.

2. J. Kenneth Galbraith, *The Affluent Society* (Boston: Houghton Mifflin, 1958).

3. Unlike many other business schools, HBS didn't experience the degree of rivalry between its Managerial Economics (ME) and POM areas during the 1960s and 1970s that beset the OR and OM groups at other schools. The reason, we suspect, is that our ME group was not a traditional OR group, in the sense that it did not attempt to cover the full range of OR topics. Under Professors Raiffa, Schlaifer, and Pratt, it concentrated primarily on statistical decision theory, so its interests did not overlap as much with those of POM (except in the case of forecasting and inventory control). At other schools, the two groups were engaged much more in head-to-head competition.

4. There were two notable exceptions: the Manufacturing Policy course taught by Wick Skinner was popular with students, as was Jim Bright's course on Technological Innovation.

5. For example, in a letter to the unit chairman, dated 22 May 1969 (and later distributed to all unit members), Professor A. Richard Dooley stated "I would have doubts about the suitability of Area course offerings in Management of Southern Baptist Churches; or Management of Professional Football Teams; or Management of Laotian Bordellos, even though I suspect that all three kinds of enterprises could be viewed as a system. . . ."

6. Memo to the unit faculty from Richard S. Rosenbloom, entitled "What's in a Name?" 21 May 1969, 1.

7. Memo to the POM unit faculty from A. Richard Dooley and C. Wickham Skinner, entitled "Dooley/Skinner POM Position Paper #4—Recommendations," 21 November 1969, 6.

8. Memo to the POM faculty from Robert W. Merry, responding to "Dooley/Skinner POM Position Paper #1," 6 November 1969, 4.

9. The four were Ron Fox, Jim Heskett, Paul Marshall, and Steve Wheelwright.

10. The subsequent demise of the required HRM course, and the OB unit's refocusing on small-group relationships and organizational leadership, in the 1990s put this issue back in the foreground—both for POM and for the School.

11. Including, in order of publication, "The Focused Factory," by Wickham Skinner; *The Productivity Dilemma: Roadblock to Innovation in the Automobile Industry,* by William Abernathy; "Link Manufacturing Process and Product Life Cycles," by Robert Hayes and Steven Wheelwright; *Management of Service Operations: Text, Cases, and Readings,* by Earl Sasser, Paul Olsen, and Daryl Wyckoff; and *Energy Future: Report of the Energy Project at the Harvard Business School,* edited by Robert Stobaugh and Daniel Yergin.

12. Among the better-known books were (roughly in order of publication) *Industrial Renaissance: Producing a Competitive Future for America,* by William Abernathy, Kim Clark, and Alan Kantrow; *Restoring Our Competitive Edge: Competing through Manufacturing,* by Robert Hayes and Steven Wheelwright; *Logistics Strategy: Cases and Concepts,* by Roy Shapiro and James Heskett; *Manufacturing: The Formidable Competitive Weapon,* by Wickham Skinner; and *The Uneasy Alliance: Managing the Productivity-Technology Dilemma,* edited by Kim Clark, Robert Hayes, and Christopher Lorenz.

13. Many of the issues addressed in these four projects were summarized in the book *Dynamic Manufacturing: Creating the Learning Organization,* by Robert Hayes, Steven Wheelwright, and Kim Clark, which was published in 1988 by The Free Press and for several years thereafter was used as the core reference text for first-year TOM.

14. Kim Clark, Robert Hayes, and Christopher Lorenz, *The Uneasy Alliance: Managing the Productivity-Technology Dilemma* (Boston: Harvard Business School Press, 1985).

15. A notable exception is Gary Pisano's work in the biotechnology sector.

16. David Upton and Richard Seet, "Pacific Dunlop China (A): Beijing," Harvard Business School Case 9-695-029; multimedia case 696-701.

17. The introduction of a new structure, incorporating three cohorts and two starting dates, into our first-year program, while fostering more innovation and better integration across courses, may well foster disintegration within the former faculty "areas." The same phenomenon has been observed in companies that have moved to broad adoption of cross-functional product development teams: their products get developed faster and more efficiently, but their functional groups tend to lose their cohesiveness and depth.

3 THE GLOBAL FINANCIAL SYSTEM PROJECT

1. We would like to thank the members of the Global Financial System project and the Finance Area at Harvard Business School, whose work we have tried to portray in this chapter.

2. See Merton (1989, 1990, 1992a, 1993, 1998) and Merton and Bodie (1992a, 1992b).

3. Crane et al. (1995).

4. As Miller (1992, 4) observes, "No 20-year period in financial history has witnessed an even remotely comparable burst of innovative activity."

5. In perhaps no other branch of economics has the implementation of theory into real-world practice been as rapid as for finance theory and the financial services industry over this period. See Bernstein (1992) for an in-depth description of how this interplay between theory and practice has brought about some of the major innovations of the last few decades.

6. This point is discussed further in Merton (1994).

7. For a comprehensive discussion of the implementation of asset securitization, see Norton and Spellman (1991), Zweig (1989), and the entire Fall 1988 issue of the *Journal of Applied Corporate Finance*.

8. See Perold (1992) for cost comparisons of using derivatives. See also Darby (1994).

9. Quantifying the gains from innovation is no easy task. However, a number of researchers have attempted to measure the size of the gains from financial innovation in the mortgage market in the form of securitization and unbundling through the creation of collateralized mortgage obligations, or CMOs. These papers find that innovation can be associated with significantly lower spreads in the mortgage rates charged to borrowers. See Hen-

dershott and Shilling (1989), Sirmans and Benjamin (1990), and Jameson, Dewan, and Sirmans (1992).

10. It is all the more perplexing because derivative securities have long been integral parts of the financial system. As discussed in Merton (1992a, 13), options, forward contracts, and futures have been around since the seventeenth and eighteenth centuries in Europe, the United States, and Japan. Among the earliest derivative securities were bank currencies (money), which "derived" their value from their convertibility into the underlying gold held in depositories.

11. A more prosaic prospect is simply the distinction in mindsets between those who focus on benefits (when new things work as intended) and those who focus on costs (when they don't).

12. See Homer (1977).

13. See de la Vega (1688).

14. For a history of nineteenth- and twentieth-century financial innovations, from a functional perspective, see Tufano (1995).

15. See the extensive listing in Finnerty (1992).

16. This feature of the neoclassical perspective has been stressed by North (1994).

17. The functional perspective on the financial system falls within the research tradition of what Williamson (1985, 16) calls the New Institutional Economics. For more on functional analysis and the functional perspective, see Bodie and Merton (1993), Crane et al. (1995), Mason et al. (1995), Merton (1993), Merton and Bodie (1993), Pierce (1993), Sanford (1993), and Scholes (1994).

18. See, for example, Hubbard (1994), Kohn (1994), Rose (1994), and Sanford (1993).

19. These data are taken from U.S. Department of Commerce, Bureau of Economic Analysis, "Gross Product by Industry, 1977–1994, 1994 Preliminary Estimates" (http://www.stat-usa.gov); "The Fortune 500," Fortune, 21 April 1996; and "Consumer Expenditure Survey of the Bureau of Labor Statistics" (http://www.whitehouse.gov/fsbr).

20. For details on this case study, see Peter Tufano and Sanjay Bhatnager, "Enron Gas Services," in Mason et al. (1995, 645–679).

21. See Harry Hurt III, "Power Players," Fortune, 5 August 1996, 94–98.

22. For details, see Tufano and Poetzscher (1996).

23. When TVA announced its plans to halt construction of nuclear plants, it explicitly noted that it would consider purchasing power from other pro-

ducers as an alternative. See "TVA Halts Nuclear Construction; Reduces Debt for 'Competitive Edge,'" *Energy Report*, 19 December 1994.

24. See Gilson and Warner (1997).

25. The well-known financial technology firm Smith-Breeden Associates, Inc., uses this approach in its Market Track Short Duration and Intermediate Duration Mutual Funds to broaden the market for its investment expertise in the mortgage market. See Merton and Moel (1997). This approach is also described in the "BEA Associates" case study by André Perold, which appears in Mason et al. (1995).

26. In evaluating the performance of an investment manager using tools such as the Sharpe-Lintner Capital Asset Pricing Model, a portfolio's "alpha" represents its excess performance after controlling for the risks borne by the portfolio. "Alpha transfer" implies the movement of this excess performance from one asset class to another.

27. Although these systems are proprietary, they tend to use categories that reflect exposures developed in risk management systems. For generic examples, see Hindy (1995) and Merton (1989, 242–247; 1992b, 450–457).

28. Much of the discussion surrounding the safety and soundness of the Pension Benefit Guaranty Corporation has focused on setting static measures, such as asset surplus requirements, and not on setting dynamic exposure limits. See Bodie and Merton (1993).

29. This section is based on Merton (1995) and Tufano (1996a).

30. See, for example, Grossman and Hart (1982), Jensen (1986), and Merton (1993).

31. See, for example, Stulz (1984, 1990), Smith and Stulz (1985), Froot, Scharfstein, and Stein (1993, 1994a,b).

32. This discussion ties into the work by Jensen (1986) on the corporate form of organization and Williamson (1985) on the boundaries of the firm. Williamson (1988) compares and contrasts his transaction cost approach with Jensen's agency approach to the study of economic organization.

33. Some of the GFS field research documents how hedging can enable firms to bear higher debt levels. For an example, see the case study "MW Petroleum (B)" by Luehrman and Tufano (1994).

34. For a detailed discussion of the allocation of risk capital in financial firms, see Merton and Perold (1993) and the supporting work in Merton (1993, 1997).

4 COMPETITION AND STRATEGY

1. See relevant passages in Jeffrey L. Cruikshank, *A Delicate Experiment: The Harvard Business School, 1908–1945* (Boston: Harvard Business School Press, 1987).

2. In Melvin T. Copeland, *And Mark an Era: The Story of the Harvard Business School* (Boston: Little, Brown, 1958), 164.

3. In Cruikshank, *A Delicate Experiment*, 170.

4. See Division of Research, *Research at the Harvard Business School* (Cambridge, Mass.: Division of Research, 1982) 58.

5. Faculty members involved in updating subsequent Business Policy casebooks included Christopher Bartlett, Norman Berg, Joseph Bower, William Guth, Richard Hamermesh, Andrall Pearson, Malcolm Salter, Howard Stevenson, and Richard Walton.

6. Kenneth R. Andrews, *The Concept of Corporate Strategy*, 3rd ed. (Burr Ride, Ill.: Irwin Custom Publishing, 1987), xii.

7. The authors are greatly indebted to Peter Botticelli and Pankaj Ghemawat, whose teaching note "Competition and Business Strategy in Historical Perspective" lays out much of this history in clear and compelling form.

8. One of BCG's leaders in developing this model was Seymour Tilles, a former lecturer in BP who had done much of the School's research into the typewriter industry.

9. Robert H. Hayes and William J. Abernathy, "Managing Our Way to Economic Decline," *Harvard Business Review* (July/August 1980): 68.

10. As of 1995, there were more than 15 graduates of the program who had served on the faculty of HBS. In addition to Porter, past and present members of the C&S group who are graduates of the program have included Pankaj Ghemawat, David Collis, Michael Enright, Anita McGahan, and Tarun Khanna.

11. Michael E. Porter, "Note on the Structural Analysis of Industries," Intercollegiate Case Clearinghouse No. 9-376-054.

12. Michael E. Porter with R. E. Caves, "From Entry Barriers to Mobility Barriers: Conjectural Decisions and Contrived Deterrence to New Competition," *Quarterly Journal of Economics* (May 1977): 241–262.

13. In 1974–1975, the General Management area, which encompassed the Business Policy course, was established. One advantage was a larger "peer group" for the Policy specialists.

14. Personal communication, 24 September 1996.

15. It was taken over by Pankaj Ghemawat, Stephen Bradley, and later by David Collis.

16. Pankaj Ghemawat, "Sustainable Advantage," *Harvard Business Review* (September/October 1986).

17. David B. Yoffie, ed., *Competing in the Age of Digital Convergence* (Boston: Harvard Business School Press, 1997).

5 Entrepreneurial Management

1. The authors gratefully acknowledge the help of several colleagues who gave us extremely useful suggestions on earlier drafts of this paper, including Norm Berg, Amar Bhidé, Diane Burton, Myra Hart, Walter Kuemmerle, Josh Lerner, Bill Poorvu, and Bill Sahlman.

2. P. Lynch *Wall Street Journal*, 20 September 1996.

3. "Who Are the Harvard Self-Employed?" *Frontiers of Entrepreneurship Research*, Proceedings of the 1983 Conference on Entrepreneurship (Wellesley, Mass.: Center for Entrepreneurial Studies, Babson College, 1983).

4. J. L. Cruikshank, *A Delicate Experiment: The Harvard Business School, 1908–1945* (Boston: Harvard Business School Press, 1987).

5. In the former category was Len Bollinger, who as an HBS researcher had lead a pioneering series of studies of the U.S. aircraft industry; in the latter category was Thornton Bradshaw, later chairman of ARCO.

6. G. F. Doriot, *Manufacturing Class Notes: Harvard Business School 1927–1966.* (Boston: Board of Trustees, French Library, 1993).

7. P. R. Liles, *New Business Ventures and the Entrepreneur* (Homewood, Ill.: Irwin, 1974).

8. This tactic of raising dedicated resources in support of a specific topic was a time-honored tradition at the School. McArthur, though, used the technique to an unprecedented extent, evidently determined to create an "entrepreneurship critical mass" that would not be subject to swings in academic fashion or staffing levels.

9. O. F. Collins and D. G. Moore, *The Enterprising Man* (East Lansing: Michigan State University, 1964).

10. J. P. Kotter, *The New Rules: How to Succeed in Today's Post-Corporate World* (New York: The Free Press, 1995).

11. D. F. Muzyka, H. H. Stevenson, and A. Larson, "Career Paths of Entrepreneurs with MBAs: A Comparative Study of Alumni from Three Graduate Programs," *Frontiers of Entrepreneurship Research*, Proceedings of the Eleventh Annual Babson College Entrepreneurship Research Conference (Wellesley, Mass.: Center for Entrepreneurial Studies, Babson College, 1991).

12. L. Bongiorno, "To B-School or Not to B-School," *Business Week*, 18 March 1996, 22–24 ff; J. Flynn and L. Bernier, "Springtime for Start-ups," *Business Week*, 24 April 1995, 38ff.

13. R. Cantillon (d. 1734), *Essai Sur la Nature du Commerce* (London: Macmillan Co., Ltd., 1931).

14. J. A. Schumpeter, *The Theory of Economic Development: An Inquiry into Profits, Capital, Credit, Interest, and the Business Cycle* (Cambridge, Mass.: Harvard University Press, 1934).

15. A. Bhidé "Bootstrap Finance: The Art of Start-ups," *Harvard Business Review* (November/December 1992).

16. D. C. McClelland, *The Achieving Society* (Princeton, N.J.: Van Nostrand Reinhold, 1961).

17. Unfortunately, those studies that focused on a seemingly high percentage of entrepreneurs who were firstborns fell victim to fuzzy statistical thinking. Almost exactly the same percentage of the general population consists of firstborns.

18. P. Kilby, ed., *Entrepreneurship and Economic Development* (New York: The Free Press, 1971).

19. H. H. Stevenson, and D. E. Gumpert, "The Heart of Entrepreneurship," *Harvard Business Review* (March/April 1985).

20. H. H. Stevenson and J. C. Jarillo-Mossi, "A Paradigm of Entrepreneurship: Entrepreneurial Management," *Strategic Management Journal* 11, Special Issue (1990).

21. Originally defined as "commitment to opportunity." The framework evolves.

22. This characteristic was added to Stevenson's original five-point model by William A. Sahlman, working with Stevenson. See, for example, "Importance of Entrerpreneurship in Economic Development," a chapter by Stevenson and Sahlman in R. D. Hisrich, ed., *Entrepreneurship, Intrapreneurship, and Venture Capital: The Foundation of Economic Renaissance* (Lexingon, Mass.: D. C. Heath, 1986).

23. R. Amit and E. Muller, "'Push' and 'Pull' Entrepreneurship," Paper presented at the Babson Entrepreneurship Research Conference (Wellesley, Mass.: Center for Entrepreneurial Studies, 1994).

24. M. M. Hart, "Founding Resource Choices: Influences and Effects," Ph.D. diss., Harvard Business School, 1995.

25. M. J. Roberts, "The Transition from Entrepreneur to Professional Management" Ph.D. diss., Harvard Business School, 1986.

26. W. J. Poorvu, "The Real Estate Challenge: Capitalization and Change," in *Real Estate: A Case Study Approach* (Englewood Cliffs, N.J.: Prentice Hall, 1996).

27. H. H. Stevenson, M. J. Roberts, and H. I. Grousbeck, *New Business Ventures and the Entrepreneur,* 3d ed. (Homewood, Ill.: Irwin, 1989).

28. H. H. Stevenson and J. C. Jarillo-Mossi, "A Paradigm of Entrepreneurship: Entrepreneurial Management," *Strategic Management Journal* 11 (1990): 17–27.

29. H. H. Stevenson and J. C. Jarillo-Mossi, "A New Entrepreneurial Paradigm," in *Socioeconomics: Toward a New Synthesis,* ed. A. Etzioni and P. R. Lawrence (New York: M. E. Sharpe, 1991).

30. Bill Sahlman, Josh Lerner, and Paul Gompers are focusing on these questions.

31. Myra Hart made these discoveries in her dissertation on founding resource choices in five entrepreneurial firms.

32. These results were obtained by Walter Kuemmerle in his dissertation research on innovation in multinational firms. Additional data on this topic can be found in W. Kuemmerle, "Analyzing Foreign Direct Investment in Research and Development: An Entrepreneurial Perspective," in *International Entrepreneurship,* ed. S. Birley and I. C. MacMillan (London: Routledge, 1995).

33. Diane Burton is examining these issues.

34. Although these resource issues are of interest to all faculty in the Entrepreneurial Management unit, they are a central focus for Bill Sahlman (deals), Myra Hart (founding resource choices), Walter Kuemmerle (information sources), Josh Lerner (venture capital), Paul Gompers (venture capital), and Diane Burton (organizational design and human resource systems). In addition, several HBS colleagues have interests in these areas, and some are actively collaborating on research or course development projects concerning these problems, broadly conceived (e.g., Kent Bowen, Marco Iansiti, and Ben Shapiro).

35. S. J. Parnes, ed., *Source Book for Creative Problem-Solving: A Fifty Year Digest of Proven Innovation Processes* (Buffalo, N.Y.: Creative Education Foundation Press, 1993).

36. J. Backman, ed., *Entrepreneurship and the Outlook for America* (New York: The Free Press, 1983); R. M. Kanter, *The Change Masters: Innovation and Entrepreneurship in the American Corporation* (New York: Simon & Schuster, 1983); and J. A. Schumpeter, *The Theory of Economic Development.*

37. Several faculty associated with Entrepreneurial Management are engaged in research or teaching (or both) on the topic of creative approaches to management taken by entrepreneurs: Teresa Amabile (innovation within established firms), Amar Bhidé (creative approaches to firm growth taken by resource-poor entrepreneurs), and Walter Kuemmerle (global entrepreneurship). A number of other HBS faculty are doing related work (e.g., Kent Bowen, Clay Christensen, Marco Iansiti, Dorothy Leonard-Barton, and Rosabeth Moss Kanter).

38. M. M. Hart, "Founding Resource Choices: Influences and Effects," Ph.D. diss., Harvard Business School, 1995.

39. E. L. Deci, *Intrinsic Motivation* (New York: Plenum, 1975); E. L. Deci and R. M. Ryan, *Intrinsic Motivation and Self-Determination in Human Behavior* (New York: Plenum, 1985); and M. R. Lepper and D. Greene, *The Hidden Costs of Reward: New Perspectives on the Psychology of Human Motivation* (Hillsdale, N.J.: Erlbaum, 1978).

40. T. M. Amabile, *The Social Psychology of Creativity* (New York: Springer-Verlag, 1983); T. M. Amabile, "A Model of Creativity and Innovation in Organizations," in *Research in Organizational Behavior,* ed. B. M. Staw and L. L. Cummings, Vol 10 (Greenwich, Conn.: JAI Press, 1988), 123–167; and T. M. Amabile, *Creativity in Context* (Boulder, Colo.: Westview Press, 1996).

41. H. H. Stevenson and M. C. Moldoveanu, "The Power of Predictability," *Harvard Business Review* (July/August, 1995); H. H. Stevenston with J. L. Cruikshank, *Do Lunch or Be Lunch: The Power of Predictability in Creating Your Future* (Boston: Harvard Business School Press, 1998).

42. Amabile is currently studying the impact of daily events occurring in project teams on their motivation, work environment, and project success (creativity and quality). Stevenson is articulating a theory of management based on the predictability hypothesis.

43. Among the more experienced in such endeavors are Joe Lassiter, Bill Poorvu, Myra Hart, Ed Zschau, Bill Sahlman, and Howard Stevenson. They have been involved as founding managers, founding investors, and founding directors of firms such as Staples, Teradyne, Wildfire, WCVB, The Baupost Group, Avid Technologies, Xcelnet, Quadra Capital Partners, and many other firms.

6 ORGANIZATIONS AND MARKETS

1. Michael C. Jensen and William H. Meckling, "Theory of the Firm: Managerial Behavior, Agency Costs and Ownership Structure," *Journal of Financial Economics* 3, no. 4 (1976).

2. Private telephone conversation, 7 October 1996.

3. Three faculty members at Rochester involved in the course have published a written and somewhat supplemented version of the Course Notes created by Jensen and Meckling (as they were left in 1989 on Jensen's departure). See James A. Brickley, Clifford W. Smith, Jr., and Jerold L. Zimmerman, *Managerial Economics and Organizational Architecture* (Homewood, Ill.: Irwin, 1997).

4. Because Baker had not yet joined the faculty at this point, his role was only informal; but he took formal responsibility for both sections of the course in 1989–1990 when Jensen was out for surgery.

5. See Michael C. Jensen and William H. Meckling, "The Nature of Man," *The Journal of Applied Corporate Finance* (Summer 1994): 4–19, and Michael C. Jensen, "Self Interest, Altruism, Incentives, and Agency Theory," *The Journal of Applied Corporate Finance* (Summer 1994): 40–45.

6. Malcolm P. McNair, "Tough-Mindedness and the Case Method," in *The Case Method at the Harvard Business School*, ed. Malcolm P. McNair (New York: McGraw-Hill, 1954), 15–24. Adapted from an address given 25 February 1953, at the first meeting of the executives registered for the 23rd Advanced Management Program at the Harvard Business School.

7. Kahneman and Tversky have documented a different, more tangential, but related set of systematic human mistakes than those on which we are focused here. They show how decision making typically depends on the "framing" of the problem and how such framing results in violations of the expected utility model that lies at the heart of much economics research. The frame is the decision maker's perception of the "acts, outcomes and contingencies associated with a particular choice." They demonstrate the human tendency to systematically overestimate the probability of low-probability events and underestimate the probability of medium- and high-probability events. See A. Tversky and D. Kahneman, "The Framing of Decisions and the Psychology of Choice," *Science* 211 (1981): 453–458; and A. Tversky and D. Kahneman, "Rational Choice and the Framing of Decisions," *Journal of Business* 59 (1986): S251–S278.

8. Examples of such economists are Ronald Coase, Oliver Williamson, Paul Milgrom, John Roberts, Gary Becker, Armen Alchian, Harold Demsetz, Bengt Holmstrom, and Sherwin Rosen.

9. George P. Baker, Michael C. Jensen, and Kevin J. Murphy, "Compensation and Incentives: Practice vs. Theory," *Journal of Finance* (July 1988).

10. Michael C. Jensen and Kevin J. Murphy, "Performance Pay and Top Management Incentives," *Journal of Political Economy* (April 1990): 225–265. This paper was the third most cited paper in economics in the period 1990–1993, as measured by the Social Science Citation Index. Related work: Michael C. Jensen and Kevin J. Murphy, "A New Survey of Executive Compensation," Full Survey and Technical Appendix to "CEO Incentives—It's Not How Much You Pay, But How," *Harvard Business Review* (May/June 1990).

11. George P. Baker, Robert Gibbons, and Kevin J. Murphy, "Relational Contracts and the Theory of the Firm" (Harvard Business School Working Paper, December 1997).

12. George P. Baker, "Pay for Performance: Causes and Consequences," *Journal of Applied Corporate Finance* 3, no. 3 (Fall 1990); Michael C. Jensen and Richard S. Ruback, "The Market for Corporate Control: The Scientific Evidence," *Journal of Financial Economics* 11, nos. 1–4 (April 1983); Michael C. Jensen, "The Takeover Controversy: Analysis and Evidence," *The Midland Corporate Finance Journal* (Summer 1986); and Michael C. Jensen, "Takeovers: Their Causes and Consequences," *Journal of Economic Perspectives* 2, no. 1 (Winter 1988).

13. George P. Baker and Karen H. Wruck, "Organizational Changes and Value Creation in Leveraged Buyouts: The Case of O.M. Scott & Sons Company," *Journal of Financial Economics* 25 (1990): 163–190.

14. Michael C. Jensen, "The Agency Costs of Free Cash Flow: Corporate Finance and Takeovers," *American Economic Review* 76, no. 2 (May 1986).

15. Karen H. Wruck and Sherry P. Roper. "Sink or Swim? Cytec Industries' Spin-Off (A)," Harvard Business School Case 9-897-053 (9/18/96), and "Sink or Swim? Cytec Industries' Spin-Off (B)," Harvard Business School Case 9-897-054 (9/18/96); and Karen H. Wruck and Michael C. Jensen, "Science, Specific Knowledge and Total Quality Management," *Journal of Accounting and Economics* 18 (1994): 247–287.

16. Karen H. Wruck, "Financial Policy, Internal Control, and Performance: Sealed Air Corporation's Leveraged Special Dividend," *Journal of Financial Economics* 36 (1994): 157–192; and Karen H. Wruck and Steve-Anna Stephens, "Safeway, Inc.'s Leveraged Buyout (A)," Harvard Business School Case 9-294-139 (6/2/94), "Safeway, Inc.'s Leveraged Buyout (B)," Harvard Business School Case 9-294-140 (6/2/94), and "Safeway, Inc.'s Leverage Buyout (C), Media Response," Harvard Business School Case 9-294-141 (6/2/94).

7 SERVICE PROFIT CHAIN RESEARCH

1. The authors are grateful to their Service Management colleagues James Cash, Jody Hoffer Gittell, Jeffrey Rayport, W. Earl Sasser, and Len Schlesinger for fundamental contributions to what is presented in this paper. We also thank Roger Hallowell, Sarah Woolverton, and Sabina Ciminero for help in this and many related projects. Jim DiCostanzo and Eric Heistand at PNC Bank provided invaluable help and insight in the creation, use, and interpretation of their company data sets. Concepts described reflect contributions over the past 20 years of former colleagues Christopher W. L. Hart, Thomas O. Jones, Christopher H. Lovelock, David H. Maister, and the late D. Daryl Wyckoff.

2. The positive relationship also exists in first difference regressions of ROI on customer satisfaction.

3. Some 243,000 surveys were mailed, with a response rate of 18 percent.

8 ETHICS, ORGANIZATIONS, AND BUSINESS SCHOOLS

1. Yankelovich and Skelly, *Corporate Priorities*, 1972; Yankelovich, Skelly, and White, release date 12 December 1979; Public Opinion On-line (database).

2. Robert A. Gordon and James E. Howell, *Higher Education for Business* (New York: Columbia University Press, 1959), 111.

3. Frank C. Pierson et al., *The Education of American Businessmen: A Study of University-College Programs in Business Administration* (New York: McGraw-Hill, 1959), 92.

4. Derek Bok, *Higher Learning* (Cambridge, Mass.: Harvard University Press, 1986), 99.

5. The discussion of entering students is based on research by Sharon Daloz Parks. See Thomas R. Piper, Mary C. Gentile, and Sharon Daloz Parks, *Can Ethics Be Taught? Perspectives, Challenges, and Approaches at Harvard Business School* (Boston: Harvard Business School Press, 1993), 17–48.

6. Thomas Hobbes, *Leviathan*, part I, ch. 13, ed. Richard Tuck (New York: Cambridge University Press, 1992), 89.

7. Ibid.

8. Robert D. Putnam, "The Prosperous Community: Social Capital and Public Life," *The American Prospect* (Spring 1993): 37–38.

9. Kenneth J. Arrow, *The Limits of Organization* (New York: W. W. Norton, 1974), 26–27.

10. W. Edwards Deming, Foreword to John O. Whitney, *The Trust Factor: Liberating Profits and Restoring Corporate Vitality* (New York: McGraw-Hill, 1994), vii, viii.

11. Some researchers argue that extra effort is more likely if employees view their employment relationship broadly as a social exchange rather than narrowly as an economic *quid pro quo* of formal rewards for specific behaviors. See D. W. Organ, "The Motivational Basis of Organizational Citizenship Behaviors," in *Research in Organizational Behavior*, ed. B. M. Staw and L. L. Cummings, vol. 12 (Greenwich, Conn.: JAI Press, 1990), 43–72.

12. For managers' views of how attention to ethics contributes to the quality of work life, see, e.g., Lynn S. Paine and Sarah Mavirnac, "AES Honeycomb (A)," Harvard Business School Case 9-395-132; Lynn S. Paine, "Martin Marietta Corporation: Managing Corporate Ethics (A)," Harvard Business School Case 9-393-016.

13. The integrity factor plays an important role in shaping reputation. See Jennifer Reese, "America's Most Admired Corporations," *Fortune*, 8 February 1993, 44ff. See also Charles J. Fombrun, *Reputation: Realizing Value from the Corporate Image* (Boston: Harvard Business School Press, 1996), 7ff.

14. See, e.g., surveys discussed in "Study Shows 67% of Adult Consumers Consider a Company's Ethics When Purchasing Products or Services," *Business Wire*, 15 November 1993; "Consumers Put a 'Surprisingly High' Priority on Clean Conduct; Public Demands Better Ethics, Says Survey," *South China Morning Post*, 9 May 1994. A British marketing consultant has dubbed this group "vigilante consumers." See Nicole Dickenson, "Consumers Get Ethical with Choices," *South China Morning Post*, 29 May 1993, supplement.

15. See, e.g., James L. Heskett, W. Earl Sasser, Jr., and Christopher W. L. Hart, *Service Breakthroughs: Changing the Rules of the Game* (New York: The Free Press, 1990).

16. On the tasks of leadership and the importance of needs and commitments in motivation, see John W. Gardner, *On Leadership* (New York: The Free Press, 1990).

17. For a dramatic example, see Lynn S. Paine and Jane P. Katz, "Problems at InSpeech," Harvard Business School Case 9-394-109.

18. Leadership theorist James MacGregor Burns argues that useful goals should elevate people to a higher moral level. See Burns, *Leadership*, ch. 2 (New York: Harper & Row, 1978). See also Christopher A. Bartlett and Sumantra

Ghoshal, "Changing the Role of Top Management: Beyond Strategy to Purpose," *Harvard Business Review* (November/December 1994).

19. Numerous studies find the root causes of corporate misconduct in the culture, norms, reward systems, and decision processes of organizations. See, e.g., Marshall B. Clinard and Peter C. Yeager, *Corporate Crime* (New York: The Free Press, 1980); John C. Coffee, Jr., "Beyond the Shut-Eyed Sentry: Toward a Theoretical View of Corporate Misconduct and an Effective Legal Response," *Virginia Law Review* 63 (November 1977): 1099–1278.

20. James Willard Hurst, *The Legitimacy of the Business Corporation in the Law of the United States, 1780–1970* (Charlottesville: University Press of Virginia, 1970). To be precise, Hurst speaks of efficiency and social responsibility as the two bases of legitimacy.

21. For an argument that a society's level of trust is critical to its well-being and ability to compete, see Francis Fukuyama, *Trust: The Social Virtues and the Creation of Prosperity* (New York: The Free Press, 1995).

22. E. J. Conry and D. R. Nelson, "Business Law and Moral Growth," *American Business Law Journal* 27 (1989): 1–39; James W. Fowler, *Stages of Faith: The Psychology of Human Development and the Quest for Meaning* (San Francisco: Harper & Row, 1982); Jeffrey Gandz and Nadine Hayes, "Teaching Business Ethics," *Journal of Business Ethics* 7 (1988): 657–669; Thomas M. Jones, "Can Business Ethics Be Taught? Empirical Evidence," *Business and Professional Ethics Journal* 8, no. 2 (1989): 84; Robert Kegan, *The Evolving Self: Problem and Process in Human Development* (Cambridge: Harvard University Press, 1981); Sharon Parks, *The Critical Years: The Young Adult Search for a Faith to Live By*, ch. 2 (San Francisco: HarperCollins, 1986); William G. Perry, *Forms of Intellectual and Ethical Development in the College Years* (New York: Holt, 1970); James Rest, "Can Ethics Be Taught in Professional Schools? The Psychological Research," *Easier Said Than Done* (Winter 1988): 22–26; James Rest et al., *Moral Development: Advances in Research and Theory* (New York: Praeger, 1986).

23. See Parks, "Is It Too Late for Young Adults and the Formation of Professional Ethics," in *Can Ethics Be Taught?* 13–72.

9 BUSINESS HISTORY

1. This chapter combines an essay by authors McCraw and Koehn with a commentary by Nelles, presented by Nelles at the October 1996 symposium. McCraw and Koehn wish to thank Professors Alfred D. Chandler, Jr., Richard

S. Tedlow, and Richard H. K. Vietor for their comments on earlier versions of the chapter. Where the first-person plural is used in the text, it means the HBS historians and necessarily does not include coauthor Nelles, who teaches at York University.

2. See Fritz Redlich, "Approaches to Business History," *Business History Review* 36 (Spring 1962): 61–62.

3. Harvard Business School Archives, Gras papers, Office Files, Case 2, N. S. B. Gras to F. T. Tout, 21 October 1927. We are indebted to Robert D. Cuff for his generosity in sharing this reference, and also for his helpful criticism of an early draft of parts of this paper.

4. Key members of this group included John Rosenblum, George Lodge, Hugo Uyterhoeven, and James Baughman.

5. John H. McArthur and Bruce R. Scott with the assistance of Audrey T. Sproat, *Industrial Planning in France* (Boston: Harvard University Graduate School of Business Administration, 1969). The principal finding of this book was that such planning had little effect on the actual conduct of French business.

6. These scholars included Edmund Learned, C. Roland Christensen, Kenneth Andrews, Joseph Bower, and Bruce Scott himself.

7. Boston: Harvard Business School Press, 1988. The introduction is on pp. 1–20, and a full bibliography of Chandler's works up to 1988, prepared by Takashi Hikino, appears on pp. 505–517.

8. Cambridge, Mass.: MIT Press.

9. New York: Doubleday, 1963.

10. For discussions of these issues, see the introduction of McCraw, ed., *The Essential Alfred Chandler*, 5–15; Louis Galambos, "Parsonian Sociology and Post-Progressive History," *Social Science Quarterly* 50 (June 1969): 25–45; Louis Galambos, "The Emerging Organizational Synthesis in Modern American History," *Business History Review* 44 (Autumn 1970): 279–290; Louis Galambos, "Technology, Political Economy, and Professionalization: Central Themes of the Organizational Synthesis," *Business History Review* 57 (Winter 1983): 471–493; and Robert D. Cuff, review of *Scale and Scope, Canadian Historical Review* 72 (March 1991): 104–107.

11. Chandler's revised dissertation was published as a book entitled *Henry Varnum Poor: Business Editor, Analyst, and Reformer* (Cambridge, Mass.: Harvard University Press, 1956).

12. In fact, he did it for two additional firms: the Burlington Railroad and the Illinois Central. But his publisher, MIT Press, advised against including these chapters in what was already a long and complex book.

13. See, as examples, Richard B. Duboff and Edward S. Herman, "Alfred D. Chandler's New Business History: A Review," *Politics and Society* 10 (1980): 87–110; Richard Dellobuono, "Markets and Managers: A Critique of Two Points of View," *Contemporary Crisis* 5 (October 1981): 403–415. Discussions of small business that either implicitly or explicitly take issue with some of Chandler's emphasis include Philip Scranton, "Diversity in Diversity: Flexible Production and American Industrialization, 1880–1930," *Business History Review* 65 (Spring 1991): 27–90; and Mansel G. Blackford, "Small Business in America: A Historiographic Survey," *Business History Review* 65 (Spring 1991): 1–26.

14. See, as examples, B. W. E. Alford, "Chandlerism, the New Orthodoxy of U.S. and European Corporate Development?" *Journal of European Economic History* 23 (Winter 1994): 631–643; "Review Colloquium on *Scale and Scope: The Dynamics of Industrial Capitalism*," *Business History Review* 64 (Winter 1990): 690–758; Leslie Hannah, "Delusions of Dominance, or The Invisible Hand Strikes Back" (Paper presented at the International Economic History Congress, Session A2, Milan, September 1994); Leslie Hannah, "The American Miracle, 1875–1950, and After: A View in the European Mirror," *Business and Economic History* 24, no. 2 (Winter 1995): 197–220, 257–262 (221–257 of this same source contain a symposium of commentaries on Hannah's paper by a number of scholars, including Chandler himself).

15. The actual MBA enrollments for sample years are as follows: 1967–1968, 21 students; 1968–1969, 20; 1969–1970, 23; 1970–1971, 25; 1971–1972, 28; 1972–1973, 26; 1973–1974, 31. Enrollment began to grow in the middle 1970s, reaching 96 in 1979–1980, after the course had been taught for several years by Alfred Chandler. It then took off in the mid-1980s. Enrollment reached 203 in 1985–1986, when Richard Tedlow first taught two sections of the course. When both Tedlow and Thomas McCraw taught it, enrollment was as follows: 1987–1988, 303; 1989–1990, 298; 1990–1991, 400; in subsequent years, in all of which some combination of Tedlow, McCraw, and Nancy Koehn taught the course, its enrollment hovered between about 330 and 385. (These data come from the records of the Registrar.) Occasionally in the late 1940s and 1950s, enrollment in the course entitled "Business History" had surpassed 200.

16. See Harris Corporation, "Founding Dates of the 1994 *Fortune* 500 U.S. Companies," *Business History Review* 70 (Spring 1996): 69–90.

17. Cambridge, Mass.: Harvard University Press, 1990.

18. Boston: Harvard Business School Press, 1986.

19. Over the years, as the seminar's structure evolved, the students were allocated a separate additional hour with the instructors, in sessions that were closed to everyone not enrolled for credit.

20. See, for example, A. M. McGahan, "The Emergence of the National Brewing Oligopoly: Competition in the American Market, 1933–1958," *Business History Review* 65 (Summer 1991): 229–284; Clayton M. Christensen, "The Rigid Disk Drive Industry: A History of Commercial and Technological Turbulence," *Business History Review* 67 (Winter 1993): 531–588; Peter Tufano, "Business Failure, Judicial Intervention, and Financial Innovation: Restructuring U.S. Railroads in the Nineteenth Century," *Business History Review* 71 (Spring 1997); Matthew B. Krepps, "Another Look at the Impact of the National Industrial Recovery Act in Cartel Formation and Maintenance Costs," *Review of Economics and Statistics*, forthcoming; Jeffrey Bernstein, "7-Eleven in America and Japan," in *Creating Modern Capitalism: How Entrepreneurs, Companies, and Countries Triumphed in Three Industrial Revolutions*, ed., Thomas K. McCraw (Cambridge, Mass.: Harvard University Press, 1997).

21. The course has had an enrollment of 50 to 80 students over the years, and has undergone two name changes: first "Capitalism Constrained," taught by Emmons, then "Managing Regulation, Deregulation, and Privatization," by Dyck.

22. The current editor is Thomas McCraw. His recent predecessors were Jack High, a visiting professor who served as acting editor for two years; Steven Tolliday; and Richard Tedlow.

23. See note 20 above for articles by Christensen, McGahan, and Tufano, who are members of the faculty. Other faculty authors include Carliss Y. Baldwin and Kim B. Clark, "Capital Budgeting Systems and Capabilities: Investments in U.S. Companies after the Second World War," *Business History Review* 68 (Spring 1994): 73–109; Michael A. Cusumano, Yiogos Mylonadis, and Richard S. Rosenbloom, "Strategic Maneuvering and Mass-Market Dynamics: The Triumph of VHS over Beta," *Business History Review* 66 (Spring 1992): 51–94; Alvin J. Silk and Louis William Stern, "The Changing Nature of Innovation in Marketing: A Study of Selected Business Leaders, 1852–1958," *Business History Review* 37 (Autumn 1963): 182–199.

24. Joseph A. Schumpeter, *Capitalism, Socialism, and Democracy* (New York: Harper, 1942), 83–84.

25. In the United States, the Business History Conference, the leading professional association, had 472 members in 1995, up from 223 in 1987 and 148 in 1978. The Economic and Business Historical Society, another professional group, had just under 300 members in 1996. Both of these associations are primarily American but include members from other countries as well.

    The field is burgeoning not only in the United States, but also abroad. There are organized societies of business historians in Canada, Britain, Germany, Japan, and New Zealand, as well as a Europewide Business History Association, formed in the mid-1990s. Superb business historians are at work in all of the countries named, as well as in France, Italy, Spain, Portugal, the Low Countries, Australia, and several of the countries of Latin America.

    The *Business History Review*'s counterpart journal in Britain, called *Business History*, has a circulation of just under 1,000. "Yearbooks" of research in business history are published annually in both Germany and Japan, and for many years the Japanese Business History Society has cosponsored an annual week-long conference held at the foot of Mount Fuji. Most of the participants are Japanese, but guests from Europe, America, and elsewhere are invited each year. Proceedings of the Fuji Conference, published in English by the University of Tokyo Press, constitute a noteworthy ongoing barometer of the rich state of the art of doing business history. (The authors thank Will Hausman, William Childs, and Geoffrey Jones for providing much of this information.)

26. There are many useful articles on the evolution of the "new economic history." An excellent retrospective, together with a look at possible additional developments, is Alexander J. Field, "The Future of Economic History," in *The Future of Economic History*, ed. Field (Boston: Kluwer-Nijhoff, 1987), 1–41.

27. D. N. McCloskey has written widely about this broad phenomenon, not only among economic historians but among most other mainstream economists as well. See, for example, the following works by McCloskey: *The Rhetoric of Economics* (Madison: University of Wisconsin Press, 1985); *The Writing of Economics* (New York: Macmillan, 1987); *If You're So Smart: The Narrative of Economic Enterprise* (Chicago: University of Chicago Press, 1990); *Knowledge and Persuasion in Economics* (New York: Cambridge University Press, 1994). See also Jack High's review article on the last-named book, in *Business History Review* 70 (Summer 1996): 262–267.

Appendix B The Global Financial System Research Initiatives

1. Some of these cases appear in Mason et al. (1995); they also form the basis for a new MBA elective, Corporate Financial Engineering.

2. For example, see Das (1994, 1995a,b, 1997), Das and Foresi (1996), Das and Baz (1996), Das and Tufano (1996), and Balduzzi, Das, and Foresi (1995).

3. See Lerner (1994a,b, 1995, 1998), Gompers (1994, 1995, 1996a,b,c), and Gompers and Lerner (1996, 1998a,b).

Index

About the Contributors

THOMAS K. MCCRAW is the Isidor Straus Professor of Business History at the Harvard Business School and Editor of the *Business History Review*. His many books include *Prophets of Regulation: Charles Francis Adams, Louis D. Brandeis, James M. Landis, Alfred E. Kahn* (1984, Pulitzer Prize, Newcomen Book Award), *Management Past and Present: A Casebook on the History of American Business* (1996, with Alfred D. Chandler, Jr., and Richard S. Tedlow), and the edited volumes *America Versus Japan* (1986), *The Essential Alfred Chandler: Essays Toward a Historical Theory of Big Business* (1988), and *Creating Modern Capitalism: How Entrepreneurs, Companies, and Countries Triumphed in Three Industrial Revolutions* (1997). His current research is on American business since 1920, the history of economic thought, and the development and effects of public policies toward competition.

JEFFREY L. CRUIKSHANK is a co-founder of Kohn Cruikshank Inc., a Boston-based communications consulting firm. He has written numerous books on subjects of interest to managers, including *Herman Miller, Inc.: Buildings and Beliefs* (1994, with Clark Malcolm); *A Delicate Experiment: The Harvard Business School 1908–1945* (1987); *Breaking the Impasse: Consensual Approaches to Resolving Public Disputes* (1987, with Lawrence E. Susskind); *From the Rivers: The Origins and Growth of the New England Electric System* (1996, with John T. Landry); *Going Public: A Field Guide to Development in Art in Public Places* (1988, with Pam Korza); and *Do Lunch or Be Lunch: The Power of Predictability in Creating Your Future* (1998, with Howard H. Stevenson). He is currently working on books about entrepreneurship and the real estate industry.

TERESA M. AMABILE is the MBA Class of 1954 Professor of Business Administration and Senior Associate Dean for Research at the Harvard Business School. Originally focusing on individual creativity, Professor Amabile's research has expanded to encompass team creativity and organizational innovation. She is the author of *Creativity in Context* (1996) and *Growing Up Creative* (1989), as well as over 100 scholarly papers, chapters, and presentations. Her recent papers include "Motivational Synergy:Toward New Conceptualizations of Intrinsic and Extrinsic Motivation in the Workplace" (1993, *Human Resource Management Review*) and "Assessing the Work Environment for Creativity" (1996, *Academy of Management Journal*).

GEORGE BAKER is a Professor of Business Administration at the Harvard Business School. He has published works on management incentives, leveraged buyouts, and organizational economics. His recent work focuses on managerial performance measurement and its effect on incentive systems and organizational structure and success. His publications include a recently finished book, with George David Smith, entitled *The New Financial Capitalists: Kohlberg Kravis Roberts and the Creation of Corporate Value*. He has also published articles in numerous journals, including the *American Economic Review*, the *European Economic Review*, the *Journal of Finance*, the *Journal of Financial Economics*, the *Journal of Political Economy*, and the *Quarterly Journal of Economics*.

CARLISS BALDWIN is the William L. White Professor of Business Administration and Senior Associate Dean, Director of Faculty Planning at the Harvard Business School. With Kim B. Clark, Baldwin is presently involved in a multi-year project to study the process of design and its impact on the structure of the computer industry, entitled *Design Rules: The Power of Modularity*. Her earlier projects include a study of capital budgeting systems in large U.S. companies: "Capital-Budgeting Systems and Capabilities Investments in U.S. Companies after the Second World War" (1994, with Kim B. Clark, *Business History Review*); and a study of optimal methods of sale in corporate divestitures: "Choosing the Method of Sale: A Clinical Study of Conrail" (1991, with Sugato Bhattacharyya, *Journal of Financial Economics*).

KIM B. CLARK, the Harry E. Figgie, Jr., Professor of Business Administration, is Dean of the Faculty at the Harvard Business School. His research focuses on modularity in design and the integration of technology and competition in industry evolution, particularly in the computer industry. He and Carliss Y. Baldwin are co-authors of a forthcoming book on the topic, entitled *Design Rules: The Power of Modularity*. Dean Clark's earlier research focused on technology, productivity, product development, and operations strategy in a variety of industries, including automobiles, steel, semiconductors, computers, and advanced ceramics. His recent publications, both co-authored with Steven C. Wheelwright, include *Leading Product Development: The Senior Manager's Guide to Creating and Shaping the Enterprise* (1995) and *Revolutionizing Product Development: Quantum Leaps in Speed, Efficiency, and Quality* (1992).

LINDA S. DOYLE is the President and Chief Executive Officer of the Harvard Business School Publishing Corporation, a not-for-profit publishing enterprise that seeks to improve the practice of management and to extend the intellectual influence of the Harvard Business School. Her previous positions include Associate Dean for Administration at the Harvard Business School (five years) and Adjunct Professor of Business Administration and Course Head for Management Communication, a required course in the MBA program (three years). She holds a Ph.D. and an M.A. in English from the University of Notre Dame, and a B.A. in English and History from Mary Manse College.

ROBERT H. HAYES is the Philip Caldwell Professor of Business Administration at the Harvard Business School. His current research is concerned with manufacturing competitiveness, technological development, and the integration of design with manufacturing. He has published widely, and three of his articles have won McKinsey Awards from the *Harvard Business Review*. His books include *Restoring Our Competitive Edge: Competing Through Manufacturing* (1984, with Steven C. Wheelwright), *The Uneasy Alliance: Managing the Productivity-Technology Dilemma* (1985, co-edited with Kim B. Clark and Christopher Lorenz), *Dynamic Manufacturing: Creating the Learning Organization* (1988, with Steven C. Wheelwright and Kim B. Clark), *Manufacturing Renaissance* (1995, co-edited with Gary P. Pisano), and *Strategic Operations: Competing Through Capabilities* (1996, with Gary P. Pisano and David Upton).

JAMES L. HESKETT is the UPS Foundation Professor of Business Logistics at the Harvard Business School. Among his publications are *The Service Profit Chain: How Leading Companies Link Profit and Growth to Loyalty, Satisfaction, and Value* (1997, with W. Earl Sasser, Jr., and Leonard A. Schlesinger), *Corporate Culture and Performance* (1992, with John P. Kotter), *Service Breakthroughs: Changing the Rules of the Game* (1990, with W. Earl Sasser, Jr., and Christopher W. L. Hart), *The Service Management Course: Cases and Readings* (1991, with W. Earl Sasser, Jr., and Christopher W. L. Hart), *Managing in the Service Economy* (1986), *Logistics Strategy: Cases and Concepts* (1985, with Roy D. Shapiro), *Marketing* (1976), *Business Logistics: Physical Distribution and Materials Management* (second edition 1973, with Nicholas A. Glaskowsky, Jr., and Robert M. Ivie), and numerous articles in such publications as the *Harvard Business Review*, the *Journal of Marketing*, the *Sloan Management Review*, and the *California Management Review*.

MARCO IANSITI is a Professor in the Technology and Operations Management Area at the Harvard Business School. Professor Iansiti's research focuses on the management of technology and product development. He has been involved in numerous studies of effective development practice in many industries, ranging from computers and microelectronics to steel manufacturing, and from software to automobiles. He has authored and co-authored more than three dozen papers, book chapters, articles, and cases. His latest book is *Technology Integration: Making Critical Choices in a Turbulent World* (1997).

MICHAEL C. JENSEN is the Jesse Isidor Straus Professor of Business Administration at the Harvard Business School. He is the author of more than 50 published papers and articles on a wide range of economic, finance, and business-related topics in scholarly journals and books. He is editor of *The Modern Theory of Corporate Finance* (1984, with Clifford W. Smith, Jr.) and *Studies in the Theory of Capital Markets* (1972). He is Founding Editor of the *Journal of Financial Economics*. He served on the steering committee of the Mind-Brain Behavior Initiative at Harvard from 1992 through 1998, and he is co-founder and President of Social Science Electronic Publishing, Inc.

NANCY F. KOEHN, an authority on business history, is an associate professor at the Harvard Business School. Her research focuses on brand creation, business strategy, and consumer behavior in the three industrial revolutions—that is, the broad range of economic, social, and organizational transitions accompanying technological innovation. She is the author of *The Power of Commerce: Economy and Governance in the First British Empire* (1994), as well as a contributor to *Creating Modern Capitalism* (1997, Thomas K. McCraw, ed.), *Management Past and Present* (1996, Alfred D. Chandler. Jr., Thomas K. McCraw, and Richard S. Tedlow, eds.), and *Macroeconomic Decision Making in the World Economy: Text and Cases* (1986, Michael G. Rukstad, ed.).

GARY W. LOVEMAN is Executive Vice President and Chief Operating Officer for Harrah's Entertainment. Before joining the company in May 1998 he was Associate Professor of Business Administration at the Harvard Business School. He was named the first recipient of Harvard Business School's Apgar Award for excellence in innovative teaching. He has authored three books, numerous scholarly papers, and five articles for the *Harvard Business Review*. Loveman serves on the editorial boards of several academic journals, including *Human Resource Management* and the *Journal of Services Research*.

ROBERT C. MERTON is the John and Natty McArthur University Professor at Harvard. His books include *Finance* (1998, with Zvi Bodie), *The Global Financial System: A Functional Perspective* (1995, with Dwight B. Crane, Kenneth A. Froot, Scott P. Mason, André F. Perold, Zvi Bodie, Eric Sirri, and Peter Tufano), *Cases in Financial Engineering: Studies of Applied Financial Innovation* (1995, with Scott P. Mason, André F. Perold, and Peter Tufano) and *Continuous-Time Finance* (revised edition 1992). His research focuses on developing finance theory in the areas of capital markets and financial institutions. A member of the National Academy of Sciences since 1993, Professor Merton received the Alfred Nobel Memorial Prize in Economic Science in 1997.

H. V. NELLES teaches History at York University in Toronto, where he specializes in the study of Canadian Political Economy and Public Memory. He is the author or co-author (with Christopher Armstrong) of *The Philosophy of Railroads, and Other Essays* (1972), *The Politics of Development: Forests, Mines and Hydro-electric Power in Ontario, 1849–1941* (1974), *The Revenge of the Methodist Bicycle Company: Sunday Streetcars and Municipal Reform in Toronto, 1888–1987* (1977), *Monopoly's Moment: The Organization and Regulation of Canadian Utilities, 1830–1930* (1986), *Southern Exposure* (1988), and a forthcoming book on the theatre of Canadian commemoration. He has been awarded the Newcomen Prize, the City of Toronto Book Award, a National Business Book Award, and the Sir John A. Macdonald Prize of the Canadian Historical Association. In 1981–1982 he was the William Lyon Mackenzie King Professor at Harvard University.

LYNN SHARP PAINE is Professor at the Harvard Business School, where she is chair of the School's general management unit and head of the required MBA ethics module Leadership, Values, and Decision Making. Professor Paine's current research focuses on management and organizational value systems, with special emphasis on ethical aspects of globalization. Author of numerous articles and dozens of case studies, she has written most recently on organizational ethics strategies. Her publications have appeared in a variety of books and journals, including the *Harvard Business Review*, the *California Management Review*, the *Journal of Business Ethics*, *Philosophy and Public Affairs*, and the *Wisconsin Law Review*. She is the author of *Cases in Leadership, Ethics, and Organizational Integrity: A Strategic Perspective*, a text and casebook (1997).

THOMAS R. PIPER is the Lawrence E. Fouraker Professor of Business Administration at the Harvard Business School. For many years during John

McArthur's deanship he was Senior Associate Dean for Educational Programs. His other assignments included early leadership of the school's program on ethics and corporate responsibility, and of its initiative to strengthen management education in central and eastern Europe. His work includes *The Economics of Bank Acquisitions by Registered Bank Holding Companies* (1971), *Case Problems in Finance* (1992, with William E. Fruhan, W. Carl Kester, Scott P. Mason, and Richard S. Ruback), and *Can Ethics Be Taught? Perspectives, Challenges, and Approaches at Harvard Business School* (1993, with Mary C. Gentile and Sharon Daloz Parks).

MICHAEL E. PORTER is the C. Roland Christensen Professor of Business Administration at the Harvard Business School. In 1983, Professor Porter was appointed to President Reagan's Commission on Industrial Competitiveness, the initiative that triggered the competitiveness debate in America. He serves as an advisor to heads of state, governors, mayors, and CEOs throughout the world. The recipient of the Wells Price in Economics, the Adam Smith Award, three McKinsey Awards, and honorary doctorates from the Stockholm School of Economics and six other universities, Professor Porter is the author of 15 books, among them *Competitive Strategy: Techniques for Analyzing Industries and Competitors* (1980), *Competitive Advantage: Creating and Sustaining Superior Performance* (1985), and *The Competitive Advantage of Nations* (1990).

NICOLAJ SIGGELKOW holds a Ph.D. in Business Economics from Harvard University. He is an Assistant Professor of Strategy at the Wharton School at the University of Pennsylvania. His current research is on the benefits of focus with respect to the creation and sustainability of competitive advantage, the evolution of systems of interconnected choices, and agency issues in the mutual fund industry.

HOWARD H. STEVENSON is the Sarofim-Rock Professor of Business Administration at the Harvard Business School. He has authored, edited, or co-authored six books and numerous articles, including *New Business Ventures and the Entrepreneur* (1993, with Michael J. Roberts and H. Irving Grousbeck), *Policy Formulation and Administration: A Casebook of Senior Management Problems in Business* (1980, with C. Roland Christensen, Norman A. Berg, and Malcolm S. Salter), and *The Entrepreneurial Venture* (1991, with William Sahlman). His latest book is *Do Lunch or Be Lunch: The Power of Predictability in Creating Your Future* (1998, with Jeffrey L. Cruikshank).

PETER TUFANO is Professor of Business Administration at Harvard Business School. His research focuses on financial innovation and corporations' use of financial engineering. His publications include "The Economics of Pooling" (1995, with Erik Sirri) in the *Global Financial System*, edited by Dwight Crane et al., *Cases in Financial Engineering: Applied Studies of Financial Innovation* (1995, with Robert C. Merton, Scott P. Mason, and André F. Perold), "How Financial Engineering Can Advance Business Strategy" in the *Harvard Business Review* (1996), and articles in the *Journal of Finance*, the *Journal of Financial Economics*, the *Journal of Applied Corporate Finance*, and the *Business History Review*, as well as in other journals and books.

KAREN H. WRUCK, Associate Professor of Business Administration at the Harvard Business School, engages in research aimed at arriving at a clearer understanding of the management practices and financial operating principles that lead to the creation of value for shareholders. Her many publications include "Information Problems, Conflicts of Interest, and Asset Stripping: Chapter 11's Failure in the Case of Eastern Airlines" (1998, with Lawrence A. Weiss, *Journal of Financial Economics*), "Organization Structure, Contract Design and Government Ownership: A Clinical Analysis of German Privatization" (forthcoming, with Alexander Dyck, *Journal of Corporate Finance*), and "Lessons from a Middle Market LBO: The Case of O. M. Scott," in *The New Corporate Finance: Where Theory Meets Practice* (1993, ed. Donald H. Chew, Jr.).

UNIVERSITY LIBRARY
INDIANA UNIVERSITY OF PENNSYLVANIA
INDIANA, PA 15705